GALANTHUS

SCILLA

CROCUS

LILY (BASE-ROOTING)

STERNBERGIA

LYCORIS
SQUAMIGERA

DAFFODIL

FOR SPRING BULBS SEE BACK ENDSHEET

THE COMPLETE
BOOK OF BULBS

BY F. F. ROCKWELL
AND ESTHER C. GRAYSON

The Complete Book of Flower Arrangement

10,000 Garden Questions Answered (Editors)

Gardening Indoors

BY F. F. ROCKWELL

Around the Year in the Garden

The Book of Bulbs

The Home Garden Handbooks

Pre-spring flower show in a sheltered nook. Tulip species bloom even before the Daffodils.

THE
COMPLETE
BOOK
OF BULBS

by F. F. Rockwell and Esther C. Grayson

A PRACTICAL MANUAL ON THE USES,
CULTIVATION, AND PROPAGATION
OF MORE THAN 100 SPECIES,
HARDY AND TENDER,
WHICH THE AMATEUR GARDENER
CAN ENJOY OUTDOORS
AND IN THE HOME.
WITH EIGHTY-SEVEN HALFTONES,
NINETEEN LINE DRAWINGS, AND
THIRTY-ONE NATURAL COLOR PHOTOGRAPHS
OF THE AUTHORS' GARDEN.

THE AMERICAN GARDEN GUILD AND DOUBLEDAY & COMPANY,
INC., GARDEN CITY, N.Y.

Library of Congress Catalog Card Number 53-7520

TO JAN DE GRAAFF who, like his father and grandfather before him, has done so much to provide gardens the world over with ever increasing beauty.

Foreword

For some reason the group of plants commonly designated as bulbs has always held a special fascination for me. A psychologist would probably ascribe it to the fact that the very first plant I ever owned was a potted Lily presented to me at an Easter church service. I remember, too, that one of my very first attempts at growing a flower was to dig up a blooming Meadow Lily from the edge of a hayfield where the clattering newfangled mowing machine would have caught it on the next round. Carefully I transplanted it to the dry, sandy patch of ground which had been given me as a garden of my very own; to keep me, as I came to suspect later, from getting under the feet—and in the hair—of the hired man who had to take care of the real gardens. Needless to say, the tall stalk and nodding yellow bells never appeared again.

At any rate, and for whatever reason, this group of plants has continued, through the years, to hold the interest which it so early inspired. It has been a great satisfaction, therefore, to watch the steadily growing popular appreciation of bulbous plants of all kinds, and to contribute, where opportunity offered, to this development.

When, some twenty-five years ago, I undertook the writing of a book devoted to bulbs, I was astonished to find that in the preceding quarter century there had appeared no American book on the subject. I have long felt that my original venture in this field was out of date, and have therefore welcomed the opportunity given me by my present publishers to prepare this new volume.

A lot of water has passed over the dam since those earlier days. Bulbous plants are no longer for the gardens of the few, but are represented, by one species or another, in almost every yard. The sale of bulbous plants has increased steadily, year by year. Where formerly practically all plants of this type were imported from Holland, Belgium, France, Japan, and other bulb-producing countries, millions are now grown in the United States. Notwithstanding the output of this comparatively new American industry, the importation of bulbs from abroad in 1951 reached the impressive figure of over 450,000,000.

The use of bulbs in American gardens is, however, in its infancy. Dozens of species and varieties, grown without difficulty and most rewarding to the grower, are seldom to be found in the average garden. The Hardy Amaryllis and the Hardy Begonia—to cite but two examples—are among the most persistent and easily cared-for garden subjects to be found anywhere, and by no means new, yet one seldom encounters them.

I should like to express here my appreciation of the assistance given me from many sources in the preparation of this volume. First and foremost to my co-author and co-worker; then to many friends, among them Jan de Graaff, internationally known for his Lily hybrids and Daffodils; Dr. George Slate, author of *Lilies for American Gardens;* Dr. Cynthia Westcott, the Plant Doctor; Dr. P. P. Pirone of the New York Botanical Garden; and Jack Grullemans of Wayside Gardens, whose excellent catalogues have played an important part in making American gardeners more bulb-conscious; to Marjorie P. Johnson, for her assistance, beyond the call of duty, in preparing the manuscript; and to Katharine Burton, for her patient co-operation in the preparation of the line drawings which accompany the text. The quotation from *The Poetical Works of Robert Bridges* is by permission of The Clarendon Press, Oxford. That from Mr. Slate's book is used by courtesy of the publishers, Charles Scribner's Sons.

It is with the hope that this new volume may bring to other gardeners something of the great pleasure that the growing of bulbous plants, outdoors and in, has brought to us, that I and my co-author pass along, within these pages, such information as we have gained.

F. F. ROCKWELL

GrayRock
West Nyack, New York

Contents

How bulbs differ from other plants; true bulbs, corms, tubers, bulbous roots, and rhizomes; the importance of knowing how they differ.

The mechanism of a bulb; what happens underground; the growth cycle and the part it plays in the culture of bulbs; reproduction—offsets, cormels, bulblets.

What bulbs need to keep them happy; exposures; sun and shade; soil, drainage; fertilizers; protection.

Getting your bulbs off to a good start; procuring good bulbs; bulb "bargains"; soil preparation; proper planting for different types; when to plant; planting depths; protection from rodents; mulching.

Round-the-year care; making use of the growth cycle; feeding; cutting; mulching; lifting; calendar of operations for hardy, semi-hardy, and tender bulbs.

Fun and profit in increasing your supply of bulbs. Propagation by offsets, bulblets, bulbils, scales, cuttings, seeds.

Importance of good culture. Overcrowding; sanitation. List of insect enemies and controls. List of diseases and controls. Insecticides and fungicides.

COLOR ILLUSTRATIONS BY THE AUTHORS

LINE ILLUSTRATIONS
By Katharine Burton

HALFTONE ILLUSTRATIONS
By the authors except as noted

PART ONE
—BULBS FOR YOUR GARDEN AND HOW TO USE THEM

Group of Daffodils naturalized under Birches. For this purpose it is best to use individual varieties or types rather than a general mixture.

CHAPTER *1. Make Your Garden*
More Beautiful with Bulbs

Why have bulbs in your garden?

First of all because a garden without bulbs is only half a garden. Bulbs provide whole groups of flowers for which there are no substitutes, not even poor ones, among annuals or perennials. The garden pictures which you can readily create with them can be achieved in no other way.

But the one clinching argument for having bulbs, and having them in abundance, is that they provide a month or more of heart-lifting color before perennials, annuals, and all but the earliest shrubs are giving more than a promise that eventually they will break the shackles of their prison-keeper Winter and again be set free to beautify the earth.

I have just come in from an around-the-garden stroll, between showers, on a day in April in one of the latest of all late springs. It would have been a disheartening trip indeed but for the cheerful flowers from bulbs and corms that greeted me along the way, just as their still earlier companions have been doing for nearly a month past.

All but the most laggard of the Tulip species—which in this spring's moisture and refrigerator temperatures seemed to be everlasting—have finally dropped their weather-beaten petals along the curving main path through the rock garden. But *dasystemon's* golden stars, tipped with white light, and the brilliant flames of *Eichleri* are still in their prime, with the dainty Candlestick and the weirdly twisted petals of *acuminata* still to carry on.

Another spot of glorious color, now in its third week, is a collection of half a dozen varieties of Early Tulips; old varieties which I used to grow when a youngster, but still as desirable as ever. So colorful are these that from the living-room windows they make a patch of sunshine even on a dreary day; and so fragrant that visitors, noticing the sweet scent, look around to see where it could come from, not realizing that there are such things as fragrant Tulips—a sad commentary, incidentally, on our general lack of knowledge concerning bulbs in a land where we are beginning to pride ourselves on our horticultural prowess.

In the rock garden there is still plenty of interest: the later-flowering sorts of such little bulbs as Grape-hyacinths, and Snowflakes, with Camassias thrusting up their tall spikes that later will bear blue and white stars set off by golden stamens, and the late Wood-hyacinths. But if this area of the garden produced not another flower from now until next spring, it would have proved worth while. In March, April, and early May it is a sort of sun trap, sloping to the southeast and protected on the northwest by Hemlocks, Pines, and Rhododendrons— the earliest of our several outdoor living rooms to become really comfortable and inviting. *And its attractiveness is due chiefly to bulbs.*

It is in the hardy borders, however, that bulbs make their most extensive, varied, and colorful displays. Here, long before the rock garden has lost its interest, the Daffodils and Tulips, in groups spaced between the various types of perennials, bring sudden life and color to the long stretches where but a few days before were only brown earth and bits of budding greenery. Many of the other bulbous flowers will help carry on here, too, through midsummer and even into autumn. The wide range of hardy Lilies begins with the dainty Coral Lily and chaste Madonna in June, continues with the towering spikes of *centifoliums* and others in midsummer, and ends with *tigrinum* and *speciosum* in August or September. The Lilies are especially desirable because their upright habit of growth gives much needed contrast to the rounded or spreading forms of most of the perennials.

And then there are the half-hardy and tender bulbous plants of many kinds from many climes. It is nice to know that after the Tall Bearded and Siberian Irises are gone there will still be the Bulbous Irises to take over and continue to make available this flower, so delightful in any of its many forms, in arrangements as well as in the garden. The exotic Ismenes and the spire-stalked Galtonias provide notes of pure white, especially welcome during the season when they are in bloom. (The heavy, strap-leaved foliage of Ismene is so useful in arrangements all summer long that it would be well worth growing even if it never flowered.)

And after these, of course, come the summer-flowering tender bulbs

—Gladiolus in all their rainbow range of colors, with the delightful little miniatures and "babies" for table-size arrangements; Dahlias in all kinds of shapes, sizes, and hues; Montbretias, fountain-like and sprightly, sending up one spike after another for a long season; Tigridias, unsurpassed in brilliancy and dramatic color combinations.

WHERE CAN YOU USE THEM?

With such a treasure chest of plant jewels to choose from, it is small wonder that the inexperienced gardener will find himself bewildered. But it is an easy matter to make a beginning and then gradually increase, in variety and numbers, the range of bulbous plants that will add so greatly to the beauty and character of your garden. Most of the hardy bulbs and many of the tender ones, when given even moderate care, will propagate themselves so readily that in a few years' time you will have, from a very modest start, all of any one species or variety you are likely to be able to use. And yet, unlike most of the more persistent perennials, they do not demand frequent taking up, dividing, and replanting.

When you are ready to add bulbous plants to your garden, the first step should be to make a survey of locations in which you can use them, and then select the kinds that will best fit into these areas. The way *not* to start is to go through the bulb catalogues, with their gorgeous close-up photographs of individual flowers, and pick out at random those which, in color and size, are most dramatically presented. Such photographs usually convey little or no conception of the habit of the plant and, as they are not in uniform scale, fail as a guide even to the size of the individual blooms.

Let us then take a walk about the place, about *your* place, and try to get an idea of where the various types of bulbs could be used to best advantage. Unless your property is of considerable size, it is not likely that you will have available all of the types of locations we shall consider, but on even the smallest place there will be several of them.

The Mixed Border

Usually the first bit of planned planting on a new place (often before trees and shrubs are put in, though it shouldn't be) is the sizable flower

border where perennials, biennials, bulbs, and annuals can all be used
—the "mixed border," in garden lingo. Bulbous plant material should
have a prominent place in such a border; is indeed essential for early
color accents, and highly desirable for medium to tall spire material
during the summer.

It is here that, on the moderate-sized place, the more familiar
bulbs, such as Daffodils, Tulips, Hyacinths, some of the more robust-
growing minor bulbs, and the more vigorous hardy Lilies, can best
be used to advantage. Here, too—though they are seldom so employed—may well go such tender bulbs as Dahlias (of moderate
size), Gladiolus, Summer-hyacinth (Galtonia), and Tigridias.

*A Tulip border edged with Pansies. Curving design of bed, with hedge at
rear, sets off the blooms to the very best advantage.*

A drawback to the use of some of these—especially Tulips and Daffodils—is the fact that the foliage should be left to mature, and during its dying-down period becomes unsightly. For this reason, on large estates where many bulbs are grown, these are often placed in a special bulb border or borders where they can be left until time to take them up; or interplanted with annuals or bedding plants to conceal the dying foliage and provide later color. In the mixed border, however, tying up the maturing foliage and using suitable perennials near and in front of the groups of bulbs will keep the foliage from being too obtrusive.

Bulbs which are best *not* used in the mixed border include low-growing sorts, such as Crocus and Grape-hyacinths, and the various delicate-flowered little fellows: Snowdrops, Snowflakes, Glory-of-the-snow, and the like. In the bare soil of the flower border, these are likely to become beaten down and mud-spattered and more or less lost amid the fast-growing foliage of larger bulbs and perennials. Being so low-growing, they display themselves to much better advantage if they are planted, where possible, at an elevation somewhat above the general ground level, as at the top of a low retaining wall.

Such bulbs as are used in the informal mixed flower border are best placed in small groups, somewhat irregular in form and at irregular distances. Otherwise they will present very conspicuous and spotty patterns when in bloom. As few as five or six Tulips or Daffodils of a single variety, or even three Lilies, will make an attractive spot of color the first season, though double these quantities are desirable. In a large border, of course, more should be used in each group, to be in scale with the general planting design.

Landscape groups

Before discussing this method of employing bulbs, it will be worth while to mark the distinction between landscape groups and "naturalizing"—a term that is too loosely used. To be really naturalized, bulbs—or any other type of plant material for that matter—should be planted in such a location and in such a way, both as to numbers and distribution, as to simulate a natural growth, unplanned by the mind, and largely untended by the hand, of the gardener; in a word, a passable substitute for a work of nature. To be convincing, the setting—the terrain and the companion plants used—must be in accord with the plants that are to be naturalized. In most cases this requires more space than many of us possess, and the use of bulbs in large quantities.

The landscape group, on the contrary, makes no pretense of having, like Topsy, "jist growed." It may occupy a space of but a few square feet. Its purpose is to create a pleasing "little picture," a high light or accent point in the general garden scheme. Its success will depend upon the gardener's skill in selecting the right thing for the right place. It *may* have the appearance of having been a happy accident of nature (which will be a credit to the gardener's cleverness), but that is not at all essential.

In the landscape group, as in naturalizing, a keen sense of composition is all-important. A circle of Daffodils set in the middle of a lawn does not constitute a landscape group: it is, on the contrary, about as attractive as a rag-bound thumb at a game of canasta. I remember, in fact, as a pre-teen-age youngster, exactly such a circle, made up of the old Pheasant's-eye Narcissus—my first introduction to any Daffodil. Delighted as I was with the flowers, I still felt that something about them was wrong. Later, when I got permission to transplant them to the base of a gray stone wall, over which an old Forsythia trailed its pendent branches, I realized what a difference a bit of background can make.

Here again the degree of success attained will be commensurate with the good taste used in selecting materials. If one desires informal effects, the garden or horticultural types of flowers will be avoided— such as the giant Darwin and Breeder Tulips, huge Trumpet Daffodils, Exhibition Hyacinths, large-flowered Gladiolus and Dahlias. Those which make the most attractive landscape groups are the species and species-hybrids of Tulips and Daffodils, small-flowered Daffodils in general, Crocuses, both spring- and autumn-flowering, and many of the Lilies.

Landscape groups are arranged according to the setting and the plants to be used. Often the soil where such a group is to be grown can be left in grass or permanently mulched. This is a great advantage in growing hardy bulbs, for the foliage always should be allowed to mature. Then a planting, which is a decided point of accent in the spring, just automatically disappears and is forgotten after the flowers fade. Landscape groups are most easily done and, on the whole, most successful when but a single variety of bulb is used.

Making a group planting is an excellent way of spotlighting some out-of-the-ordinary or unusually attractive species or variety. During its period of bloom it may attract more attention in the garden than a whole border full of larger flowers competing with each other. *White* flowers, showing up more conspicuously against their green or dark backgrounds than most colored flowers, are especially effective in group plantings.

One word of caution! A group planting is an exclamation point! The too free use of kinds that flower at the same time will, like a page of print sprinkled with exclamation points, defeat its own purpose! If care is taken to provide for bloom *at intervals through the season,* a large number of landscape groups can be arranged even on a small place.

Naturalizing

Where a sufficient area is available and local conditions are suitable, many of the hardy bulbs make extremely satisfactory plants for naturalizing. Daffodils in particular, because of their permanency, their freedom from insect injury and disease, and the fact that they bloom early in spring, while sunshine still floods the ground under deciduous trees, are ideal for the purpose.

One need not possess acres of ground to have a satisfactory naturalized planting. Wherever a bit of woods or meadow, a natural slope or a rocky bank, a few old fruit trees, a bit of stream or a pool suggests a suitable setting, bulbs of one sort or another can be used to create an intriguing view.

What has already been said about selecting appropriate types and varieties for landscape groups applies also, but with even greater force, to naturalized plantings. The effect desired simply will not come off if the flowers planted look foreign to their setting. This by no means implies that only native material should be used. One does not think of a field of Dandelions or of roadside Day-lilies covering a bank as being exotics, although both are immigrants from other lands. The point is that they *look* as though they belonged naturally where one finds them. Just so with the simpler types of Daffodils, the Tulip species, the Grape-hyacinths, the Lilies, and the many other bulbs and bulbous plants which are well adapted to naturalizing.

Another highly desirable, if not essential, quality required in plants for naturalizing is that they be permanent or self-perpetuating. An advantage possessed by many bulbs adapted for use in naturalized

Daffodils naturalized in the landscape. Scattered planting, with areas left unplanted, is more pleasing than a solid mass of bloom.

plantings is that they pretty much take care of themselves, increasing in numbers by division and by self-seeding, while on the other hand they do not spread so rapidly and vigorously as to drive out everything else—a serious fault of many perennials.

The prime objective in naturalizing is to get a finished planting that will look natural. There are two rules which must be observed if this

is to be accomplished. The first is to avoid using too many species, or even varieties of a single species, in one area. The second is to avoid placing the bulbs in anything approaching a regular pattern. A naturalized planting need not involve a very heavy original outlay. Bulbs will have to be used, of course, in greater numbers than would be required for planting small groups in borders. But many of the older and least expensive varieties are perfectly satisfactory, and most of them will multiply rapidly. If one is content to have a somewhat thin effect for three or four years, the allotted spaces will soon fill up. On the other hand, the wise gardener will not be tempted by cheap mixtures containing many varieties offered for naturalizing. Daffodils are frequently sold in this way. Even if the bulbs are good, the result is a hodgepodge that looks anything but natural. The "naturalizing" of a collection of varieties is a compromise which the collector may be willing to make. If he takes pains to keep varieties of the same general type together, the result will not be so regrettable —from the artistic point of view—as otherwise it might.

In foundation plantings

On the small property, where lack of room presents a problem, another possibility is to place bulbs in, or just in front of, the foundation planting about the house and garage. Often such plantings are composed entirely of dwarf evergreens—although in most instances a combination of evergreen and deciduous shrubs would be better. In either case, almost any of the spring-flowering bulbs (except the very low-growing ones) can be used to add interest and color. They should be planted in groups rather than in a straight line or border, as they often are. The maturing foliage can usually be pretty well concealed under low branches or by pot-grown annuals set in to provide color later in the season.

In the rock garden

The very term "rock garden" is likely to scare off the beginner with a small place or limited means. The picture of a rock garden that comes to mind is based upon what has been seen in books, magazines, or at botanical gardens and flower shows—rock gardens, to be sure, but rock gardens on a much grander and more elaborate scale than is at all essential. A rock garden is primarily a garden made among rocks, and such a garden can be made on an area of a few square yards and with very few rocks. Your real rock-garden enthusiast may condescendingly refer to such a setup as a "rockery" rather than a rock garden, but that does not change the fact that it provides growing conditions and a setting quite different from those in the flower bed or border.

The point is stressed here because many of the smaller spring bulbs find conditions more to their liking, and are displayed to much better advantage, when they are planted among rocks. If there is available a natural outcrop or a stony slope or bank, so much the better; but wanting that, a rock garden of some sort can usually be provided without too much expense or labor. If it must be constructed on a level surface, suitable shrubs (especially evergreens, either broad-leaved or coniferous) and some small trees will help to camouflage that fact and also to give the plants shelter from prevailing spring winds.

Among the bulbs especially suitable for growing among rocks are the species and species-hybrids of Tulips and Daffodils, and the smaller bulbs already mentioned. Others will be found in the tables on pages 330–32.

Where the rock garden is sufficiently large, or a bank or sloping wall may be utilized to provide height somewhat above surface level, the smaller bulbs can be enjoyed not only for their general effect but for the beauty of the individual flowers, much of which is lost when they must be looked down upon at one's feet. By all means provide, if possible, a rock setting for some of your bulbs.

One might continue almost indefinitely concerning the garden possibilities of this greatly varied group of bulbous plants for gardens large or small. A pool, a stream, a winding path through a bit of woods—these and a dozen other locations not already discussed present alluring possibilities. And the wonderful part of it is that the initial expense for almost any of these adventures need not be great. With few exceptions, the colony of plants increases more or less automatically once you get a start.

In a word, you cannot have a garden so beautiful, so interesting, or so varied as it might be until you accept the help that bulbs so generously proffer, and learn to master, in some degree at least, their use as garden material and the simple essentials of their welfare.

Having made something of a survey of the value of bulbous plants in the garden, let us take a look at what they can do in providing beauty and interest within the house; for here you can enjoy them, in one form or another, from the first week in January to the last in December.

The three ways in which bulbs serve to provide enjoyment indoors are (1) as cut flowers for decoration; (2) forced in pots for winter bloom; and (3) as house plants that are grown indoors the year round, except for their summer vacation in the open.

As cut flowers the spring bulbs provide an ample supply for decorations at a time when few other flowers are available. They last well and combine charmingly with branches of such early shrubs as may be in bloom (or may readily be forced indoors), adding needed color and emphasis in arrangements. Later in the season the summer-flowering types, including the many July and August Lilies, furnish tall spikes to accompany the annuals and perennials in bloom at this season. And from midsummer on, Gladiolus, Dahlias, Montbretias, and others are available during that period when perennial borders usually have little to offer until the Chrysanthemums come in. If one has a cold frame, Daffodils, Early Tulips, and many of the other hardy spring bulbs, grown in pots, flats, or directly in the soil, may be had for cutting a month or more ahead of the same varieties in the garden. With a small greenhouse the flowering dates of some sorts may be advanced to New Year's or shortly thereafter.

Forced bulbs for flowering indoors constitute one of the easiest and most certain of all types of flower growing. Everyone, even the city apartment dweller, is familiar with the Paperwhite and the similar yellow-flowered Soleil d'Or Narcissi which can be bought in dime stores (the name still lingers, though its meaning has long since

Forced bulbs of various kinds add color and cheer to the indoor garden from Christmas time to Easter. Growing them is not difficult.

ceased!) and grown in pebbles or bulb fiber and water, without benefit of soil. A number of others, including Hyacinths, Colchicums, and Crocuses can be treated in the same way.

Those which are grown in soil or compost—Tulips, Daffodils, and a whole group of the early hardy bulbs—require little more work, for they are merely potted up in late fall, stored away in the dark at a cold temperature (like so many packages of food in a freezer), and then brought into the house, one or a few at a time, to flower. In this way it is possible to have, from January to April, as much of a bulb garden indoors as you can provide space for. And in addition to this

*Paper-white
Narcissi, most
popular of bulbs
for flowering
indoors, may be
grown in pebbles
and water; but they
do better, and last
longer, in soil.*

*Veltheimia, excellent
long-lived house
plant, thriving in a
kitchen window.
This flower spike
began to open on
December 20, was
photographed a full
month later.*

winter show, most of these bulbs, after being forced, can be transferred to the garden and there will establish themselves and flower during succeeding years.

Winter-flowering tender bulbs make satisfactory house plants or greenhouse subjects to be grown in pots the year round, or placed out of doors during summer and brought in again in late autumn. Best known of these perhaps is the Amaryllis (Hippeastrum) with its giant, spectacularly colored blooms. In other days varieties of Amaryllis and Oxalis, with its cheerful, simple flowers and shamrock-like leaves, were to be found in almost every farmhouse collection of house plants, "swapped" among neighbors and passed on to every daughter who was setting up housekeeping on her own. They are still deservedly popular.

Florists' Cyclamen, a favorite gift plant, continues in bloom for weeks if kept in a cool (40° to 50°) temperature, and can be saved for another season.

For porches and window boxes

If you are a flower lover who has little or no outdoor space, you will find several of the summer-flowering bulbs most helpful in the decoration of a porch, or in window boxes outside or inside the house. Some of these are grown in pots, urns, or tubs and moved into the cellar or a cold room for their dormant resting period during the winter; others are planted directly in the soil and in late fall taken up, dried off, and wintered in much the same way as Gladiolus or Dahlias —the very dwarf varieties of which, in fact, do well in large window or porch boxes.

Some of these accommodating house and porch bulbs grow well with a considerable amount of shade. The Tuberous-rooted and Multiflora Begonias are among these. Others, such as the Fairy-lilies (Zephyranthes), prefer full sun.

In the small greenhouse

The possession of a greenhouse, even a very small one, increases tremendously the pleasure which may be had from bulbous plants. With "glass" one can enjoy many kinds that cannot be handled in the house or that are not practical to attempt. Also, bulbous plants wanted for house decoration can be cared for in the greenhouse until they come into flower, and returned to it afterward. Thus such window space or other locations as may be available for plants can be constantly replenished with blooming material. In our own small greenhouse, for instance, bulbs are brought in and started into growth under a bench, grown on to flowering stage on a bench, then transferred— as many as we have room for—to living room, dining room, or kitchen. After flowering they are returned to under-bench space in the greenhouse, where the foliage is allowed to mature. But even without a greenhouse a very satisfying number may be grown.

So you see that, though you may possess little garden space, there are many ways in which you can have a lot of fun growing bulbous plants. And as most of them may be kept from year to year, the expense of having them is very reasonable indeed.

Now let's take a somewhat closer look at the many different types of bulbs you can select to suit the various purposes for which you may wish to use them.

Up to this point we have talked only in a very general way about bulbous plants and what they can do to help make the garden more beautiful and to bring cheer and color into the home. We have spoken of "hardy" bulbs and "tender" bulbs, without providing any definition of just what those terms mean; and of summer-flowering and winter-flowering ones just as though they might be different varieties of the same species. It is time now to observe more closely the members of this great group of plants and to learn something of the habits, possibilities and limitations, advantages and disadvantages of each.

This knowledge is essential for two reasons. It is necessary to enable us to know *where* and *how* to use the different types about the garden or indoors; and it also helps us to *grow* them successfully after we have decided which bulbs we would like to use.

The botanists' system of arranging bulbous plants in groups or categories is to classify them according to family relationships. Of more immediate importance to the amateur, however, is information concerning their behavior in his garden, his window, or his greenhouse.

He will want to know, first of all, whether they are hardy, semi-hardy, or tender: whether they can be left in the ground without protection in winter; whether they will come through if they are protected; whether they must be taken up and stored over the winter in a frostproof place or must be grown as pot plants the year round.

He will want to know also the season of the year when each blooms —spring, summer, autumn, or winter. And of course the size or height of the plant will be a determining factor in where to place it in the garden.

Let us take a quick glance at some of the more familiar bulbous plants and get an idea of how they fit into groups based on the characteristics indicated above.

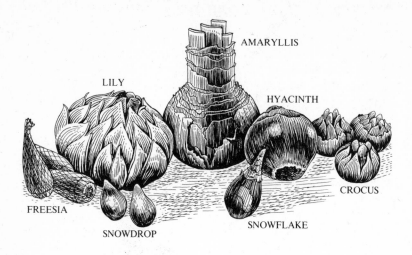

LILY
AMARYLLIS
HYACINTH
CROCUS
FREESIA
SNOWDROP
SNOWFLAKE

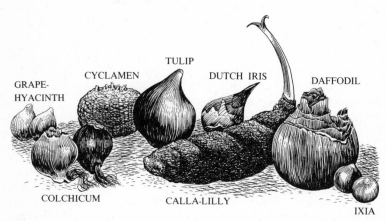

GRAPE-HYACINTH
CYCLAMEN
TULIP
DUTCH IRIS
DAFFODIL
COLCHICUM
CALLA-LILLY
IXIA

PLANTS SOLD AS "BULBS"

HARDINESS

If by the term "hardy" we mean capable of living out of doors through the winter, it is obvious that many plants are hardy in the

South which are not hardy in the North. The term as applied to plant material in general designates a species or a variety that will survive out of doors, without protection, in sections where the temperature drops to zero or occasionally well below. It is not an exact and definite term, for many plants commonly survive in areas where temperatures drop lower than those encountered in other areas where frequently the same plants perish during the winter. The reason for this, of course, is that temperature is only *one* factor of the several involved. Some of the others are: protection by snow that remains for most of the winter; exposure to high winds; the amount of moisture in the soil (determined by rainfall and drainage conditions); and the degree to which new growth has matured as it goes into the winter.

Hardy

When we speak of a hardy bulb, therefore, we refer to one which, once planted and established, under normally good conditions will survive in cold climates—in our Northern tier of states, for instance, and up into Canada. Most of the spring-flowering bulbs are hardy. This group includes the "Dutch" bulbs—Tulips, Hyacinths, Crocuses, Narcissi (Daffodils)—with a few exceptions—Muscari (Grape-hyacinths), Galanthus (Snowdrops), Leucojums (Spring Snowflakes), Scillas, and others. Another large group of the really hardy bulbs takes in most of the Lilies, such as Regal, Madonna, Turkscap (*Martagon*), Meadow (*canadense*), and the new hybrid sorts. In addition to these there are many native bulbous plants, such as Jack-in-the-pulpit (*Arisaema triphyllum*), Dogtooth-violet (Erythronium), Camassia, and Calochortus (Mariposa-lily). The last named, however, is often temperamental in Eastern gardens.

Semi-hardy

This group includes those which, while hardy in somewhat milder climates, or in moderate winters, or under unusually favorable conditions in the North, still cannot be relied upon to withstand near-zero temperatures unless given adequate protection. Well-known examples of these are the cluster-flowered Narcissi (Paperwhite and Soleil d'Or, and the Poetaz varieties), Anemones, Ranunculus, and Bulbous Irises.

These are hardy, in general, in the latitudes of Philadelphia, Louisville, Oklahoma City, and south, and on the West Coast to Portland and Spokane.

Tender

This group, again, includes those bulbs which will not tolerate hard freezing and can be left in the ground only in warm climates. In chillier sections they must be taken up when early frosts kill back their foliage and stored over winter, or treated as pot plants and taken indoors. Among the tender bulbs are such popular ones as Dahlias, Gladiolus, Cannas, Montbretias, Tigridias, Tuberous-rooted Begonias, Ismenes, and Galtonias (Summer-hyacinths), all of which are stored; and, usually grown as pot plants, Amaryllis, Calla, Amarcrinum, Caladium, Eucharis, and Gloriosa.

SEASON OF BLOOM

There is some bulb which may be had in bloom, outdoors or in, almost any week in the year. Few of us, however, can have any very complete collection of bulbous plants, and hence it becomes important to make sure that those we do procure will give us as wide a spread as possible in time of flowering. We can classify them roughly, so far as blooming season is concerned, into four general groups: spring-, summer-, fall-, and winter-flowering. If a few species or varieties are selected from each of these groups, with a very moderate investment one can enjoy flowers from bulbous plants pretty much the year round.

Spring-flowering

This group is made up chiefly of the "Dutch" bulbs, so called because Holland has been the main source of supply for them. Far from being natives of Holland, they came originally from many parts of the world. The Dutch bulbs include Tulips, Daffodils, Hyacinths, Crocuses, and numerous smaller flowering species—Snowdrops, Grape-hyacinths, Squills, and others.

In addition to these, there are such of our own natives as Trillium,

Jack-in-the-pulpit, Spring Beauty, and Camassia. All of these, and the Dutch bulbs mentioned above, are perfectly hardy.

There are also a few semi-hardy bulbs that will give spring bloom in the Northern states if grown in frames or under specially favorable conditions: Anemones, Ranunculus, Brodiaea, for example.

Summer-flowering

The summer-flowering (June to September) bulbs include two distinct types, some reliably hardy and some that, except in warm climates, must be taken up and wintered over in storage.

Among the former, the hardy Lilies comprise by far the most important single group. They provide, in the various species and hybrids an almost uninterrupted succession of bloom.

In addition to the Lilies, among the hardies are the Hardy Amaryllis (*Lycoris squamigera*), the Hardy Begonia (*B. Evansiana*), the Blackberry-lily (*Belamcanda chinensis*), Lily-turf (Liriope), and a few others that are hardy in milder climates.

The tender bulbs which provide our summer gardens with flowers are numerous and include several species in which the named varieties run into the thousands. Dahlias lead in diversity of form and coloring, with Gladiolus a close second. Popular, too, are Tuberous-rooted Begonias, now grown by the thousand where they used to be grown by the dozen. Others are Cannas, Tigridias, Montbretias, Tuberoses, Caladiums, Zephyranthes, and the less well-known but well worthwhile Ismene (Peruvian-daffodil), *Lycoris radiata,* Galtonia, Acidanthera, and Chlidanthus.

Still another group of summer-flowering bulbs includes several species usually grown in the greenhouse or indoors, but which can be set out in the ground during warm weather, or kept out of doors (or on a porch) in pots or tubs. Typical of these are the dramatic blue Lily-of-the-Nile (*Agapanthus africanus*), the Amazon-lily (*Eucharis grandiflora*), Glory-lily (Gloriosa), Gloxinia, and Amaryllis.

Fall-blooming

For most of our fall-blooming bulbous plants we come back again to the hardy group. Hardy bulbs which bloom in autumn are, incidentally, one of the most useful and most neglected of all groups of plant material.

Among these we have a fine array of Crocus species and varieties—sufficient in themselves to provide a whole garden of color, in a final defiant thumbing-of-the-nose at oncoming winter. And then there are the Crocus-like Colchicums, and *Sternbergia lutea* to add a touch of gold.

Late-planted Gladiolus (you can put them in up to the Fourth of July), Montbretias, and Tigridias will carry on into the fall; and of course the Dahlias, Cannas, and Tuberous-rooted Begonias will keep on flowering until Jack Frost cuts them down.

Winter-blooming

Here again we have two distinct groups—the tender bulbs for house or greenhouse that normally bloom in winter (in the Northern Hemisphere), and the spring-flowering hardy ones that can be forced into winter bloom.

Among the former are such bulbs as Achimenes, Amaryllis, Calla, Clivia, Cyclamen, Gloriosa, Moraea, and Veltheimia. Among the latter are practically all of the spring-flowering hardy bulbs, though with some (Darwin Tulips, for instance) it is necessary to use *early* varieties. Many catalogues indicate which varieties are most suitable for forcing.

HEIGHT

To plan for the most effective use of bulbs of any kind in the garden, one must have a knowledge of their heights. Otherwise very dramatic or very lovely delicate kinds may be almost completely hidden from sight behind taller ones, or lost among more robust-growing companions. Typical examples of such possible misplacement are most of the Tulip and Daffodil species and many of their hybrids.

Tall

Some of the taller kinds—2 feet or over—are a few of the late Tulips, Cannas, Dahlias (except dwarf types), Gladiolus, Galtonia, most of the Lilies, Tuberoses, and the towering Foxtail-lilies (Eremurus), some species of which reach a height of 8 feet or more. All of these should be kept well to the back in border plantings or in mixed landscape groups.

Medium

For the middle border use species and varieties of medium height—12 to 24 inches. Into this group fall most of the garden Tulips and Daffodils, Camassias, Bulbous Irises, the dwarf Lilies, Wood-hyacinth (*Scilla campanulata*), *Fritillaria meleagris*, Jack-in-the-pulpit, and Solomon's-seal, among the hardy ones. Some tender bulbs of medium height are Montbretias, Tigridias, Tuberous-rooted Begonias, Caladiums, Callas, and Moraeas.

Low

Along or near the front of the border, for edgings along paths, in the foreground of naturalized plantings, or by themselves where ground-carpeting masses of color are wanted, and in rock gardens, the various low-growing bulbs find their places. Here there is a wide choice indeed: Crocuses (spring- and autumn-flowering), Colchicums, almost all of the minor Dutch bulbs (Grape-hyacinths, Snowdrops, Snowflakes, Squills, Scillas, and the like), Lily-of-the-valley, and Lily-turf (Liriope). Several of the Tulip and Daffodil species and their hybrids are less than a foot tall—some under 6 inches. Then, too, there are the Erythroniums for shaded places, and the early-blooming Winter-aconite (Eranthis).

So it becomes amply evident that whatever your limitations of space, your local conditions or requirements, you can find a goodly number of bulbous plants ready to accommodate themselves to your needs and to grace your garden with additional beauty.

In the specialized lists of bulbs (beginning on page 321) you will find more complete and detailed information, arranged to help you select just the species and varieties that will best provide the flowers you want for any location or season.

Now let's see how to get the best results from these accommodating bulbs once you have planned to add them to your garden.

CHAPTER *4. What Is a Bulb?*

The amateur gardener, starting out on this great adventure into the world of plant life and the management of growing plants, quite naturally assumes that anything he purchases from a bulb catalogue, or picks out at the dealer's intriguing display of bins and trays in the section of the store devoted to bulbs, will be a bulb.

Like Alice in Wonderland, however, he will not have traveled far into this strange new realm before he discovers that not everything is exactly what at first it seemed to be, and that there are many complications to be unraveled. When he innocently asks his better half, who has been attending garden-club lectures, how deep he should plant the Gladiolus bulbs, or if it is yet warm enough to put the Dahlia bulbs in the ground, he is likely to be informed that these are not bulbs but, in the one case, "corms," in the other, "tuberous roots."

His reaction to this information may be: "I don't give a damn what they are called. All I want is to grow some good flowers."

The point he fails to realize is that to grow good flowers, and particularly to keep on getting good flowers *after the first year,* he must have some knowledge of the growth habits, the life cycle, of the plant that is to produce the good flowers he wishes to grow. It may surprise him to learn, for instance, that the Daffodil bloom which he hopes to display proudly to his friends or perhaps win a blue ribbon at his local flower show begins its career some ten to twelve months before it opens its white or golden petals to "take the winds of March with beauty."

BULBS, CORMS, AND TUBERS

Bulbs, corms, and tubers are alike in one particular. They are all in reality *buds* (or underground roots or stems bearing buds), in a state

TYPES OF BULBS

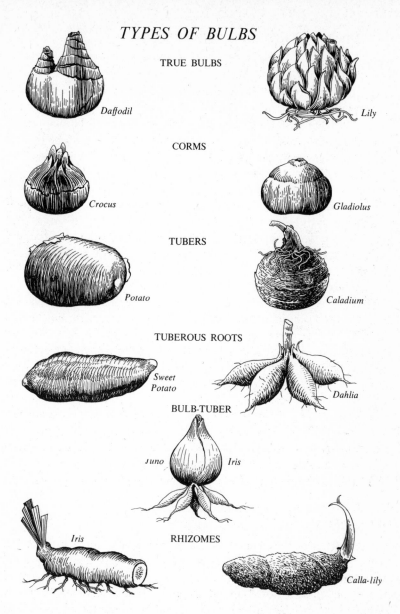

TRUE BULBS

Daffodil

Lily

CORMS

Crocus

Gladiolus

TUBERS

Potato

Caladium

TUBEROUS ROOTS

Sweet
Potato

Dahlia

BULB-TUBER

Juno   Iris

Iris   RHIZOMES

Calla-lily

of dormancy, awaiting, to resume growth, only the right season or the
proper conditions of temperature and moisture. In this respect they
resemble the leaf buds and flower buds on your Forsythia or Lilac
bush. In many other respects they differ from such buds: they are

formed underground; they are self-contained—that is, each is the nucleus of an entire plant, not just a part of a plant; and they are so constructed as to serve as storehouses of food that will support the plant for a considerable period when it renews growth. (Hyacinths grown in pebbles and water, and Colchicums that will bloom even if pinned up on a curtain in the window, are examples of bulbs and corms capable of producing flowers, when growth is renewed, with no additional supply of food.)

Unlike the bud on a shrub or tree, these bulbous, underground buds produce new sets of roots without an intervening stem or trunk that remains a permanent part of the plant's structure. In shrubs and trees the reserve food supply is stored in branches, trunks, canes, and roots; in perennials (which die back to the ground) it is in the crowns and in the roots, which in numerous species are so enlarged or swollen as to resemble bulbs, but still remain only parts of a larger organism.

Without getting into botanical technicalities, it may be explained that the food stored in any underground root, stem, or bud, to be carried over the dormant period as a reserve supply, is first taken up by the feeding roots, carried to the leaves to be elaborated or proc- essed, and then returned to dormant-season storage quarters. In a word, the foliage plays a very vital part in preparing the reserve food supply.

The practical point for the gardener to learn from all this is that the bulb, corm, or tuber cannot develop normally to its full size, or its maximum flower-producing capacity, unless the leaves of the plant are allowed to complete, under favorable conditions, their full growth.

That is lesson number one in the culture of all bulbous plants.

True bulbs

Coming from the general to the more specific application of the word "bulb," we may define a true bulb as being an underground stem with a growing point (or bud) surrounded by fleshy layers of tissue containing a stored-up food supply. These layers may be closely wrapped around the growing point or bud at the center, as is the case with an Onion, a Daffodil, or a Tulip. Or they may be loosely placed, fleshy scales, as in a Lily. All of these are true bulbs.

In the case of all of these, too, the layers or scales are held together at the base by a disk of hardened stem tissue known as the "plate."

When growth is renewed, new roots develop from around the edge of this plate. If you have ever grown Onions, you know how, when the foliage dies down, the roots at the base of the Onion bulb also die off, so that the slightest pull will remove the Onion from the soil. It is then in its dormant state, and if properly "cured" and stored may be kept through the winter. (Onion "sets" are merely very small Onions which, because of late planting and overcrowding, have not attained their normal size. They are, however, true bulbs, just as fully grown specimens are.)

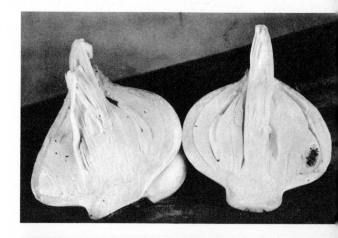

Cross sections of Daffodil bulb show complete embryo flower developed at center. Dark spot (extreme right) is new offset forming.

Conical sections of Tulip bulb, showing thick fleshy tissue. Embryo flower, well developed, apparent at center—right.

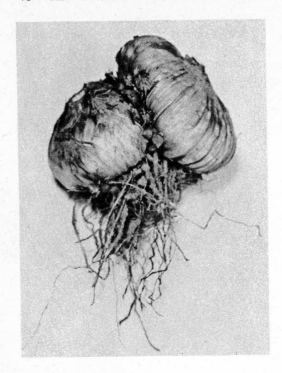

Second-year
Gladiolus corm at
harvesting. Group
of cormels have
developed near
bases of large corms.

Corms

A corm differs from a true bulb in that it is made up of a solid mass of fleshy tissue. Usually incipient buds on the top surface of the corm are visible, indicating where new growth will start. As with true bulbs, there is a distinct bottom or basal plate around the edge of which roots start when growth is renewed. Unlike a true bulb, however, a corm is a temporary storehouse for food and withers and disintegrates as this food is used up. A brand-new corm (sometimes two or more) forms on top of the old one. Gladiolus and Crocuses are typical corms.

Tubers

A tuber, like a corm, is composed of solid tissue but does not have a basal plate: it is really a modified stem. Like corms, also, tubers

*The onset of spring: Daffodils bring the first masses of color;
as they pass, the Tulips take over.*

ABOVE: *Daffodils at GrayRock, naturalized on a terraced slope to provide the most effective display.* BELOW: *Against purplish-gray stones, the brilliant colors of Single Early Tulips bring warmth and cheer to the rock garden.*

have discernible "eyes" or buds that develop into new growth shoots. In some cases they shrivel and disintegrate as the new plant matures. Potatoes, Caladiums, and Elephant's Ears (Colocasia) are typical tubers.

Tuberous roots

These resemble tubers in that they are made up of solid tissue and do not have basal plates. Unlike tubers, however, they are formed of *root* tissue instead of stem tissue; in other words, they are modified roots. The Dahlia, usually called a tuber, is more accurately a tuberous root. In some instances the tuberous root has eyes or buds at intervals over its surface; in others the eyes are limited to the neck of the tuberous root, where it is joined to the old plant stem. The former type can be cut into numerous pieces (each with an eye), all of which will grow—as with the Sweet Potato. On the contrary, a Dahlia root, unless it carries a piece of the old stem bearing an eye, will not sprout at all.

Still another form of tuberous root may be called a bulb-tuber, as it is an unusual combination of a real bulb with short, fat tuberous roots attached to it. The Juno Iris is an example. It is quite different from the more generally known Bulbous Irises—the English and Dutch Irises of the catalogues—which are true bulbs. The long, fleshy roots of Ismene bulbs persist through the dormant period (in the ground or in perfect winter storage) and are important in aiding the new growth. To a less extent, the same is true of many Lilies.

Rhizomes

Forming a sort of halfway link between tubers and perennial roots are rhizomes. A rhizome consists of solid tissue (stem tissue), but instead of being rounded in shape, like a tuber, it is elongated and often branching. In some cases—as with Bearded Irises and Rex Begonias—rhizomes grow just in or along the surface of the soil; in others—Calla-lily and Solomon's-seal, for instance—the rhizomes form underground. Another characteristic of most rhizomes is that the roots develop along the lower surface, while the leaves and flower stalks rise from buds (eyes) on the upper surface.

Rhizomes of Calla-lilies during dormant period after foliage has matured and died. Flower buds will develop with new leaf growth.

So you see that the term "bulb" as employed in the trade, and even by many gardeners, really covers several groups of plants, many of which are not, accurately speaking, bulbs at all. They do have some common characteristics. The most important of these, from the gardener's viewpoint, is this: in their resting or dormant period they become self-contained bits of suspended plant life that will survive for weeks or months without benefit of soil or moisture. They thus lend themselves particularly well to being transported long distances or stored for long periods with little attention.

When—after the proper resting period—soil, moisture, and a congenial temperature are provided, they are ready and eager to take up active growth again and reward the gardener's efforts with beauty in a thousand forms and many colors, and at any season of the year he may elect to have them serve him.

But just as there are *structural* differences among true bulbs, corms, tubers, tuberous roots, and rhizomes, there are also differences in the *way they grow* during their life cycles. And so our next step, in progressing toward the goal of achieving success with bulbs, is to get some understanding of their habits, and particularly of *what goes on underground* during the periods when ordinarily we give them no thought or attention. And that is quite as fascinating, if not as spectacular, as what goes on above it.

CHAPTER *5. How Bulbs Grow*

Plants adapt themselves to the conditions under which they have to grow. This is not to say that if you set out in a hot dry place a species that ordinarily grows in a bog it will at once change its structure and its method of life to conform to its new environment. On the contrary, it will probably perish quickly.

But by gradual evolution during hundreds or thousands of years, each species has developed a structure and a time for growing and for resting which fit into the conditions of soil, moisture, temperature, and seasonal changes that constitute its natural habitat.

The changes which the plant undergoes from the time it starts into active growth until it begins again the following year are known as its *growth cycle*. The growth cycle includes what happens underground and even the changes which may take place within the plant itself, as well as those obvious changes which you see taking place before your eyes aboveground.

These changes are far more extensive than the gardener is likely to suspect. When we carelessly speak of a plant's being in a "dormant" state, we usually mean that it is not making any visible growth aboveground. But its roots may be in active growth, and most important changes may be going on in its physical structure and in its chemical composition. The most unobservant gardener cannot fail to notice, for instance, the difference between a branch of a flowering shrub in late fall, when it enters its so-called dormant period, and the same branch, still "dormant," just before its buds break into leaf or flower. If he is a bit more observant, he will know that the same spray, cut and placed in water indoors, in December will remain dormant; while cut in March or April it will—often within a matter of days—burst into bloom. What has happened during the interim? The growth cycle, in nature's secret, potent ways, has continued at work.

Stages in development of a Hyacinth grown in plain water. Embryo flower spike, already formed within bulb, draws its sustenance from the bulb.

Placing a bulb in the ground, you think of it as a dormant thing which can be forgotten until next spring, when—according to the habit of bulbs—it will start to grow. What really happens is something quite different. When planted, it immediately sends out roots and, somewhat later, a stem or stems from the top. In most cases the top growth will remain safely underground until spring, although it may have pushed up several inches to a point just below the surface of the soil. Or, as with the familiar Madonna Lily, it may form a rosette of foliage in the fall that persists through the winter.

Clump of Daffodils, dug several weeks after planting, shows vigorous root development while top growth remains practically inhibited.

Not all bulbs, however, follow this pattern. Colchicums and autumn-flowering Crocuses will often bloom without having been placed in the ground at all, even in a paper bag on a shelf. And if they are then planted they will produce roots, but sometimes no foliage until the following spring.

These infinitely varied growth patterns, could we trace them all back, would be found connected with the conditions existing where the various genera and species developed. In sections where summer months are hot and rainless, making vegetative growth impossible, they have come to adapt themselves to such conditions—like Fenestrarias, the "windowed" plants of South Africa, which have learned to live largely underground, with merely a peephole to admit a sufficient amount of sunlight to keep them alive. In our own gardens, where we bring together bulbous plants from all over the world, we cannot expect to reproduce all the variations of soil, climate, and treatment which best suit the individual genera and species. But the more we do know about their normal environments and growth habits, the closer we can approximate their maintenance in the style of living to which they are accustomed. Fortunately for us, most of them are willing to co-operate and strive to do their best under such conditions as we can provide.

METHODS OF REPRODUCTION

The annual growth cycle of a plant that lives for more than a year is but part of its longer life cycle from birth to death. This brings us

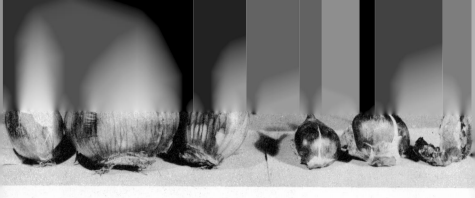

LEFT: *Original bulb of Daffodil has produced two offsets or "splits" which readily separate from it.* RIGHT: *Original Tulip bulb has disintegrated, leaving merely a husk; the three bulbs are new growths.*

to the matter of the method of *reproduction* employed—of how it perpetuates itself. Bulbs, corms, tubers, tuberous roots, and rhizomes, under favorable conditions, can go on producing new plants asexually —that is, without the production of seeds. Some bulbs do this by "division"—that is, the original bulb splits up, forming small new bulbs which in time separate themselves from it. (The Daffodil and the Madonna Lily are familiar examples of this type.) Others increase by "multiplication"—the old bulb or corm disintegrates, leaving in its place several new ones of various sizes. Tulips, Crocuses, and Gladiolus are examples of this type.

In the case of some tubers, the old tuber disappears, leaving a cluster of new tubers in its place. This happens with stem tubers and root tubers—the white Potato and the Dahlia are examples. In others, such as the Tuberous Begonia and the Gloxinia, the original tuber persists, producing additional eyes but not splitting up to form separate new plants.

Rhizomes, during the annual growth cycle, may branch, each branch producing a new eye or growing tip; or they may continue as single horizontal fleshy roots, each year's new growth starting at the tip of the old rhizome. Bearded Iris and False Solomon's-seal are examples of these two types.

Bulbils and cormels

In addition to what we may term direct propagation from the bulbs, corms, or tubers planted in our gardens, there are other, indirect means by which the plants propagate themselves. The first of

Very small Tulip bulbs (left) produce merely one big leaf, no flower. The following season they will bloom and begin to form new bulbs, as at right.

Clump of Daffodils toward end of season's growth. Foliage still attached, but at this stage they can be lifted, separated, and replanted.

these, of course, is the production of seeds: but with that, for the moment, we are not concerned.

Some of the Lilies, in addition to forming offsets underground, also develop secondary aerial bulbs, called *bulbils,* in the axils of the leaves. These sprout readily and, when grown on for a year or more, produce flowering-size bulbs. The Tiger Lily and certain of its offspring, like the Mid-Century Hybrids, are examples of this type of reproduction. Bulbils are occasionally formed also by Tulips.

Cormels are miniature corms, formed at the ends of fleshy stems sent out from the base of a corm. They are pointed, hard-shelled, and quite different from the new corms which form at the surface of the old one. Like bulbils, they must be grown on for at least one season before being capable of producing a flower. The Gladiolus is a typical cormel bearer.

IMPORTANCE OF FOLIAGE DEVELOPMENT

Attention has already been called to the fact that many of the true bulbs, especially those flowering in early spring, contain completely formed flowers when they are planted in autumn. (See page 47.) The food supply to support the amazingly rapid growth and production of flowers in the spring is drawn largely from the bulb. The same is true of early-flowering tubers and corms.

With such plants as these, the growth cycle is not drawing to a close when they reach the flowering stage. It is, in fact, just getting into its stride. The production of the following spring's bloom depends entirely on what happens *after* this spring's flowering.

The foliage constitutes the factory in which is processed the food to be stored up in the growing bulbs, corms, or tubers. If the foliage is not allowed to mature, or if it is starved for lack of adequate nourishment in the soil, the growing bulb underground is bound to suffer as a result.

GROWTH CYCLES

Growth cycles, in diagrammatic form, of a few typical bulbs, corms, and tubers are presented on the following pages: 135, 161, 171, 197, 217, 227, 240, 251, 255, and 276.

CHAPTER 6. *Cultural Requirements*

The horticultural varieties of bulbs, many of which are of such mixed ancestry that no one knows just what species and sub-species went into their making, are of course better adapted to uniform garden conditions than are the original wild kinds from which they have descended. Most of the Tulip species, for instance, will thrive in soil so dry that their giant-flowered descendants would quickly perish if planted alongside them.

But bulbs are, on the whole, extremely adaptable to growing under widely diversified conditions. Tulips, Daffodils, Hyacinths, Crocuses, and a host of others gladden the hearts of winter-weary gardeners from Maine to British Columbia, and from far above the Canadian border down to our southernmost states, where temperatures do not go low enough to provide the required period in cold ground during which root systems are developed before the tops make growth. Dahlias, originally from Mexico, and Gladiolus, hailing from South Africa, thrive side by side over the same areas.

Notwithstanding their general tolerance of growth conditions, however, they do have individual preferences and also vary greatly in their tolerance of conditions other than those under which they will do their best. The wise bulb gardener will learn to depend, for his chief garden effects and for flowers for cutting, upon the species and varieties which really like the conditions he can provide. At the same time he will find it worth while to grow some of the others, both for their intrinsic beauty and for the thrill which any gardener feels when he succeeds in bringing through a difficult subject.

Soil

So far as the physical character of soil is concerned, the majority of bulbs are less particular than many other plants. With few exceptions they do well in fairly heavy clay, loam, or sandy loam, provided the proper nutrients are available. The preferred soil for most bulbs, however, is a medium sandy loam, which does not remain wet and sticky after heavy rains, nor, on the other hand, dry out too quickly. The relatively small areas usually required for bulb plantings —except where they are naturalized on a relatively large scale— can readily be brought to a condition that will result in good normal growth.

The basic treatment for heavy clay soils is the addition of sifted cinders, such as will pass through a ¾-inch screen. (Soft-coal ashes, which form a soggy mass when wet, only aggravate the condition instead of improving it.) Very coarse sand or fine gravel serves the same purpose as the cinders. A layer of at least 2 inches, and preferably more, should be dug in. A more thorough job of mixing will result if half the amount is spread and dug well under and the balance then spread and cultivated in.

The chief trouble with light sandy soils is that they dry out too quickly. The basic treatment here is to add well-rotted stable manure or compost; or, if these are not available, peatmoss. All of these are moisture holders and help greatly in maintaining an adequate supply of water in sandy soils. Any of them can be applied in a layer 3 inches or so deep and forked in to a depth of 8 inches. These humus-forming materials are also valuable in improving clay soils, making them more open.

The physical condition of both clay soils and sandy soils is bettered by the addition of ground raw limestone (agricultural lime). The only condition, in our experience, where lime will not prove beneficial is on alkaline soil (with a pH of 7 or over) in which plants that prefer such a soil are to be grown.

Drainage

Tolerant or indifferent though most bulbs may be as to soils, when it comes to *drainage* it is quite a different story. With very few exceptions they simply refuse to do well in soils that retain a water level close to the surface. Water that the roots can reach is all right—as witness the bulb fields of Holland with their drainage ditches maintaining a water level at a fixed depth below the surface; or the more familiar example of a Hyacinth growing in a vase filled with water just *up to* the base of the bulb, or Paperwhite Narcissi in pebbles that hold them just above the water in the bottom.

Any place in your garden that remains wet for long periods after rain, or becomes more or less of a bog during winter and early spring, is no place for the general run of bulbs.

The task of remedying poor drainage conditions is often more difficult than that of improving the soil. If possible, it is better to side-step it by planting bulbs only where the drainage is naturally good. If this cannot be done, you may as well face the fact that you have a difficult job on your hands—and then do it thoroughly to start with. Such makeshift efforts as putting a handful of sand under each bulb, as is frequently advised, will accomplish little or nothing. Even excavating the soil to a depth of 2 or 3 feet and putting in a layer of small stones or some similiar drainage material may prove to be wasted effort, for unless the water which collects in the space thus provided can drain off to some lower level, nothing is gained.

The first step in correcting poor drainage is to discover its cause. It may be due to a layer of hardpan—compacted clay subsoil—through which surplus water from the topsoil above cannot percolate. Often it is possible to break up such a hardpan subsoil with a pick, thus permitting the water to pass down to more open soil below. The most certain method of correcting poor drainage, however, is to install drain tile as described in the following chapter.

Sun and shade

Most of the spring-flowering bulbs like full sun—the more the better. This does not, however, restrict their planting to areas that are in full sun the year round. As they bloom before deciduous trees and shrubs have donned summer raiment, they get plenty of sun at this season of the year even in locations where there may be considerable shade later on. This is not the case under evergreens or to the north or northwest of hedges, buildings, or fences. The *foliage* will continue to develop, after the flowering season, with little direct sunshine; but shade so dense that it results in thin, weak foliage is of course to be avoided.

The gardener should learn that there is a great difference, so far as plant growth is concerned, between "high" shade and low shade. The foliage of many types of plants will function normally without

Exposure is an important factor in determining time of bloom. Here Tulips from the same bag, planted the same day, are in full flower along south wall of house, while along west wall they are still in bud.

direct sunshine if the *light* is sufficiently strong. To get an idea of the difference there is between high shade—from branches well above the ground—and low shade, under shrubs or low-growing tree branches, make a few tests with your camera light meter. You will find the light reading from two to five times as high under the former condition as under the latter. The growth of the plants themselves, however, is the surest test. If the foliage remains vigorous and green until it matures and the second year's flowering seems all right, you can be pretty sure you have nothing to worry about.

Another advantage of high shade is the much better air circulation near the surface of the ground. Bulbs, in common with most other plants, like to breathe freely. A confined, dead atmosphere not only makes them unhappy, but also creates conditions favorable for many diseases, especially blights and mildews.

A list of bulbs which prefer shade, or at least tolerate it, will be found on page 327.

Protection

In the culture of many bulbous plants, protection in one form or another is very important. It may be needed for purely mechanical reasons, to keep flower stems from being broken or knocked down by high winds, and to prevent low-growing flowers from being disfigured by spattering mud.

Or protection against too low temperatures may be required for kinds that, in any particular locality, are on the questionably hardy list. In the latter case it will enable you to grow a number of very desirable subjects that otherwise would be too uncertain to be worth while.

Fortunately the early spring-flowering bulbs leave the gardener little to worry about so far as the frost-hardiness of buds and flowers is concerned. We have had Snowdrops, blooming in late January, come out as cheerful and smiling as ever after nearly a month's incarceration in frozen snow and ice. Even Daffodils in bloom have reappeared, uninjured, from under a fleecy blanket of April snow.

Mechanical injury from driving March and April storms is another matter. Protection by low evergreens or shrubs, a hedge or a fence, will frequently save tall Tulips or Daffodils from being damaged when those in the open take a beating or are completely wrecked.

Ground covers of growing plants and mulches of various sorts provide a degree of protection against low temperatures for bulbs that are on the danger line as to winter-hardiness. They also minimize the alternate freezing and thawing of the surface soil, which in bare ground will sometimes damage newly planted small bulbs that are not covered deep and may be literally heaved out onto the surface. The greatest value of ground covers and mulches, however, is that they provide a

Protection from moles, weeds, and drought. Wire screening (at back of bed), extending 8 inches into soil, forms underground barrier. Mulch of buckwheat hulls keeps down weeds, conserves moisture.

background against which the little bulbs show up to greater advantage and prevent the mud-spattering from heavy rains that so frequently disfigures them.

The Lilies—a most important group among bulbous plants—appreciate protection of another sort: they benefit by having a not too dense carpet of creeping or low-growing plants about their feet through which the flowering stalks can push up to the light and air. Such ground covers—or, in place of them, a suitable permanent mulch—will keep the soil about the roots several degrees cooler than it would be if fully exposed to the sun.

Summing up the requirements of hardy bulbous plants, then, it may be said in general that:

They are not particular as to soil, provided it is not so heavy and sticky as to interfere physically with growth.

They do want quick and thorough drainage, with a water level below the bulbs in the soil.

They do like, especially until they are through flowering, full sun or the ample light provided by high shade.

They do not require winter protection from low temperatures, but are greatly benefited by protection from spring winds, driving rains, and spattering mud.

CHAPTER *7. Planting*

In the entire circle of the year's garden operations there is none more pleasurable than that of bulb planting. Here indeed are happily met the time, the place, and the undertaking. And added to these is the assurance that one's efforts will end in success. In no other type of gardening can the operator be quite so certain that the results of his work will come up to his expectations.

On one of those crisp, sunny Indian-summer days, after early frosts have cut down all but the hardiest of annuals and left the perennials sere and brown, you gather up your bags of bulbs—each with its previously prepared label—your strongest trowel, and favorite dibber. Then begins the happy ritual of getting into the ground these little brown and tan bombs, of various shapes and sizes, which, with the coming of spring, each in accord with its own built-in timing device, will explode into a pattern of heart-lifting beauty.

It is to be assumed that your ground has been prepared well in advance and your bulbs ordered sufficiently early so that they are now on hand. Then you can pick your weather for planting and do as much or as little of it at one time as you prefer. The planting period extends from mid-August until the ground freezes too hard to be dug. This will vary, in normal seasons, from mid-October in the general latitude of New York, Cleveland, or Kansas City to two or three weeks earlier farther north, and several weeks later farther south and along the Pacific coast.

Some bulbs—such as the Madonna Lily, autumn-flowering Crocus, Colchicum, and Winter-aconite—are available considerably in advance of the general run of Tulips, Daffodils, and small-flowered spring bulbs. With few exceptions—Tulips being the most important one—it is best, as a general rule, to get the bulbs into the ground as soon as possible after receiving them.

In any event, all bulbs, corms, or tubers should be opened immediately upon receipt and carefully examined. If complaints are to be made, now is the time to make them. Bulbs purchased from a reputable dealer, at a fair price, seldom give any cause for dissatisfaction. If they cannot be planted for a week or longer, keep the bags containing them in flats or on a shelf in a cool, well-ventilated place where the air is not dried out by artificial heat. If the only storage place available is very dry, keep the bags covered with moist peatmoss or wet newspapers. *Any condition causing the bulbs to shrivel will injure them.* Any cut or bruised bulbs should be immediately dusted with sulphur, Arasan, or some similar fungicide. Rats, mice, and squirrels are extremely fond of most bulbs. (Daffodils are an exception to this rule.) Protection from rodents is necessary, therefore, when bulbs are stored for even a short period.

START WITH GOOD BULBS

Before discussing the actual planting of the bulbs, let us take a moment to consider the question of the *quality*. What constitutes a good bulb, and how is it to be distinguished from a poor one?

Of course there *are* such things as bulb bargains, just as there are sometimes bargains in most of the other things one buys. But "bargain bulbs" are something else again, and the gardener will do well to mark the distinction clearly.

Genuine bargains in bulbs may be had by taking advantage of preseason offers from reliable· dealers. The logical reason for such bargains is that it actually costs the dealer less to handle your order. Advance orders help him to determine accurately what quantities of bulbs to buy, and sizable orders can be packed by the grower before shipping, thus saving the dealer the expense of rehandling them. And one can buy small-sized bulbs (but large enough to bloom) at lower prices than top-sized ones. But usually these are available only in mixtures and will not produce top-size flowers the first season.

Another opportunity to get good bulbs at a bargain sometimes comes late in the season, when reliable dealers find themselves with surpluses to dispose of. Such bulbs may or may not be in first-class condition—but the buyer can pretty well determine that for himself by tests to be described later on.

ABOVE: *Grape-hyacinths, among the easiest of all bulbs to force, provide a note of bluebird blue in the winter garden indoors.* BELOW: *Unsurpassed in fragrance indoors is the deep orange Tulip General De Wet.*

Indicative of the great range in size and form among Daffodils are the Giant Trumpet Golden Harvest and the dainty species, N. triandrus albus

Irena Baranova, a well-proportioned Daffodil in the Large Cup class.

Bargain bulbs—the kind offered at absurdly low prices in extravagant newspaper and radio advertising during the height of the planting season—are an entirely different commodity.

Not all bulb bargain hunters are inexperienced. I have known gardeners who would not for a minute consider 15- or 25-cent Rose plants, but to whom 100 Tulip bulbs for less than $2.00 (with other bulbs thrown in as a premium for cash with order) seemed to be an irresistible bait.

What makes a good bulb?

The quality—and the value—of a bulb does not depend upon size alone. There are cases in which size is a controlling factor in what you will get for your money, but these are exceptions to the general rule. Assuming that a bulb of a given species or variety is of a size capable of producing normal flowers, the other factors affecting its "goodness" are:

Firmness: The layers of tissue or the scales, if it is a true bulb (such as a Tulip, Daffodil, or Lily), or the flesh, if it is a tuber, corm, or rhizome (such as a Dahlia, Crocus, or Calla), should be plump and fairly hard. In the case of true bulbs, the layers or scales should be firmly adpressed, so that there is little or no feeling of squashiness or looseness when it is compressed in the hand.

Weight: Most good bulbs present a distinct effect of being fairly heavy. This of course goes along with firmness, but even bulbs (of the same kind, of course) that feel equally firm may vary considerably in weight.

Condition: The skin or coating (in the case of Tulips, Hyacinths, and others) should be smooth, bright, and free from mechanical injuries. Some varieties of Tulips shed their coats readily, and if the flesh beneath is not badly bruised, no injury may result; but as a rule badly skinned bulbs have been carelessly handled and will show corky spots or even fungus growth on the scales. Such are to be avoided.

With most bulbs, the base or basal plate (the corky layer or disk at the base, which holds the layers or scales together) is most likely to show injury from disease—such as the basal rot of Daffodils. Any indication of trouble here means that the bulb may rot or disintegrate after it is planted. Mechanical injuries (cuts or bruises) will usually heal if dusted with flowers of sulphur, Arasan, or Spergon.

The quality of any bulb depends, first, upon how it was grown; secondly, upon how it is handled after harvesting. Assuming good, true-to-name stocks to start with, careful culture and a reasonably favorable season will produce good bulbs. But after they are once removed from the ground, almost anything can happen. Improper or careless curing may result in soft or even diseased bulbs. Overheating in transit, as in the hold of a vessel, or poor storage facilities may blast the embryo flower, so that the bulb, while it will grow, fails to produce a bloom the first season after planting.

Then there is the matter of grading. Imported bulbs of most species are graded on a basis of centimeters (cm.) in circumference. In catalogues they are often listed as "top size"—a rather loosely applied term. Really top-size Tulips, for instance, are 11 to 12 cm. for some types and varieties and 12 cm. or over for others. Extra-size bulbs are larger than top or first size. As a rule, it is best to know the centimeter size if one is ordering by mail. Species and species hybrids of many bulbs—Tulips and Daffodils in particular—are not graded by circumference because the normal bulb sizes vary so greatly that such grading would mean little.

Bulbs of many kinds will flower satisfactorily even though smaller than extra, top, or first size. Sometimes these are offered as "bedding" size. With Hyacinths, for instance, the largest bulbs (18 cm. and over) are less desirable for garden planting than the "miniatures" (14 to 15 cm.) and the bedding (15 to 16 cm.). The very large bulbs are used for show purposes (usually forced) and produce very tall, dense spikes that under garden conditions are readily broken by wind or rain and are much less graceful than the more slender and more open spikes of the same varieties from smaller bulbs. (The term "Miniature Hyacinths" is a misleading one, for they are not a miniature type at all but merely the same varieties in smaller bulbs.)

The proper handling, curing, packing, and transporting of bulbs constitute a large part of the cost of getting them into the hands of the gardener in first-class condition. This should be kept in mind by the purchaser when he is making a comparison of price.

Bargains? Beware!

Bulbs that are offered for sale at far below the average prices quoted in the catalogues of reliable seedsmen and bulb dealers should

ABOVE: *When you buy bulbs, consider quality. Here are good Tulip bulbs (left) compared to "bargain" bulbs costing exactly the same.* RIGHT: *The result: one puny flower from the 100 "bargain" bulbs; an armful from the top-size ones.* BELOW: *And the harvest: from the top-sized bulbs, more than twice as many as were planted; from the bargain bulbs, fewer than were planted—and all runts.*

put the purchaser on guard. If he can actually see and handle the bulbs, he can judge for himself so far as size and condition are concerned. With many kinds, such as Tulips, Daffodils, Hyacinths, and Crocuses, he can even see if they will flower. A perpendicular cut through the center of the bulb will reveal the embryo flower, completely formed. If it is blackened, dried up, or lacking, he knows that, although the bulb may grow, he can get no bloom from it the first year. (See illustration, page 47.)

But if the bulbs are to be purchased by mail, sight unseen, that is a horse of another color—and usually a very dark one. Thousands of bulbs, described as "flowering size" but so small or so poor that they will not produce normal flowers the *first* season after planting, are annually sold.

An old Chinese proverb says that a picture is more convincing than a thousand words. The photographs show the results obtained from one of these bulb bargains (Tulips) and a much smaller number of mixed Tulips at standard prices, costing exactly the same, obtained from a reliable seed house.

After being weighed and photographed, the bulbs were planted adjacent to each other and given the same care and treatment. The bargain lot produced exactly one flower, weak-stemmed and undersized. After the foliage died down, the bulbs of both lots were carefully harvested and again weighed and photographed. The results show plainly which lot could be counted upon to make the better showing the *second* season. These pictures speak for themselves. Look at them carefully and then decide for yourself how much of a bargain the too cheap "bulb bargain" really is.

PROVIDING PERFECT DRAINAGE

In discussing the cultural requirements of bulbs, we stressed the fact that, with very few exceptions, one of the most important is thorough drainage.

If the soil where you are to plant lacks good natural drainage, it can be improved in this respect without too great expense or labor. Such improvement is thoroughly worth while, for once done it will be permanent, enabling you to get better results for years to come.

If your soil is heavy and wet, but sloping, a thorough breaking up

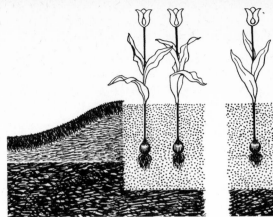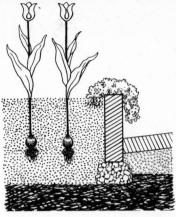

Two methods of making a raised bed on poorly drained soil: left, with turf; right, with edging of boards, brick, blocks, or stones.

of the subsoil will usually do the trick. This involves throwing out the soil from the area to be planted, down to the hard, impervious subsoil—generally not more than 1 to 2 feet below the surface—and then thoroughly breaking this up with a pickax. As the removed soil is returned to its place, sifted cinders (from which both large clinkers and soft fine ash have been removed) can be added to the bottom layer to make it more porous. Stable manure or other rough humus material has the same effect, but the results are less permanent.

If the only space available for planting bulbs lies low and cannot be sufficiently well drained by the method suggested above, two other courses are open. The first is to raise a bed or border 6 to 12 inches above the general soil level, the sides being held in place by stones, sod, bricks, or thin cement blocks. Stones are preferable, as they make a more natural setting for the flowers in the bed. A grass bank requires frequent cutting, and boards or cement blocks are unsightly even when camouflaged with edging plants that trail down over them.

The second method is to install drainage tile. A single line of 4-inch agricultural tile placed 18 to 24 inches below the surface will drain an area 10 to 20 feet wide if the soil above the tile is fairly porous. The drain tiles (available at any building-supply house) are laid end to end with open joints. The drainage ditch is dug with a slope, from the highest point to the exit from which the water will run off, with a pitch of 6 inches or more to 100 feet. A layer of sand, gravel, or cinders along the bottom of the trench makes it easier to lay the tile on a uniformly even slope. Strips of tar paper or of old burlap bags placed over the joints prevent soil from silting into the tile after the trench is filled in. Test the system before refilling to make certain that everything is working properly. If there is no low spot to which the water from the tile can drain off, it may be necessary to dig a dry well—merely a wide, deep hole filled with stones, with a layer of soil over the surface—into which it can flow.

It is not often that any of these measures for improving drainage will have to be resorted to. They have been given emphasis because, in the growing of bulbs, inadequate drainage, where it is encountered, may be the one obstacle preventing success.

SOIL PREPARATION

Preparation of the soil for growing bulbs differs little from that of preparing it for vegetables, Roses, or perennials. The soil should be in good mechanical condition, so that it will readily admit water and air and be well supplied with such nutrients (plant foods) as are needed to support vigorous growth.

There are, however, two respects in which the ordinary procedure of preparing soil for planting may have to be departed from.

The first of these is in the use of stable manure. Unless it is so thoroughly decomposed as to have become humus, *stable manure should never be used where it will come into contact with dormant bulbs, tubers, or corms in the soil.* Also, stable manure should not be used as a mulch over any bulbous plants subject to botrytis or fungus diseases. This applies particularly to Tulips and to Lilies, the two groups most frequently injured seriously by botrytis.

The second is the possibility of having the soil too rich. Most horticultural varieties of bulbs—types or clones which gardeners have developed through the years—accept a rich diet or may even insist upon it. The familiar Giant May-flowering Tulips are an example; to produce solid top-size bulbs from year to year, they must be grown in heavily fertilized soil. Many of the natural species, however, do better with a moderate or even a rather lean diet. Overfed, they may be injured and in any event are not improved, for their charm lies largely in their delicately refined proportions.

With these two warnings in mind, we may proceed to the preparation of the soil for planting.

Unless it is already in good tilth—friable and well supplied with humus and plant food from previous working—digging it over twice will prove the best way to get it into shape.

Mark out the area to be prepared, and then clean off the surface, removing weeds or other small growth. If it is in sod, skim off the surface, an inch or so deep, leaving bare ground, saving the turfs to go into your compost heap—or to surface the sides of the bed, if it is to be a raised one, as illustrated on page 69.

Then with spade or fork—some gardeners prefer the former implement and some the latter—dig the bed over to a depth of 8 inches or more. To do a good job, remove all soil from a strip 12 inches wide across one end of the bed, leaving an open trench. Turn the next strip over into this, inverting it, breaking up lumps, and throwing stones and roots to the surface. This will leave a second open trench into which the next strip can be turned. This procedure is continued to the end of the plot or border being prepared, leaving an open trench at that end. Next stones and roots are removed and the surface roughly leveled. A prong hoe is better than a rake for this job, as it will catch any debris down to 3 inches or more below the surface and is more convenient for breaking up any remaining clods of soil.

After this first digging, any manures, humus materials, or fertilizers to be used are spread on the surface. The bed is then dug over again, in the reverse direction, but to the same depth. This mixes the added materials thoroughly through the soil and *gets them down deep,* where the bulb roots will be searching for food. This second digging will go quickly and leave the soil loose and mellow, so that the work of planting will be a pleasant task, accomplished in a small part of the time it would take in hard, ill-prepared ground.

Humus and fertilizers

In addition to having the soil in good mechanical condition for planting, we need of course to provide the ingredients—plant foods and plant-food activators—that will enable them to make vigorous growth.

Humus: There are very few soils, either clay, loam, or sandy, which are not materially improved by the addition of a large amount of humus or of humus-forming materials. Real compost—not soggy, half-rotted leaves and grass clippings—is ideal, but seldom is the compost heap sufficiently large to supply the quantity needed. Well-rotted cow manure is even better, but that, in most sections, is difficult to procure. Commercially prepared humus is excellent but not always available at a reasonable price. (Not all so-called humus is good; much of the black-as-your-hat soil that is peddled locally from trucks is of little value.) The material most widely available and most uniform in quality is horticultural-grade peatmoss. This we have used for years in the preparation of bulb beds and have yet to find anything better. The ordinary application is a layer 2 to 3 inches thick, spread evenly over the surface. Rotted cow manure can go on at the same rate, commercial humus somewhat less.

Lime: Like humus, lime is not considered a direct plant-food element, but—in common with humus—its addition to the soil usually results in more vigorous growth. This is due both to improvement of the mechanical condition of the soil, and to making more available for use by plants the chemicals already in the soil. *The use of lime is generally beneficial even when it is not required to make the soil less acid.* If a soil test shows reaction of less than pH 6, it should be used to reduce the acidity, except for bulbs which require a definitely acid soil.

The form of lime generally employed, and the one which should be used when applied at the same time with fertilizers or just before bulbs are to be planted, is raw ground limestone, commonly known as agricultural lime. The rate of application is 5 to 15 pounds per 100 square feet. If a large area is to be covered, it is well to use a mechanical spreader such as those available for sowing lawn grass.

Fertilizers: Bulbs, like other types of plants, require the three essential elements—nitrogen, phosphoric acid, and potash—and the minor or trace elements which, in most soils, are available in sufficient amounts.

In general, we prefer to use organic fertilizers rather than chemical ones for bulbous plants, especially when preparing the soil for planting. Commercial growers use chemical fertilizers freely; there is a considerable saving in cost, and they are better equipped to get even and thorough distribution throughout the soil. In commercial work, too, applications are likely to be made much longer in advance of planting.

Nitrogen, for bulbs planted in the fall, is relatively less important than for most bulbs or plants set out in spring. In soil which has been under culture during the summer—as in the hardy border—there is likely to be a sufficient residue. In newly prepared ground, manure (if it has been applied) or one of the commercial dehydrated manures— such as Driconure or Bovung—will provide all that is needed. There is also a small amount of nitrogen (about 2 to 4 per cent) in bone meal, used principally to supply phosphoric acid. Nitrate of soda, dried blood, and other quick-acting high-nitrogen fertilizers, excellent for many purposes, not only are unnecessary but will be largely wasted if used in fall bulb plating. Apply dehydrated manures at the rate of a minimum of 10 pounds per 100 square feet, and two or three times that amount on poor soil.

Phosphoric acid is supplied by bone meal, which can be had in several forms. That usually sold by seed houses is steamed. The raw ground bone contains more nitrogen but is slower-acting. We use the two mixed half and half, 5 pounds per 100 square feet. Another source of phosphoric acid is superphosphate, which may be had in grades containing either 22 or 50 per cent phosphoric acid. Three to 4 pounds of the former per 100 square feet, or half that amount of the latter, is a moderate application.

Potassium is of particular value in providing strong stems and good flowers and also in developing firm, heavy bulbs for the following year. Unleached wood ashes and tobacco stems supply potash in moderate amounts—(3 or 4 per cent) and can be used generously— up to 15 pounds or more per 100 square feet. As ashes are not always available, the usual source of potassium is muriate of potash. This contains 50 per cent of potassium and is applied sparingly—½ to 1 pound per 100 square feet. In most soils there will be sufficient potash present for the initial root growth, and this element can be provided in the general fertilizer applied the following spring.

Our own method of fertilizing new beds before planting is to apply (after the first rough digging) the lime, bone meal, and wood ashes, finishing up with the dried manure, and then forking these all in deep. If the soil is dry and planting is not to be done at once, the bed is given a thorough watering to settle it and to start the breaking down of the fertilizer materials in the soil. If chemical fertilizers are employed, soil preparation and watering well in advance of planting are even more important.

In preparing spots for group plantings, much the same procedure is followed, but on a smaller scale. Where bulbs are to be naturalized

Planting in groups: soil is dug out to proper depth, bulbs placed irregularly, hole filled, area marked off, labels put in place.

in very poor soil, it may be advisable to loosen it by thrusting in a fork and working it back and forth to open up small holes. The plant foods are then spread on the surface and washed in as thoroughly as possible with a heavy watering.

PLANTING

There are two methods of actually getting the bulbs into the ground. The first is to remove the soil to the desired depth, set the bulbs in place on the exposed surface, and then replace the soil.

The second is to make a hole in the soil, with trowel or dibber, for each individual bulb, placing it at the bottom and filling in soil over it.

The former method, which was in vogue when Tulips and Hyacinths found favor in formal landscaping for the creation of "design" gardens laid out in geometrical patterns of contrasting colors, is now seldom practiced. In making designs it was important that all the bulbs should be spaced at accurately regular distances and flower at the same height and at the same time. Excavation planting (see photograph, page 75) assured such results. In the more informal landscaping of today, in mixed borders, decorative groups, and naturalized plantings, such uniformity is not only unnecessary but distinctly undesirable.

Whether excavation or surface planting is to be done, each lot of bulbs should be laid out before the actual planting is begun. For a formal bed, it is helpful to prepare a planting stick, with notches or

Planting in formal or display beds: soil is removed, bottom leveled and marked off, and bulbs placed in exact design.

Planting from surface: soil is prepared to proper depth, bulbs spaced as wanted. Bulbs are planted individually, beginning with those nearest the operator.

pegs the desired distances apart for accurate spacing. For an informal planting, the spacing may be estimated, and results are more pleasing if any regular pattern is avoided. In naturalizing, best effects are achieved by scattering the bulbs more or less at random, somewhat closer together at the center, or at one side of the colony, and thinning out toward the edge, as though they had spread from an original small group. Seeking to avoid any possibility of getting a regular pattern, some gardeners even throw the bulbs back over one shoulder and plant them where they fall.

Depth

The depth to which the bulbs are covered varies with species and varieties, with the soil, with the exposure, and to some extent with how one wants them to behave. Details may be found under the notes on individual genera and species.

Here are some general rules to follow where more definite information is lacking.

Planting depth (from *top* of bulb to soil level): 2 to 3 times greatest diameter of bulb for large bulbs—2 or more inches in diameter; 3 to 4 times greatest diameter of small bulbs.

Distance apart: for large bulbs, 1½ to 2 times the planting depth; for small bulbs, 2 to 3 times the planting depth.

In light sandy soils, planting may well be somewhat deeper—an inch or two—than in average soil, especially in sunny exposures. Extra-deep planting will delay flowering to a slight extent but not nearly so long as some writers have claimed. Planting in a northern exposure is a much more effective way to delay flowering. Gardeners who make something of a specialty of exhibiting Daffodils, for instance, can well make two plantings of important varieties, thus extending the period of bloom of each sort for a week or more.

With the soil well prepared—as it always should be—before planting is begun, the best tool for planting is a trowel, or trowels, for more than one shape of trowel will be found convenient if bulbs of different types are being set out. The large-bladed trowel with a long one-piece shank is best for large bulbs such as Tulips, Daffodils, Hyacinths, and Lilies, while a narrow-bladed "Slim-Jim" is much handier for small bulbs. Notches cut in the trowel handles, indicating varying depths from the soil's surface to the tip of the trowel, are helpful in planting.

For large groups in a bulb border, mark off areas with lime (line at upper left corner); place bulbs and label before beginning to plant. RIGHT: *Planting large bulbs in turf is facilitated by use of a special planting tool which removes a plug of sod that can later be replaced. (These are Colchicums.*

For planting in turf there is available a planter which removes a circular piece of sod and a core of soil beneath it. After the bulb is planted, soil and sod can be returned. Under certain conditions this is a useful tool.

If the soil is newly prepared and loose, it may be advisable to use a wide piece of board on which to stand or kneel when distributing the bulbs and planting. With a pointed stick the area for each variety can be marked off. The label is then put in place and the bulbs distributed on the surface. Planting then proceeds, working from the front to the back of the area, so that any packing of the soil occurs over bulbs already planted.

A word about labels may not be amiss at this point. Most bulbs will remain for many years, and the time to provide *permanent* labels is when they are planted. Ordinary wood labels are likely to be heaved out of the soil during the first few weeks after planting, and even if they last until spring, it is almost certain that many of them will be broken off. Substantial metal labels cost more but are well worth the difference.

If the soil is dry, by all means give a thorough watering as soon as planting is finished. Rapid development of roots will anchor the bulbs firmly in place and thus lessen the danger of injury by heaving.

Mulching

Whether or not newly planted bulbs should be mulched is a much debated question. It cannot be answered by an unqualified yes or no. Here are the facts upon which, in any particular case, to base your decision:

The really hardy bulbs—Tulips, Daffodils, Crocuses, and the general run of early spring-blooming bulbs—do not need protection from hard freezing once they are established. If, however, they are planted very late, mulching is beneficial in two ways: it extends the period during which root growth can develop in the soil, and it keeps the surface of the soil frozen and thus prevents heaving. A mild winter, with alternate freezing and thawing, is more likely to be injurious to newly planted bulbs—and to other plants, for that matter—than a very severe one.

For sorts that are not reliably hardy, mulching is of course desirable. The cluster-flowered (Polyanthus) types of Narcissus, Galtonia, Montbretias, Bulbous Irises, Anemones, and Ranunculus can, by providing thorough mulching, be grown outdoors in many sections where usually they are not grown. (See pages 235–37, 254, 287.)

C A U T I O N : In any event, however, mulching should never be put on over newly planted bulbs until the soil has frozen an inch or so deep. Otherwise it affords an ideal place for mice, shrews, and other rodents to nest, thus providing them with both board and lodging in one convenient package.

As to materials for mulching bulbs, we consider evergreen boughs at the top of the list. We make it a practice to gather up unsold Christmas trees (arranged for in advance), since in our locality late December or January is as early as mulching is likely to be needed. The branches are readily applied, lie flat, don't blow away, catch and hold light falls of snow, and present a pleasant appearance during most of the winter; and in spring they can be removed in a matter of minutes. Pine needles are excellent and of an unobtrusive color, as are also buckwheat hulls, sold under the trade name of Multex. Dry leaves will answer but usually must be held in place with branches and boards.

Another use for mulching is to *keep from freezing* ground that has been prepared for bulbs that cannot be obtained until late in the season—many of the hardy Lilies, for instance. After the planting is done and the soil has frozen an inch or two, the mulch can be replaced, but it should be removed in spring before growth starts.

With planting completed, you can hang up the fork and rake, put away the trowels, and look forward to the most exciting spring in your garden that you have ever experienced.

CHAPTER *8. Culture*

We have already stressed the fact that bulbs, corms, and tubers are among the most easily grown of all decorative plants. There are, of course, some exceptions, and not every bulb will find everywhere conditions to its liking. The ease with which many bulbous flowers can be grown frequently leads to neglect by the gardener. If a plant can take care of itself, why bother?

Furthermore, much of the life of most bulbous plants goes on while the tops are dormant, and then it's the old story of "out of sight, out of mind."

But if you want your bulbs to provide their maximum beauty in the garden and in your home, then you must co-operate by giving them at least a reasonable amount of attention. So let us investigate what may be done to assure better than average blooms and to secure the permanence of your bulb plantings.

The first principle to be kept in mind, and one which cannot be stressed too often, is this:

Assure vigorous, healthy, and well-matured growth of the foliage, and the flowers will take care of themselves.

Whatever you do in the way of culture, then, should be aimed at this objective. If you can produce a crop of good strong bulbs, the bulbs will produce the blooms. With bulbs that you buy and plant, the bulb grower has already done this job for you, so your first crop of flowers is assured. After that it is up to you.

CULTIVATION

For our first lesson in cultural requirements, let us go back to the humble Onion. This succulent and delicious true bulb, which is usually grown from "sets" (small, immature bulbs), is considered one of the easiest and surest crops for the beginner *if* the plants are kept free of weeds. If they are not, the crop will be a failure no matter how rich the soil.

So the initial step in growing good bulbs is to make sure that they do not suffer from too much competition with weeds and grasses. As soon as the tops have made 3 or 4 inches of growth in the spring, the surface of the soil should be gone over lightly with a small hoe, or with a claw weeder, to break up the hard crust which will have formed during the winter and to destroy all sprouting weeds. As the spring-flowering bulbs make very rapid growth, one thorough cultivation is usually sufficient to keep them clean until the foliage shades the soil thoroughly. After flowering, they may need a second going over, but usually this is not required. The handiest tool I know of for cultivating among bulbs which grow close together and are spaced irregularly is the small triangular-bladed "all-purpose" hoe.

With tender bulbs planted in the spring, cultivation is given as soon as the plants are large enough to be readily distinguished. It should be repeated at intervals so long as weeds threaten serious competition.

First spring operation is to clear the bed of weeds and loosen surface. The "all-purpose" hoe, with ▽-shaped blade, is ideal for this job.

Plant food is applied while growth is still small, and worked lightly into surface. A low-nitrogen, slow-acting fertilizer is best for bulbs.

FERTILIZING

Maintaining the food supply of most bulbs (other than those grown in pots as house plants) is an easy matter.

Our method with the hardy spring-flowering sorts grown in bulb beds or in a mixed border is to make one application in early spring, immediately after cultivation to eliminate weeds. If we get time for it, a second application is made in late summer or early autumn, when new roots are beginning to develop underground. We feel that the second application is desirable but not essential, especially if the plants have made normally vigorous growth after flowering.

The fertilizer we use is a mixture of three parts (by weight) of dehydrated manure, such as Driconure or Bovung, and one part of bone meal. This supplies nitrogen and phosphoric acid and a moderate amount of humus. It is scattered between the sprouting plants at the rate of 8 to 10 pounds per 100 square feet. To this is added once every two or three years, to maintain the potash content in the soil, wood ashes at the rate of 10 to 15 pounds per 100 square feet, or muriate of potash, 1 to 2 pounds per 100 square feet. In many soils, however, most bulbs will thrive without applications of potash.

Many bulb plantings are maintained in good condition with general-purpose chemical fertilizers, such as those with an analysis of 5–10–5 or 4–12–4. Only in very exceptional cases is it necessary to use a quick-acting high-nitrogen fertilizer like tankage or nitrate of soda. If the foliage is weak in growth and lacking a healthy, normal green color, a nitrogen application may be advisable. Trying it first on a few plants in liquid form (one tablespoonful of nitrate of soda to a 10-quart watering can) will indicate in the course of a few days, by the response of the plant, if the trouble is due to lack of nitrogen.

If any chemical fertilizer is used, exercise care to prevent it from lodging on the foliage; or, better, give a thorough watering immediately after applying.

MULCHING

The advisability of mulching after planting has already been discussed. (See page 78.) This applies to mulching for winter protection. Mulching *as a part of general cultural practice* is quite another matter. In bulb literature other than that concerning Lilies, there is little on this point. Even with Lilies it is the desirability of using a ground cover of growing plants, rather than actual mulching materials, that is stressed.

Most bulbs are benefited by mulching. Put it on before foliage begins to spread. Buckwheat hulls, shown here, last for two years or more.

So far as Lilies are concerned, there is small doubt that mulching is beneficial. (See Chapter 15.) In regard to the hardy spring-flowering bulbs and summer-flowering bulbs in general, we feel certain that mulching could advantageously be used to a much greater extent than has been the general practice.

There are three distinct advantages to be derived from mulching: weed control, conservation of moisture, and prevention of defacement of the flowers from mud spattering.

We have emphasized repeatedly the importance of *growing a good crop of foliage*. This applies to all types of bulbs, corms, and tubers. Preventing the competition of weeds, which use plant foods, moisture, and sunshine needed by the bulbs, is decidedly a step toward this end. Weeds can of course be controlled by cultivation, as they are in the commercial plantings of bulb growers. As bulbs are grown about the home, in borders, groups, or naturalized, cultivation is difficult and fraught with some danger of injury to the plants aboveground, or to roots below. Adequate mulching, which can easily be maintained year after year once it has been established, is an answer to the weed problem.

Soil under a mulch tends to remain moist. For most species of bulbous plants, the amount of water received in home-garden plantings is more likely to be too little than too much. The few exceptions include some of the wild species which, in their native habitats, get a real sun baking in the soil during a rainless period. (This applies especially to many of the Tulip species and to some of the Bulbous Irises.) But even with these a mulch can work both ways, for some materials prevent ordinary rains from penetrating the soil. We have never experienced unfavorable results with any of the bulbous plants we have mulched. If the drainage is what it should be, there is no need to fear excessive moisture from mulching.

Mulching materials are of many kinds. What the gardener will use depends largely upon what is available. In recent years we have leaned more and more to pine needles, which we can gather locally. They have the advantage of being easily applied, of "staying put," and of remaining loose and open enough to admit water and air readily. They are not favored as nesting headquarters by rodents and, having much the color of soil, are not conspicuous. Buckwheat hulls, now generally available as a commercial mulch, have the same good qualities; no other commonly obtainable material makes quite so neat a mulch or more closely resembles good brown soil. Rough compost, about half decomposed, is good but may contain weed seeds that are still viable. We prefer digging this into the soil, in preparing beds for planting, rather than using it as a mulch.

Of quite different consistency, but also useful, are peatmoss and sawdust. The former, if put on too thickly, has the double disadvantage of becoming almost impervious to rain if it gets completely dry, and of tending to remain wet and soggy if it becomes thoroughly soaked. It is better when mixed into the upper surface of soil. Sawdust, if of a sufficiently coarse grade, remains porous, and it practically inhibits weed growth. It has been used extensively by Dr. George Slate of Geneva, N.Y., in his experiments with Lilies and Daffodils, and he recommends it most highly.

Excelsior is particularly good for any plants—bulbous or otherwise—which retain green top growth through the winter. Bog- or salt-marsh hay and straw, while desirable for many uses, are not particularly good for bulbous subjects, being unsightly and likely to attract rodents.

Mulches used for winter protection are put in place only after the soil has frozen an inch or more. Summer mulches we like to put on in beds or borders just after the spring cultivation, weeding, and feeding, or after flowering. For naturalistic plantings, they may be applied at any time.

Loose, springy mulches, such as pine needles, hay, or hardwood leaves, can be 3 to 5 inches thick; more compact materials—buckwheat hulls, sawdust, or peatmoss—about half that depth.

WATERING

In most sections of the United States there are in any year periods during which growing plants will be greatly benefited by occasional watering. Mulches help to conserve the reserve of moisture already in the soil but cannot add moisture to it.

Many a gardener makes the mistake of assuming that, since spring-flowering bulbs grow and bloom during a season when rain is likely to be plentiful, there is nothing to worry about so far as these are concerned. But an early hot dry spell may result in premature dying of the foliage of Daffodils, Tulips, and other spring subjects, with the result that the bulbs do not fully develop. And the *next* spring's flowers will suffer for it.

The extensive bulb plantings of Holland are grown on soil where the water table remains constant, not far below the surface, within easy reach of thirsty roots. Commercial bulb growers in America provide irrigation for their vast fields in order that they can be sure to produce full-size bulbs that in turn will bloom satisfactorily the first season after they are planted.

The home gardener no less than these expert plantsmen should, within the limits that it is possible for him to do so, make provision for giving his bulbous plants additional water when they need it. The fact that they may be able to survive without it should not satisfy him.

When and how should water be supplied?

As a general rule, water in generous amounts is needed most by bulbous plants from the time the flower buds begin to develop until they come into bloom. In the case of those which do not develop their foliage fully until after flowering—Daffodils, Tulips, and most of the early spring bulbs—the supply of moisture should be plentiful until the foliage has had a chance to mature. With the relatively few species that mature their foliage first and bloom at a later period—Lycoris, Colchicums, autumn-flowering Crocuses, for example—the important period for abundant moisture is *while the foliage is growing*. Most bulbs of this type will come to flower even in bone-dry soil.

For most bulbous plants, the method of watering is not especially important. We use irrigating machines of the type that turns from side to side, applying the water in a fine rain, and slowly, so that the soil can be thoroughly saturated without making the surface a mass of mud. In exceptional cases, where it is desirable not to wet flowers or foliage, the porous canvas-hose "soil-soaker" is the answer, or water may be allowed to run slowly from the open hose. As in all watering, the aim should be to get the soil thoroughly moist to a depth of several inches. Mere sprinkling is likely to do more harm than good.

Tulips are one of the exceptions to overhead watering; if there is any danger of "fire" (botrytis) being present, overhead watering may help to spread it. Another exception is Tuberous Begonias; the large flowers may become spotted or even break off as a result of careless heavy watering, and foliage may spot or "burn" if exposed to strong sunshine while wet.

The gardener who grows bulbs on a scale at all extensive will find it a paying investment to extend pipes to strategic points, so that watering can be done conveniently and quickly. As this part of his water system is used only during the summer months, pipes need be buried only 2 or 3 inches deep. They should of course be laid on a slight grade to allow for draining when shut off in fall.

PROTECTING FLOWERS

With spring-flowering bulbs, and to a lesser degree with summer- and autumn-flowering ones, much of the beauty which the gardener has been waiting for weeks or months to enjoy is lost as the result of a sudden windstorm or a driving, mud-spattering rain. This possibility should be anticipated and all practical means taken to prevent it.

For low-growing plants, such as Hyacinths and the minor spring bulbs, and most of the species of Tulips and Daffodils, a mulch of some sort is the best protection. Buckwheat hulls or peatmoss (moistened as it is applied, to prevent blowing) are particularly good here; a very light covering will prevent splashing. Even the taller-growing Daffodils and Tulips are not safe from mud spattering if they are growing in bare soil.

Many of the taller summer bulbs—Dahlias, Lilies, Summer-hyacinths—are subject to injury from being whipped about or broken by windstorms. Planting them in a protected location will do much to lessen this danger; but the use of supports to which the plants are secured is more certain, and especially advisable where flowers are wanted for show purposes. Bamboo stakes, which are available in lengths up to 8 feet, are commonly used for this purpose. We have found heavy (8- or 9-gauge) galvanized-wire stakes both more convenient to use and less conspicuous. They have a distinct advantage, too, in that they sway slightly in a heavy wind, thus making less likely the breaking of the plant's stem. With reasonable care they last indefinitely.

In staking Lilies or other tall plants—we have had the Summer-hyacinths go over 5 feet—tying should begin when they are about two-thirds grown. Good-sized soft twine or raffia is used, a knot being tied tight around the support and then a loose loop tied around the plant stem. Many gardeners now use one of the several plant-ties, such as Twist-ems, in place of twine or raffia. Very tall plants should be secured, as they grow, at two or more points.

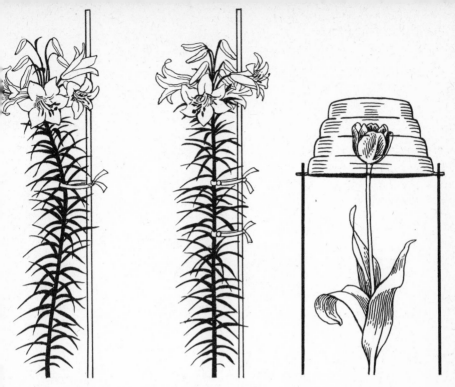

LEFT: *Supporting a tall plant: (left) wrong—one loop at one point;* *(right) correct—double loops at two or more points.* RIGHT: *Protection for individual bloom: plastic dome supported on stakes.*

Low-growing plants which have a tendency to make numerous side shoots—such as semi-dwarf and bedding Dahlias—can be inconspicuously supported with small twiggy branches of Birch, Gray Dogwood, or something similar. Whatever method of support is used, the important thing is to provide it early. A plant which has once fallen or blown over, even though it may not be broken, can never be made to resume a natural appearance when it is tied up.

Flowers being grown for show purposes will of course be given special attention in regard to preserving the blooms in perfect condition; otherwise the results of meticulous care during a whole year may be lost in an hour's heavy rain.

A not-too-difficult method of protecting low-growing plants, such as Tulips and Daffodils, is to make cones of celloglass. These are tacked to barrel hoops. Light pointed stakes—the sticks from peat-moss bales serve excellently—to which the barrel hoops are nailed, hold them firmly in position at the desired height. Such a miniature waterproof tent makes a good covering for a fair-sized group of bulbs.

Daffodil border eight years old. Annual fertilizing has maintained vigorous growth, but plants are getting overcrowded. Therefore replanting is in order.

With longer stakes, the same type of protection can be used for individual stalks of Lilies, Gladiolus, or similar tall plants. As these cones permit free circulation of air about the flowers, they can be kept in place much longer than paper or cellophane bags tied around the flowers, which are sometimes used.

For beds or for plants grown in rows, stout stakes with wires stretched between them make a support for plant-protection cloth or for light wood frames covered with celloglass. The ideal way to grow Daffodils and Tulips for show purposes is in a deep, unheated frame. Thus, in addition to protection from the weather, timing can be controlled to some extent. Where the show schedule calls for flowers grown in the open, such methods, however, are not permissible.

CUTTING

The cutting of the flowers of bulbous plants is an important point in their cultivation. There is some disagreement as to how much the development of seed pods affects the growth of bulbs underground after flowering, but it is well established that it does reduce the size of the bulbs produced. It is the universal practice of commercial bulb growers to remove the flowers. Some allow the buds to develop sufficiently to be cut for sale, as this brings a by-product income. It is considered better for the bulb crop, however, to remove them before blooming or just as soon as they show enough color to be "rogued" —a term applied to the pulling up of all plants that are not true to the variety or the type being grown.

In the garden, flowers that are wanted for decoration should be cut as soon as they are safely beyond the tight bud stage. According to species and variety, most of them will then remain in good condition from a couple of days to a week or more. Too often they are left until they have passed full bloom, and then cut and brought in, without benefit of hardening, to fade or collapse within a few hours.

In cutting flowers of bulbous plants which have thick, fleshy stems with leaves attached, such as those of Tulips, Gladiolus, or Lilies, most of the foliage should be left to grow. Foliage is the mechanism which manufactures food to be stored in the old bulb or corm remaining in the ground, or in the new ones being formed. Bare-stemmed flowers— Daffodils, Ismenes, Amaryllis, and the like—are cut to the ground.

To have them last well in bouquets and arrangements, cut flowers early in the morning or late in the afternoon, plunge the stems at once into deep fresh water, and store for several hours or overnight in a dark, cool place—the cooler the better, down to 40 degrees. If straight stems are wanted, they should be kept vertical or nearly so. Most fleshy stemmed flowers will tend to turn upright at the tips—even in the dark—if they are placed with much of a slant or if laid horizontally in boxes. Flower arrangers often take advantage of this fact to secure desired bends or curves in stems.

Blooms that are left to finish their allotted span of life in the garden should be snapped off as soon as they fade. The few exceptions are those which produce attractive seed pods, berries, or fruits—such as an occasional Lily or Iris, Jack-in-the-pulpit, Blood-lily (Haemanthus), or Blackberry-lily (Belamcanda).

CARE OF FOLIAGE

For reasons already explained, the foliage of all plants producing bulbs, corms, or tubers should be encouraged to keep growing as long as they will. This means maintaining soil moisture, and possibly additional feeding, after the flowering period is over.

In the garden such foliage growth is often a nuisance. Gradually yellowing Tulip leaves, the sprawling, messy green ribbons of Daffodils, and the great bunches of herbage of Colchicums do offer something of a problem.

For the sake of the bulbs—and *next* year's bloom—the foliage should be left intact. Long, strong foliage, such as that of Daffodils, can be tied with green raffia into fairly compact knots; or the foliage itself can be plaited or twisted together. Seedlings of fast-growing annuals—either home-grown or purchased—can be planted in front of and between groups of Tulips. Dwarf Marigolds and Zinnias, such as the Mexican type, bedding Petunias and dwarf Dahlias are a few of those which are excellent for this purpose. We like especially the too-little-known Star of Texas (Xanthisma), which withstands early frosts and goes on cheerfully producing its hundreds of starry golden flowers long after the others have been cut down.

In a mixed border, the well-planned placing of certain perennials adjacent to groups of bulbs can do much toward making their ripening foliage inconspicuous.

Where for any reason the unsightly foliage must be removed—as was often the case with Tulips and Hyacinths in the days of "design" beds in formal gardens—the bulbs can be lifted immediately after flowering and replanted. If they are just carelessly heeled in and forgotten, the foliage will die back almost immediately; but if taken up with adhering soil, planted close together in a trench in partial shade, with plenty of peatmoss in the soil, *and kept watered,* they will attain much nearer normal development. The bulbs may be smaller than normal, but perfectly usable. However, if the work of salvaging them must be done by hired labor, the cost, with Tulips, is likely to be little less than that of purchasing new stock.

REPLANTING

With the most easily grown hardy bulbs, the time will arrive when, through normal increase, they have become so overcrowded as to give fewer and inferior blooms. This stage can be postponed by good care and generous fertilizing, but not indefinitely. And putting off replanting only makes it more difficult when it is undertaken, with a larger percentage of undersized bulbs.

The period until replanting becomes necessary varies greatly with different types and species, and even with varieties. Some Daffodils, for instance, are giving us satisfactory bloom after eight years, while others make such dense clumps that they should be taken up and divided every three or four years. Others, such as the Hardy Amaryllis (*Lycoris squamigera*) and the Colchicums, which propagate slowly, can be left undisturbed almost indefinitely.

The work of replanting is best undertaken at the beginning of the dormant period, just after foliage has died down, but while it and new offsets, cormels, or bulblets are still attached to the bulbs. Using a broad-tined digging fork, thrust it down deep in a vertical position, well away from the clump (to avoid spearing any of the bulbs); then lift the clump out, turning it partly over to expose the bulbs on the surface of the forkful of soil. Grasping the foliage at the base with the left hand, after the soil is thoroughly loosened, often enables the operator to lift the clump out neatly, with small bulblets or cormels adhering to the parent plant. Separating the bulbs from the soil, place each lot in a flat with a label. Stack these flats crisscross to

Operation "lifting." Bulbs are taken up while dead foliage still is attached to them. After drying-off period in cool shed, they will be cleaned and separated, and then replanted or stored.

provide free ventilation in an open shed or garage. With the exception of Daffodils, *they should be carefully protected from mice or other rodents.*

With proper storage conditions, bulbs of most sorts can be kept out of the ground for many weeks. If they are of a type developing offsets—Daffodils, for instance—these will separate from the "mother" bulbs much more readily after they have cured for a considerable time. However, in replanting for one's own use, there is little object in doing this, except in cases of varieties which it is desired to increase rapidly.

In replanting hardy bulbs of any kind, we like to get them back into the ground as soon as possible. In this we do not make an exception even of Tulips. Immediate replanting has several advantages: it permits root growth to start again whenever the bulb is ready to break dormancy; it saves the bother of storing over a long period; and it greatly lessens the danger of losing or mixing up labels.

The bulbs, corms, or tubers you take up will be of varying sizes. All are good for replanting, but of most kinds there will soon be more than you can accommodate. Then it becomes necessary to select the largest and best; the smaller ones can be grown on in a nursery row, used for naturalizing, or discarded.

In general it is best not to replant in the same spot. This is especially true of Tulips, which are subject to fire-blight disease, and of Lilies. Needless to say, the soil for replanting should be just as thoroughly prepared as for planting new bulbs.

Tender bulbs that are grown in the garden, of course, must be replanted annually, so there is little danger of their becoming overcrowded. But it can happen. The inexperienced gardener who sets out, intact, a clump of Dahlia roots which he has carefully preserved through the winter will find himself with a dense growth of stalks and foliage and few and inferior blooms. The same is true of Cannas, Ismenes, and others that tend to remain in clusters unless separated. Separation should be done, where necessary, with a knife.

But while most hardy bulbs increase in number as rapidly, or even more rapidly, than the gardener wishes them to, there are occasions when he will want to hasten the process. Or, once he has become an enthusiast, he may even wish to try his hand at developing new varieties of his own. And so, in the following chapter, we shall consider the intriguing matter of propagation.

CHAPTER *9. Propagation*

Much of the pleasure to be had in growing any plant is to know how to increase your stock of it. With the propagator's skills at your finger tips, you can afford to purchase many things that might otherwise seem too expensive. Starting with an individual plant, which in itself scarcely would make a worth-while display, you can, with no additional outlay, soon possess as large a planting as you wish.

Then, too, it is always nice to feel that you have a few surplus plants of choice things to spare for a friend or neighbor, or to swap for some desired plant that you do not yourself possess.

With no helping hand save that of old Ma Nature, many bulbs, corms, and tubers increase so rapidly that they soon present an embarrassment of riches. There are others which come along nicely with just a little encouragement from the attentive gardener. A few, however, are really obstinate in their wish to remain the sole representative of their kind in your garden. With these, very persuasive measures must be used—even to the extent of putting them under the knife. Many kinds that normally self-propagate at a slow rate can be increased much more rapidly when special methods are used to hurry them. A knowledge of such methods, indispensable to the commercial grower, is also of definite advantage to the amateur.

METHODS OF REPRODUCTION

Members of the great group of bulbous plants have many ways of propagating themselves. Increase by seeds is known as sexual propagation; other means, such as the formation of offsets or of bulbs and bulblets (see page 96), are termed asexual. A basic difference between the sexual method and all asexual methods is that plants raised by the former are seldom entirely uniform, while the latter are. Very literally they are chips off the old block. All the Louis XIV Tulips in the world, all the Jersey Beauty Dahlias or Hyperion Day-lilies are direct descendants of the one original plant of each of these varieties— just as all the Koster's Blue Spruces are pieces, through successive generations, from the original seedling which old Peter Koster selected, because of its exceptionally fine color, from a batch of seedlings of Colorado Blue Spruce. Such a family, descended from a *single* parent, is known as a "clone."

Seeds

The method of reproduction most familiar to gardeners is of course the growing of plants from seed. *Species* of plants "come true" from seed; horticultural varieties seldom do. If, for instance, you plant seeds of the Regal Lily, the resulting seedlings will be Regals. They may vary somewhat in height, time of bloom, shape of the flowers, but they will all be Regals. If you sow seeds from a named hybrid Lily, however, you will get a great variety of plants, most of which will be definitely not the same as the parent variety. The same would be true with a species Tulip, such as *Kaufmanniana,* the seedlings of which would all be *Kaufmanniana,* and a named horticultural Tulip, such as General de Wet, the seedlings of which would vary like those of a hybrid Lily's seedlings.

In addition to the fact that garden varieties of bulbous plants do not come true from seed, there is another drawback which deters both commercial growers and home gardeners from using seeds, except infrequently, as a means of propagation: that is the length of time required to get plants to blooming size. There are a few, such as the dwarf bedding Dahlias and Tuberous Begonias (if started in January or February), which will flower the first season; but most bulbous plants require two or three years, on up to five or six—as with Daffodils, for instance. Growing bulbous plants from seed, therefore, is in general a matter of concern chiefly to the hybridist, professional or amateur, interested in developing new varieties.

Asexual methods

For the sake of making a distinction between two different types of asexual propagation, we may say that bulbous plants increase them-

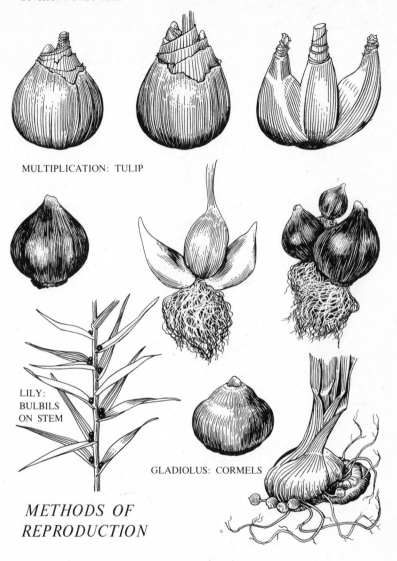

DIVISION: DAFFODIL

MULTIPLICATION: TULIP

LILY:
BULBILS
ON STEM

GLADIOLUS: CORMELS

*METHODS OF
REPRODUCTION*

selves by *multiplication;* or may be increased, at the hands of the gardener, by *division.*

To illustrate: if you plant a 60-watt Tulip bulb in October, you may dig up, the following June, a couple of 40-watt bulbs and two or three 25-watters. If you plant a single Daffodil bulb, you will find, after three or four years, a whole shovelful of individual bulbs of various sizes. In neither case will you have had anything to do with the matter.

If, on the contrary, you plant a Dahlia in the spring, you take up in the autumn a clump of many fleshy roots, but they will all be joined to one stem; and the only way you can get more than one plant is to divide this clump by cutting the stem into sections—each with an "eye" and attached to a root. If you plant a Tuberous Begonia tuber, you take up in the fall the same tuber—grown larger, perhaps— and that is all you will ever get, no matter how many times you replant it. But this tuber can be divided by cutting it into sections, each with an eye or bud.

Under "division" we might also place the propagation of bulbous plants by stem cuttings. Not many of them are subject to increase by this method, but there are a few. Dahlias and Tuberous Begonias are examples.

PROPAGATING OPERATIONS

So much for the several methods of propagation. Let us now take a look at the way each of them is put into practice. In describing these operations, typical examples of each are used. Where variations from these exist, they are mentioned in the cultural methods for each genus or species given in succeeding chapters.

Seed

In catalogues comparatively few bulbous plants are offered in the lists of seeds. In gardens many of them produce seed freely, and the amateur who wishes to try his hand at raising his own plants will find plenty of material to work with.

In general, bulbous plants are no more difficult to grow from seed than are those of other groups,—except for one thing. That is the time element. It does involve a great deal more attention and work, and considerably more space, to carry through to maturity a plant requiring several years than one which will reward the grower with its first flowers within a season or two. And the chances of loss through injury or accident are correspondingly increased. These facts the grower should face before embarking on the venture of growing bulbs from seed.

As in sowing seeds of any sort, it is advisable to use a prepared mixture rather than ordinary garden soil. We have found entirely satisfactory our regular seed mixture of one part each of soil, compost (or leafmold), and peatmoss, with sufficient sand added to give it a slightly gritty texture. This is run through a half-inch mesh screen. For extremely fine seed, such as that of Tuberous Begonias, a half-inch layer or more of very finely sifted compost, or of peatmoss or sphagnum alone, is used on top of the regular mixture.

The time for planting seeds will depend upon the type of seed and upon the facilities available. As a general rule, the sooner they are sown after gathering, the better. Seeds of most hardy sorts, ripening in summer or autumn, are usually sown in flats or in a frame. Many of these seeds will not germinate until the following spring, or even the second spring after sowing. Seeds of tender types are best started in a greenhouse in January or February; or a month or two later, when the weather has moderated sufficiently, in a hotbed or cold frame.

The seeds that germinate quite promptly—Dahlias, Cannas, Ismenes, Tuberous Begonias, Gloxinias, and some Lilies, to mention a few—are started in pots, bulb pans, or flats, with a half inch or so of coarse drainage material under the prepared soil. Those which require a long period to germinate are better sown in substantial flats, 4 inches deep, with an inch of drainage material in the bottom; or directly in a frame.

Seeds of some species will not germinate, or will give only partial germination, until after freezing. These may remain in the soil a year or more before sprouting. Daffodils and Tulips are examples. Some Lilies germinate but make only a bulblet the first season, no leaf ap-

Ismene seeds sprouting.

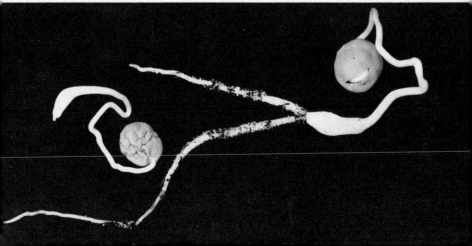

pearing above the soil until the following season. It is evident, therefore, that seeds of this character should be sown where they can be both kept track of and protected until ready for their first transplanting.

As a rule, the earlier transplanting can be done, the better. By the time there is sufficient top growth to make it possible to handle the seedlings, the root system will have made a good start—often a surprisingly vigorous one. The smaller the plant, the less the shock in transplanting it; and if seedlings have come up thickly, the longer they remain untransplanted, the greater the danger of loss by damping off or other diseases.

The first transplanting is usually made into flats, as they occupy much less space and require much less attention than individual pots. Some vigorous, rapid-growing plants, such as Dahlias and Cannas, can go directly into 2½- or even 3-inch pots, and then either into 4s or into the open ground.

The soil mixture used is similar to that in which the seed was started, but with a larger proportion—about one half—of soil, with bone meal added at the rate of a pint to a bushel of the mixture. An inch layer of rough compost or old, thoroughly rotted manure in the bottom of the flat will improve drainage and provide a happy feeding area for growing roots.

The seedling plants are set 2 to 4 inches apart each way, according to the type of plant being grown. Plants with cotyledons (seed leaves) are set deep enough so these are just above the soil; others, slightly deeper than they have been growing. Flats are best watered from the bottom, and provided with shade from hot sun for a week or so. If even with shading the seedlings wilt, mist-spray the foliage two or more times daily, but never enough to make the soil soaking wet.

Lilies and other hardy bulbs are often carried over the first winter in the seed flats, with the protection of a frame. Let them freeze, and then mulch or shade to keep them frozen, and thus avoid alternate freezing and thawing which might bring them to the surface.

Tender subjects, such as Dahlias, Gladiolus, Tuberous Begonias, Ismenes, etc., are of course taken up and stored in the usual way over the winter (see page 220), to be replanted the following spring. *Small-sized bulbs, corms, and tubers being grown from seed should be given special care in packing and an occasional examination during the storage period to make sure that they are not drying out and shrinking.*

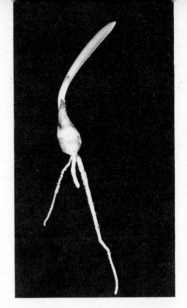

Ismene seedling;
first true leaf,
and bulb beginning
to form.

Bulbs that have begun to shrivel can be restored to their original plump, firm condition, if the process has not proceeded too far, by being placed in damp peatmoss or vermiculite for a few days. After this they should be repacked as before for storage.

Offsets

An offset—sometimes called a "split" or a "spoon"—is a small bulb which develops within the mother bulb, as with the Narcissus; or at the base of the mother bulb, as with the Ismene. Starting as a bud, it gradually increases in size until it breaks away from the mother bulb and is on its own, to produce, in time, its own progeny. The mother bulb remains, to become a grandmother or a great-great-grandmother bulb.

Nature often comes to the assistance of the gardener, but where offsets are involved the gardener can be of assistance to her, becoming, in a sense, a green-thumb midwife. For the offset baby bulbs, left undisturbed, become a dense clump, with even more offspring coming along to increase the overcrowded conditions, until finally there is not space or food enough underground, nor sufficient air or sunshine above it, for all of them to develop properly.

Here the gardener steps in, takes up the old clump, and separates, grades, and replants, so that all the progeny will have a full opportunity to grow as they should.

LEFT: *Veltheimia—offset originating on old bulb.* RIGHT: *Haemanthus (Blood-lily)—offsets originating from fleshy stolons.*

The time from planting the original bulb until replanting is necessary varies with species, varieties, and growing conditions. But if it is desired to increase the number of plants as rapidly as possible, then, with few exceptions, the lifting, separation, and replanting should be done every year or every second year.

For purposes of propagation it is best to plant both large bulbs and young offsets in rows in very well-prepared soil, in the vegetable plot or the cutting garden, where they can be cared for, cultivated, fed, and, if necessary, watered. Small offsets can be grown quite close together; Daffodils, for instance, 2 to 4 inches apart, in rows 18 to 24 inches apart. Replanting immediately after digging (after the foliage has died down), or as soon as the stock can conveniently be cleaned, separated, and graded, is advisable for most types of hardy bulbs.

New bulbs or corms

New bulbs or corms, such as those produced by Tulips, Crocuses, and Gladiolus, differ from offsets in that the original bulb or corm, at the end of the season's growth, will have dried up or disintegrated entirely, leaving a new bulb, or several of them, in its place. Some of these new bulbs will be as large as the original bulb, or at least of flowering size. Usually others are much smaller and require growing on for a season or two before reaching flowering size. In some in-

Madonna Lily bulbs as dug—from original planting of six bulbs.

stances these new bulbs are formed at the end of underground roots or runners, at a distance from the parent bulb or below it (as the "droppers" of Tulips and Crocuses), and to secure all of them, great care in digging is required.

With new bulbs, as with offsets, if they are hardy, replanting can be done at once or delayed. If tender, they are stored over winter for spring planting.

Cormels or bulblets

Cormels or bulblets (see illustration, page 97), which in some species are produced along with the new bulbs or corms, are embryo forms, much smaller in size, which must be grown on for from one to three years before they become flowering-sized bulbs. They may develop in large numbers—we have had Gladiolus of some varieties produce as many as thirty to forty from one corm—and thus they offer a means for very rapid propagation.

The trick in successful propagation with bulblets and cormels is to keep them in good condition through the winter, so that a thick and vigorous stand will result when they are planted. Storing dry in paper bags is sometimes recommended, but we have been more successful in using *slightly* moist peatmoss or vermiculite. Here again an occasional examination is advisable. Cormels of Gladiolus and Montbretias, once thoroughly dried, become almost as hard as buckshot. A soaking of 24 to 48 hours in tepid water before planting will both hasten and increase new growth.

The bulblets and cormels may be sown like peas, in a broad, flat-bottomed furrow, and covered about 3 inches deep. Avoid weedy soil, as they must be kept clean to allow the grass-like juvenile foliage to get a good start. When the foliage dies down, dig, dry off—without too much exposure to hot sun or to wind—and later clean, grade, and store for winter.

The number of new bulbs or bulblets produced may in some cases be increased by artificial means. With Lilies, for instance, removing the flower buds before they open often results in the production of more bulbs and bulblets than would otherwise form. Sir Daniel Hall reported that, with some varieties of Tulips, the production was increased 300 per cent by disbudding. (See page 160). Some growers claim that bent stems bear more bulblets, and plant bulbs on their sides to obtain a crook at the base of the stem. Removing and layering the stem is a more certain process.

Bulbils are tiny aerial bulbs which form along the stems or in the leaf axils of some species or varieties of plants. Some Lilies, notably

Madonna Lily bulbs—separated and graded for replanting.

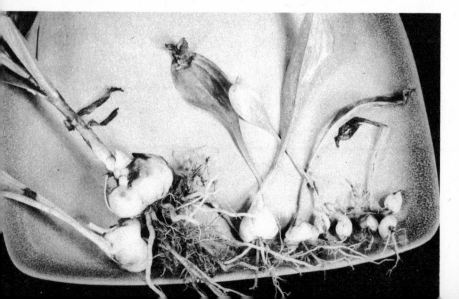

Lily (L. Maxwilli bulbiferum) *with bulbils formed in axils of leaves.*

Lilium tigrinum, regularly produce bulbils, and they occasionally occur in Tulips. They may be planted as soon as readily detached from the parent stem, in deep flats or directly in a frame.

Increase by division

In the several methods of propagation discussed above, the gardener's part has been a minor one. In those that follow he assumes the leading role, and nature becomes *his* assistant. The technique starts with an operation, in which some section of the parent plant is removed. This piece is then induced to form roots and becomes a new plant.

Simplest of the several methods of attaining this end is that in which the bulb, tuber, corm, or rhizome is cut into two or more pieces, these being planted directly, just as the original would have been. A universally known example of propagation by division is the Irish Potato. Other typical ones are Dahlias and Cannas. Many cormous plants, ordinarily grown from seed or from small corms or cormels, can be

Ismene: bulb at center (against pot) as dug; others separated. Fleshy roots are left on in storage.

increased by dividing a large corm. Gladiolus and Crocuses are examples.

In making the divisions it is essential that there be a growing point (a bud or "eye") on each piece. With cormous plants there must also be a section of the basal plate. Make the cuts with a clean sharp knife. It is good practice to dust over the cut surfaces with powdered charcoal or with one of the seed and bulb disinfectant powders, such as Floral Dust or Arasan. In any event, they should be allowed to dry sufficiently to form a slight film of scar tissue over the cut before being planted. If they are to be started in pots, flats, or a frame before being set out in the open or repotted, a rooting medium of soil, peatmoss, and sand will be of advantage.

Not a flock of geese, but new corms of Colchicum—variety The Giant. (See page 255.)

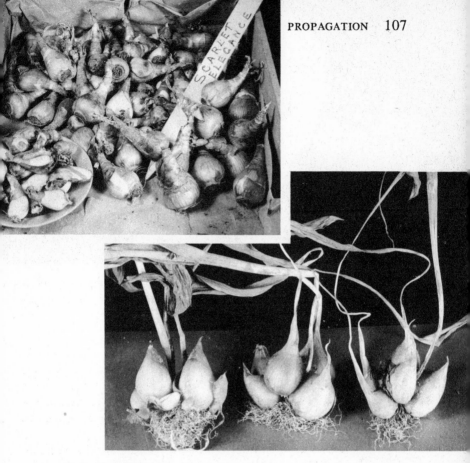

ABOVE: *Daffodils, cured, separated, and graded for replanting. (See illustration page 106.)* BELOW: *Tulips as dug. They must have rich soil to make full-size new bulbs.*

Scales

Some of the true bulbs can be propagated rapidly by an operation known as "scaling." Many Lilies are often grown in this way. Any good gardener can succeed with it, even though it may sound a bit mysterious to one who has not tried it.

The thick fleshy scales are removed from the outside of the bulb, care being taken not to bruise them unduly and to retain the base of each. If the heart of the bulb is left intact, that can be replanted for further growth.

Propagation of Lily by scaling. Scales are placed on sand, or mixture of sand and vermiculite. Plastic dome protects from rain and rodents. Heart of bulb (at left) can be replanted for further growth.

The scales are then set in rows in a flat, in sand or a sand-peatmoss mixture, and covered about 2 inches deep. *Excellent drainage is essential!* Or they may be placed directly in a frame. Keep covered against rain, *and only moderately moist,* for 20 to 25 days, until miniature new bulbs begin to form at the bases of the old scales; then moisture can be somewhat increased.

As a temperature of 60 degrees or thereabouts should be maintained, a greenhouse or other space where the temperature can be controlled is helpful. In a humid atmosphere a temperature of 75 to 80 degrees has given quicker results.

New baby bulbs forming at bases of scales and sending out vigorous roots.

When scales are started in February or March, the flats are then plunged out of doors in April or May and left undisturbed until the bulbs are planted out the following spring. Light is not necessary while the new bulbs are forming. If one must depend on a frame, the early and mid-season varieties can be scaled. The operations should be done as soon as the plants have bloomed. The lovely June-flowering Madonna Lily is readily propagated by scaling.

Stem-layering

Easier and quicker than scaling, but producing fewer new plants, is the method known as stem-layering. This develops bulblets in greater numbers than they would normally form, or where they could not form at all under normal conditions.

Stem-layering is accomplished by removing the stem from the bulb, just as the last flowers wither, by giving it a *quick* pull or jerk with a twisting motion. Don't try to be gentle about it, or you're likely merely to uproot the plant. A foot placed near the base of the stem, if the soil is light or sandy, will be an additional safeguard. The stems so gathered are heeled in, to about one third their length, in well-drained sandy soil or a half-and-half mixture, by bulk, of sand and peatmoss. Placing the stems on a slant will permit covering them with sash in an ordinary cold frame—an advantage with late-flowering varieties, as they can be held over in the frame until spring. When these heeled-in stems of early varieties have withered, they can be cut back to the soil, and the bases of the stems, with the newly formed bulblets still attached, set out in a nursery row to grow on for another year before being transplanted.

A modification of this method is to cut the stem back to 1 or 2 feet, remove all leaves, and layer in sand or sand-peatmoss, covered a couple of inches deep, in a frame until the bulblets have formed.

Cuttings

Very few of the bulbous plants lend themselves to propagation by cuttings, but two notable exceptions are Dahlias and Tuberous Begonias.

In the case of the former, the roots—usually in undivided clumps, just as they were dug in the fall—are started in March or April in the greenhouse or in a frame. Deep flats, filled with a peatmoss-sand mixture, will accommodate them. The new shoots, grown in full sun but fairly cool so the stems will be firm and short-jointed, are allowed to form four or five sets of leaves. Then they are cut *just* below the second node, leaving the first set to form side shoots. (If cut between nodes, the stems will root, but the resulting plant will never form tuberous roots to carry over winter.) The cuttings, with the lower leaves shortened about one half, placed in sand or sand and peatmoss, root easily and produce husky plants soon ready for potting or for setting out of doors.

Leaf cuttings of Gloxinias, like those of their relative, the African Violet (Saintpaulia), root readily. Mature leaves are taken, with all of the stem, and inserted a couple of inches deep in sand or sand-peatmoss. Baby plants start near the base of the stem and are grown on in small pots until ready for shifting to a larger size.

Scooping

A type of propagation which is sort of halfway between cuttings and scaling is practiced with some bulbs. Commercial growers employ it in propagating garden Hyacinths, as these increase but slowly by offsets.

A cone-shaped incision is made through the base of the bulb, leaving the scales (layers of fleshy tissue) exposed at the cut edges. The hollowed-out bulb is then placed in sand, covered 2 or 3 inches deep, and stored for about three weeks in a temperature of 60 to 70 degrees, to callus. The bulb is then placed in any dark, cool place, such as a cellar or under a greenhouse bench, where the small new bulbs form. At the approach of autumn these are removed and planted 3 to 4 inches deep and protected, after the soil begins to freeze, with a mulch of hay or pine needles.

A modified form of scooping, easier to follow, is to cut a couple of deep grooves at right angles across the basal plate. In this process, known as "scoring," the subsequent treatment is the same as for scooping. There will be fewer baby bulbs, but they will average larger in size.

In trying any method of propagation for the first time, it is advisable to start on a small scale. Do a little experimenting as soon as you can, just to get the swing of it, and then you'll be ready, when the occasion arises, to go about the job with confidence.

Taken by and large, bulbous plants are less troubled by insects and diseases than those of most other groups. Unfortunately, however, some of the most important, such as hardy Lilies, Gladiolus, and Dahlias, present problems. Catalogue compilers and some writers are given to minimizing the difficulties to be encountered, but the gardener who wishes to make reasonably sure of success with his bulbous plants may as well in the beginning face the fact that he will have some troubles to contend with.

Glancing through this chapter, the reader may get the impression that the statement above puts the case, to say the least, very mildly. But he can find reassurance in the fact that he will probably never encounter in his own garden more than a fraction of the troubles discussed, and even those which do plague him will not all appear in any one season. He will not by any means fight against hopeless odds. Both plant pests and diseases are more likely to be of serious danger to the commercial grower, handling bulbs by the hundreds of thousands, than to the gardener with his few dozens.

OVER-ALL PRECAUTIONS

Three definite measures the gardener can take to minimize greatly his troubles with pests or diseases:

Sanitation

The first is to keep his bulb plantings *clean*. Many weeds are host plants for insects or diseases, either during the summer or as sheltering material for their over-wintering stages. Fallen petals or foliage, old plant stalks—any miscellaneous litter in general—may serve the same purpose. Dead, dying, or diseased leaves on plants should be removed and burned. Don't let them lie around until dry; if necessary, sprinkle a little kerosene over them before applying the match, or bury them with quicklime. A basket—frequently disinfected—kept handy for the particular purpose of gathering such material will do much toward making sure that it actually is accomplished.

Observation

Cultivate the habit of *looking* for anything abnormal in the growth of your plants. A curled leaf that might pass unnoticed for days unless your eye was kept peeled for just such an abnormality may shelter a colony of aphids that has not yet begun to spread to other parts of the plant. *At this point* such an initial "cell" of some insect pests may be eliminated by removing a few leaves or with a few squirts from a spray gun. Not all insects, of course, are so easily controlled as are aphids. Most diseases will have obtained a strong start before their symptoms become apparent. Prompt identification of the trouble, however, and the removal and destruction of one or a few diseased plants will often prevent the infection of others.

Prompt action

The third step in the successful control of any pest or disease is to lose no time, once it has been identified, in applying the proper remedy or control. A day or two may mean all the difference between success and failure.

To this end it is well to have on hand the insecticides or fungicides most likely to be needed and equipment for applying them properly. Most gardeners make the mistake of economizing too much on sprayers and dusters. The very cheap ones not only fail to do a good job, and require an inordinate amount of time to operate, but also waste expensive material and quickly wear out; in the course of a few years they have actually cost considerably more, rather than any less, than good equipment.

Many of the insecticides and fungicides you are most likely to need for bulbous plants you probably have already on hand for garden use. A general list of the various sprays, dusts, and disinfectants is given on pages 121–22.

c a u t i o n : In using any insecticide or fungicide, *follow manufacturer's directions accurately.* Failure to do so may result not only in poor results but also in actual injury to plants—or to you!

PESTS

APHID, GREEN PEACH: a pale yellowish-green, soft-bodied sucking insect. Attacks many bulbous plants, feeding on the under sides of the foliage. It is dangerous, also, because it transmits mosaic disease.
Control: rotenone, nicotine sulphate, or pyrethrum.
Attacks: Crocus, Dahlia, Lily, Tulip.

APHID, LILY: yellow and black. One form is found only on Lilies (see Chapter 15). Another, *Myzus circumflexus,* feeds on terminal buds and shoots of many bulbous plants, turning the foliage yellow and deforming them. Also transmits mosaic disease.
Control: rotenone, nicotine sulphate, or pyrethrum.
Attacks: Anemone, Cyclamen, Freesia, Iris, Lily, Oxalis.

APHID, MELON: small, dark green, brown, or black. Feeds on under sides of foliage, which curls and turns yellow. Transmits mosaic disease.
Control: rotenone, nicotine sulphate, or pyrethrum.
Attacks: Begonia, Cyclamen, Lily.

APHID, POTATO: pink and green, wingless. Feeds on succulent young foliage.
Control: rotenone, nicotine sulphate solution, or pyrethrum.
Attacks: Gladiolus, Oxalis.

APHID, TULIP BULB: small, whitish, powdery, with black head. Colonies appear on foliage, in leaf sheaths of growing bulbs, especially under glass, causing discoloration and distortion of leaves. Found also on bulbs in storage or in the ground.
Control: soak Tulip bulbs in nicotine sulphate solution (1½ teaspoons to 1 gallon of water) with soap or in pyrethrum solution for ½ hour before planting. Spray foliage of growing plants with nicotine sulphate.
Attacks: Gladiolus, Iris, Squill, Tulip.

BORER, EUROPEAN CORN: flesh-colored caterpillar, 1 inch long with black dots. Enters stems and shoots, causing upper portions to wilt. Hole is visible where borer entered.
Control: cut below affected part, or dust stalks with DDT as preventive. Burn all dead refuse in fall.
Attacks: Dahlia, Gladiolus.

BORER, STALK: brown caterpillar, 2 inches long, with white stripes. Attacks plants as does the European corn borer (above).
Control: as for European corn borer.
Attacks: Dahlia, Lily.

BUG, TARNISHED PLANT: inconspicuous brown bug, ¼ inch long, flattened, oval, mottled. Sucks plant sap, causing drooping and malformation of shoots and buds.
Control: dust with methoxychlor, DDT, pyrethrum, or sulphur; or spray with nicotine sulphate solution. Keep weeds down. Burn trash in autumn to prevent wintering over. Difficult to control.
Attacks: Dahlia, Gladiolus.

CATERPILLAR, CONVICT: black, 2 inches long, with cream bands around body. Leaves are skeletonized; stalks eaten.
Control: lead arsenate.
Attacks: Amaryllis, Hymenocallis, Narcissus.

CUTWORMS: soft, fat, whitish, brown, or green worms. Attack newly set young plants, cutting the stem at or near ground level. Usually can be found coiled in the surface soil near where damage has been done.
Control: place tar-paper collars around newly set plants or young shoots. Distribute poisoned cutworm bait in the evening around infested areas. A new control is Lindane.
Attacks: Dahlia, Gladiolus.

FLY, LESSER BULB: wasp-like, about size of common house fly.
FLY, NARCISSUS BULB: resembles small bumblebee. Bulbs attacked are reduced to a soft brown decayed mass.
Control (for both): see Chapter 11, page 150.
Attacks: Amaryllis, Daffodil, Galtonia, Hyacinth, Hippeastrum, Lily, Tulip.

LEAFHOPPER, POTATO: see Chapter 16.

LEAF ROLLERS, CANNA: mostly in the South. There are two forms, the larger being a greenish caterpillar with dark orange head and narrow neck; the lesser, a yellow-white caterpillar, becoming greenish. Both roll the leaves, the caterpillar being found inside.

Control: hand-pick, or crush insects inside leaves, or spray or dust with DDT in early summer.

MEALYBUGS: small, oval, scale-like sucking insects covered with woolly white substance which extends beyond their bodies. Affected plants appear unthrifty; with white woolly tufts at joints and axils.

Control: under glass, fumigate with Cyanogas. Indoors and outdoors, paint individual colonies with small brush or cotton swab attached to a matchstick dipped in rubbing alcohol, or spray with rotenone.

Attacks: Amaryllis (Hippeastrum), Begonia, Calla, Cyclamen.

MILLIPEDES: round, wiry, hard-shelled worms up to 1¾ inches long (with 100 to 400 legs), which coil up like watch springs. Feeding on soft or decaying bulbs of all kinds.

Control: bait; 2 quarts dry bran; 1 ounce Paris green; 1 cup molasses mixed with 1 quart water. Place in piles around greenhouse or under shingles or grass clippings in garden beds; or drench soil with 1–1000 dilution of bichloride of mercury (deadly poison).

MITE, BULB: minute whitish mite. Burrows in roots, especially of rotting bulbs; seldom encountered in home garden.

Control: discard rotting bulbs. Prevent rotting by storing bulbs at 35 degrees. Dip slightly affected bulbs in nicotine sulphate solution (see aphid, Tulip) at 122 degrees for 10 minutes; or in hot water at 110 degrees for 2½ hours; or dust bulbs with Floral Dust or 2 per cent nicotine dust and store for several days in closed paper bags.

Attacks: Amaryllis, Calla, Crocus, Freesia, Gladiolus, Hyacinth, Lily, Narcissus, Tulip.

MITE, CYCLAMEN: minute whitish pest (too small to see with naked eye). Causes stunting of plant, especially at growing tips; malformation of leaves; blackening and distortion of buds.

Control: destroy badly infested plants. In greenhouse spray with TEPP aerosol bomb (deadly poison). Spray with 1–200 rotenone solution. Avoid contact between affected and healthy plants. Remove and burn all foliage and treat corms by soaking for 15 minutes in water at 110 degrees. Two new commercial controls are Marvel and Di-Mite.

Attacks: Cyclamen, Gloxinia, Tuberous Begonia.

NEMATODE, ROOT-KNOT: microscopic worm; male thread-like; female white, swollen, size of pin point. Causes knots or galls on feeding roots, yellowing of foliage, wilt, die-back.

Control: treat fallow soil with DD mixture, or with Soilfume Caps, 2 weeks before planting. Punch holes 10 to 12 inches apart, 5 to 6 inches deep; use ⅓ ounce DD or 1 Soilfume Cap per hole. Steam-sterilize greenhouse soil.

Attacks: Begonia, Cyclamen, Dahlia, Gladiolus, Tuberose.

NEMATODE, STEM AND BULB (Eelworm or Ring Disease): seldom found in home garden. Microscopic thread-like worm, this nematode lives in soil and decaying vegetable matter. Infestation causes irregular markings along leaf edges, stunt, failure to bloom. Leaves are twisted, with yellowish swellings. When bulb is cut, it shows black rings.

Control: soak bulbs 3 to 4 hours in water at 110–112 degrees, with formaldehyde added at the rate of 1 pint to 25 gallons. Replant at once. Destroy badly infested bulbs. Disinfect all equipment by dipping in water with formaldehyde added, 1 part to 9 of water; sterilize soil with Soilfume Caps, tear gas, or DD.

Attacks: Amaryllis, Anemone, Chionodoxa, Daffodil, Galanthus, Galtonia, Hyacinth, Iris (Bulbous), Muscari, Tulip.

RODENTS: chipmunks, mice, moles, rabbits and other rodents are enemies of many garden bulbs, and it is not an easy task to keep them under control.

Control: introduce Cyanogas into holes, either by pouring the powder in and closing the hole or, better, by using a pump gun (made by the Cyanogas Company) which forces gas through the entire run. Keep a cat which is a good mouser and moler. Plant Tulips in wire baskets, or edge Tulip beds with ½-inch hardware cloth sunk 8 inches below ground and extending 2 inches above. Mole-knots, bombs, or traps give partial control.

Attack: Tulip, Crocus, and other minor bulbs, Gladiolus and other Irids.

SLUGS: resembling snails without shells; chewing creatures which hide in the dark (usually under old boards or other debris) by day, and feed at night, eating foliage and leaving a slimy, silvery trail behind them.

Control: trap slugs under old shingles or thin boards under which they will be found by day. Remove any other litter under which they may hide. Use one of the poison baits containing metaldehyde sold under various trade names, such as Snarol.

Attacks: Dahlia, Lily, and other bulbous seedlings.

THRIPS, GLADIOLUS: tiny black or brown winged insects to $\frac{1}{16}$ inch long. Cause silvery streaks in foliage, followed by browning and dying leaves; deformed flowers, streaked white. Dormant corms become sticky, corky, browned.

Control: after drying corms, from which all foliage and stems are removed, dust thoroughly with 5 per cent DDT before storing. In growth: start spraying, with 1 to 2 tablespoons of 50 per cent wettable DDT per gallon of water, when foliage is 6 inches high. Repeat every 10 days until color shows in buds.

Attacks: Amaryllis, Daffodil, Freesia, Gladiolus, Iris (Bulbous).

THRIPS, GREENHOUSE: tiny blackish-brown insects $\frac{1}{24}$ inch long, with network of lines over head. Infested leaves look silvery or papery; wilt; die-back; leaves drop off or are marked with reddish-brown dots.

Control: dust with pyrethrum or spray with DDT as above.

Attacks: Alstroemeria, Amaryllis, Begonia, Calla, Cyclamen, Dahlia, Gloxinia, Hymenocallis, Nerine.

THRIPS, LILY BULB: see Chapter 15, page 208.

THRIPS, ONION: yellow to brown, tiny insects $\frac{1}{25}$ inch long. Infestation is marked by whitish blotches on foliage, then distortion of leaf tips, followed by withering and browning of the plant, which falls to the ground.

Control: spray with DDT, starting when plants are very young. Repeat weekly. Dust corms of Gladiolus with 3 to 5 per cent DDT before storage.

Attacks: Dahlia, Gladiolus.

WIREWORMS: dark, smooth, hard-shelled wiry worms (the larval form of click beetles), which feed on roots, corms, or bulbs. They are most prevalent in recently cultivated land which has been in sod.

Control: an old-fashioned method is to place cut potatoes, pressed 3 or 4 inches into the soil at 3-foot intervals, in an infested area. After a week or so dig them up and destroy the worms which are found attached to them. A new control is Lindane.

Attacks: Dahlia, Gladiolus.

DISEASES

BLIGHT, GRAY MOLD (*Botrytis cinerea*): symptoms vary with plants attacked.

> Amaryllis: grayish mold on foliage; mostly in South, outdoors after a chill.
>
> Anemone: rotting of crown.
>
> Tuberous Begonia: dead spots on flowers and leaves, rapidly enlarging, turning dark and covered with grayish mold.
>
> Dahlia: dark spots covered with grayish mold on buds and blooms.
>
> Gladiolus: see Chapter 17.
>
> Lily: grayish mold on leaves, but see Chapter 15 for more serious botrytis blight caused by *Botrytis elliptica.*
>
> Narcissus: occasionally troublesome, causing grayish mold on leaves.

Control: gather all infected leaves or flowers into bag as soon as noticed, and burn. Burn plants which show rot of crowns or bulbs. Provide good ventilation and wide spacing of greenhouse plants. Avoid syringing. Spraying with Bordeaux mixture will help in most cases.

BLIGHT, LILY (*Botrytis elliptica*): see Chapter 15.

BLIGHT, NARCISSUS FIRE (*Botrytis polyblastis*): see Chapter 11.

BLIGHT, NARCISSUS LEAF SCORCH and RED BLOTCH OF AMARYLLIS: tips of Narcissi appear to be suffering from frost injury for several inches and are separated from the healthy part of the leaf by a yellow margin. Secondary infection consists of very small yellowish or watery spots which become scabby and dark reddish-brown. These spots may also appear on stems and flower petals. On Amaryllis (Hippeastrum) red spots appear on leaves, stems of flowers, and flower petals. Leaves and stems are deformed.

Control: presoak affected bulbs 1 hour. Then soak for 30 minutes in a 1–750 solution of mercuric chloride before planting. Discard seriously affected bulbs. Disease is spread by syringing and heavy watering.

Attacks: Amaryllis, Crinum, Eucharis, Haemanthus, Hymenocallis, Leucojum, Narcissus, Nerine, Sternbergia, Vallota, Zephyranthes.

BLIGHT, SNOWDROP (*Botrytis galanthina*): causes black dots to appear on outer scales of bulbs.

Control: remove affected scales before planting.

BLIGHT, SOUTHERN (*Sclerotium Rolfsi*): also known as "mustard seed fungus" because of characteristic mustard seed-like sclerotia attached to white threads of mycelium found in soil around rotting roots and bulbs. The sclerotia are first white, then turn tan or brown. Often first sign of trouble is sudden wilting and yellowing of the plant. A closer examination will show sclerotia and mycelium threads in the soil, often at the surface. Bulbs and roots will be partially or completely rotted. Most prevalent during warm and rainy weather.

Control: destroy affected bulbs and the soil about them as soon as noticed. A 1–1000 solution of bichloride of mercury can be poured into and around the hole from which plant was removed and over nearby growing bulbs. Add nitrogen to soil by use of organic matter or nitrogenous fertilizers. Successful control has been reported with Floral Dust.

Attacks: Amaryllis, Canna, Gladiolus, Narcissus, Ornithogalum.

BLIGHT, TULIP FIRE (BOTRYTIS BLIGHT) (*Botrytis tulipae*): see Chapter 12.

MILDEW, POWDERY: see Chapter 16.

MOSAIC, DAHLIA: see Chapter 16.

MOSAIC, IRIS: this disease so far is confined to the Pacific coast, where plants attacked show mottled foliage and dwarfing, with flower colors darker than normal; transmitted by Potato and Peach aphids.

Control: keep free of aphids. Destroy diseased bulbs.

Attacks: Babiana, Iris (Bulbous).

MOSAIC, LILY: see Chapter 15.

MOSAIC, NARCISSUS: see Chapter 11.

MOSAIC, ORNITHOGALUM: causes young foliage to become mottled light and dark green; mature foliage gray or yellow. Stems are marked and blotched. Transmitted by the Cotton, Lily, and Peach aphids.
   Control: as above for Iris Mosaic.
   Attacks: Galtonia, Hyacinth, Lachenalia, Ornithogalum.

RING DISEASE: see Stem and Bulb Nematode, page 116.

ROT, BASAL, OF NARCISSUS: see Chapter 11.

ROT, BASAL FUSARIUM, OF NARCISSUS: see Chapter 11.

ROT, BLUE MOLD: causes brown, sunken lesions on corms in storage; edges of lesions are water-soaked, greenish. Blue mold develops when moist.
   Control: dry rapidly at 80 degrees for two weeks after digging; then store in cooler temperature.
   Attacks: Crocus, Gladiolus, Montbretia, Scilla.

ROT, BROWN, OF GLADIOLUS: see Chapter 17.

ROT, DRY FUSARIUM, OF GLADIOLUS: see Chapter 17.

ROT, FUSARIUM, OF LILY: brown rot occurs at base of scales next to basal plate of bulb. Affected scales fall away.
   Control: soak bulbs 30 minutes in formalin solution, 1–50. Soil can be disinfected with formalin or chloropicrin (tear gas).
   Attacks: Crocus, Freesia, Lily.

ROT, FUSARIUM YELLOWS, OF GLADIOLUS: see Chapter 17.

ROT, NARCISSUS SMOULDER: see Chapter 11.

SCAB, GLADIOLUS: see Chapter 17.

SMOULDER, NARCISSUS: see Chapter 11.

VIRUS DISEASES: see Mosaics, pages 119–20.

WILT, SPOTTED (VIRUS) : foliage becomes spotted, streaked, or ringed with
  yellow, brown, or purple, followed by death of leaves.
  Control: destroy affected bulbs or corms. Disease is transmitted by
    thrips. To destroy these, dust bulbs with DDT. (See Thrips,
    page 117.)
  Attacks: Amaryllis, Begonia, Calla, Dahlia, Gloxinia.

YELLOWS, FUSARIUM: see Chapter 17.

INSECTICIDES AND FUNGICIDES

ARASAN: a duPont disinfectant for the treatment of seeds.

BLACK LEAF 40: see nicotine sulphate.

BORDEAUX MIXTURE: zinc-copper fungicide. Leaves a bluish-white residue
  on foliage. Must be freshly mixed to be effective.

CALOMEL: mercurous chloride, used in the control of diseases on tubers,
  corms, and bulbs.

CERESAN: a duPont disinfectant for bulbs, especially Narcissus.

CHLORDANE: an insecticide effective against thrips, wireworms, and other
  soil-borne insects. Sold under various trade names.

CHLOROPICRIN (TEAR GAS) : used as a soil fumigant. Sold under various
  trade names. Fumes in low concentrations cause weeping.

CYANOGAS: insecticide and rodenticide which forms a deadly gas on contact with air and moisture. To be used with great caution.

DD MIXTURE: a soil fumigant for control of root-knot nematodes, wireworms, and other soil-borne pests. Contact with human flesh may
  cause serious burns.

DDT: insecticide used to control beetles, borers, leafhoppers, thrips, and
  some other pests. Toxic to man.

DI-MITE: trade name for a contact control for mites and red spider.

DITHANE Z-78: trade name for a fungicide spray or dust based on dithane,
  used to control blights and other plant diseases. Other Dithane
  fungicides sold under various trade names.

FERMATE: an organic fungicide used to prevent botrytis blight and other
  plant diseases.

FLORAL DUST: effective against both pests and diseases of many kinds.

FORMALDEHYDE: an organic fungicide used as a soil fumigant and, in solution, to clean up infected bulbs, corms, and tubers. Also available in dust form.

LEAD ARSENATE: an insecticide which acts as a stomach poison. Available
  as a dust or in wettable form. Poisonous to man.

LINDANE: an insecticide especially for soil-borne insects and household pests. Sold also under various trade names, as Isotox.

MERCURIC CHLORIDE: (Corrosive sublimate.) Deadly poison used for disinfecting soil and seeds. Used in 1–1000 solution. Corrodes metal.

NICOTINE DUST: nicotine sulphate in dust form—an insecticide effective against sucking insects. Poisonous to man.

NICOTINE SULPHATE: an insecticide effective against sucking insects. Available everywhere as Black Leaf 40. Poisonous to man.

PARADICHLOROBENZENE: a fungicide, used as a fumigant. Creates fumes poisonous to man.

PARATHION: an organic insecticide available as a dust, wettable powder, or in aerosol bombs. Highly toxic to man.

PARIS GREEN: an insecticide used chiefly in poison baits. Poisonous to man.

PARZATE: see Dithane.

PYRETHRUM: insecticide derived from pyrethrum flowers. Available as spray or dust. Non-poisonous to man and animals.

ROTENONE: insecticide made from derris root. Available as a spray or dust. Non-poisonous to man and animals.

SEMESAN: seed and bulb disinfectant and plant stimulant.

SOILFUME CAPS: soil fumigant put up in convenient capsule form. Used for nematodes and wireworms.

SULPHUR: available in many forms. Lime-sulphur is used as an insecticide and fungicide. Zinc-sulphur dust controls mildew and other diseases, mites and tarnished plant bug. Wettable sulphur is available for use in sprays.

TEAR GAS: see Chloropicrin.

TEPP: used to control mites. Available as dust, spray, or in aerosol bombs. *Use with caution*. Poisonous to man.

Caution! IN USING ANY INSECTICIDE OR FUNGICIDE, FOLLOW MANUFACTURER'S DIRECTIONS ACCURATELY. Failure to do so may result not only in poor results but also in actual injury to plants, or DANGER TO HUMAN LIFE.

PART TWO
—THE MORE IMPORTANT
GROUPS OF BULBS

Holland's Glory, a beautiful new, not-too-double, pale primrose Daffodil that is slightly fragrant and excellent for cutting.

CHAPTER *11. Daffodils*

"Take the winds of March with Beauty"

All winter our pleasantest dreams of the coming of spring are built around the certainty that the golden sunshine of Daffodils will cascade down our garden slopes, break in creamy foam against stone terrace walls, and run off in rivulets along paths and into flower borders. Whatever the weather, bugs and germs, the unkindly hand of late winter, or just plain sulks may do to other flowers, we know that the ever-dependable Daffodils will come through with colors flying.

Sounds as though we must have bought them by the thousand? Not a bit of it; not even by the hundred. They have all come from original plantings of from three to a dozen bulbs, and the only propagation we have done is an occasional replanting. Remember the old story about the blacksmith and the king's horse—one penny for the first nail, tuppence for the second, fourpence for the third, and so on? Daffodilian progression—that's the answer. Every year now we add a few bulbs of each of a few new varieties, in the hopeless attempt to keep somewhere near up to date, and give away hundreds of old bulbs. As a garden investment, no other bulbs can equal the dividend-paying Daffodils!

No other flower in the world is quite so universally and definitely associated with any one season, nor so completely embodies in its characteristics the atmosphere and essence of a season. Nature has made the Daffodil a perfect symbol of that time of year when all hearts feel the upsurge of new hopes and ambitions; when, as a poet has put it, "the hounds of spring are on winter's traces . . . and the hoofed heel of a satyr crushes the chestnut husk at the chestnut root." And— something to thank the Lord for—not all the hybridizers in the world have been able to so change the Daffodil as to give it other forms or other seasons of bloom that would destroy this age-old association.

KNOW YOUR DAFFODILS

Yes, everyone knows the Daffodil; but it is astonishing how few, even among gardeners of considerable experience, realize the wide range of types to be found in *Narcissus* species, nor for how long a season they will flood the garden with cheerfulness if but given the chance to do so.

We are not referring now to varieties—of which there is a plethora that threatens to submerge even the experts—but to those differences in flower form, in habit, and especially in time of bloom that distinguish one type or class from another. Gain first some knowledge of types, and worry about varieties later.

This is not merely a matter of botanical interest. We all wish to enjoy Daffodils as long as we can have them. At best they haste away too soon, and the last dancing blossoms have faded before "summer is y'cummin' in." And to have them for six weeks or more instead of the two or three which in most gardens covers their span of bloom, one must plant types other than the big Trumpets and the giant Incomparabilis and Leedsi varieties which get most of the display space in catalogues.

But it is not alone to have a longer-flowering season that you should be familiar with the several types. In addition to differences in season of bloom, there are differences in size, height, and general habit of growth that are all-important when it comes to placing Daffodils about your garden. The Giant Trumpet that makes such a bold display in the mixed border would be entirely out of character and out of scale in the rock garden, or in an intimate sheltered little nook where one of the low-growing informal species hybrids might make, during its fairly long stay, the most delightful close-up in all your spring pictures. And, according to the types or varieties used, a naturalized planting may look really natural, or about as much so as a plastic Christmas tree. In height Daffodils range from the 6 or 8 inches of several of the species (such as *bulbocodium* and *triandrus albus*) to the 18-inch stems of some of the more robust new Trumpets and Large-cups; and flowers vary from thimble size, singly or in clusters, to blooms 5 or 6 inches in diameter.

The new classification

The latest reclassification of Narcissi is somewhat simpler than the previous one. For the average gardener, however, with no particular desire to grow Daffodils for show purposes, the chief importance of any classification is to emphasize the fact that there exists such a remarkable range in size, form, and (with the more recent introductions) even in color.

To make it easier to follow, the official classification is here put down in abbreviated form, presenting only the eleven main divisions.

In this new classification the "Leedsi," "Incomparabilis," and "Barrii" designations, formerly so confusing, are discarded, and the varieties they included are regrouped as "Large-cupped" and "Small-cupped."

DIVISION I—*Trumpet:* the trumpet (or corona) as long or longer than the perianth (outer petal) segments; one flower to a stem.

DIVISION II—*Large-cupped:* cup (or corona) more than one third, but less than equal to, the length of the perianth segments; one flower to a stem.

DIVISION III—*Small-cupped:* cup (or corona) not more than one third the length of the perianth segments; one flower to a stem.

DIVISION IV—*Double:* double flowers. (*See comments below.*)

DIVISION V—*Triandrus:* hybrids with *N. triandrus* characteristics clearly evident.

DIVISION VI—*Cyclamineus:* hybrids with *N. cyclamineus* characteristics clearly evident.

DIVISION VII—*Jonquilla:* hybrids with any of the characteristics of the *N. jonquilla* group clearly evident.

DIVISION VIII—*Tazetta:* hybrids with characteristics of any of the *N. Tazetta* (Poetaz) group clearly evident.

DIVISION IX—*Poeticus:* hybrids with characteristics of *N. poeticus,* without admixture of any other.

DIVISION X—*Species* and *Wild Forms:* all species and wild, or reputedly wild, forms and hybrids.

DIVISION XI—*Miscellaneous:* Narcissi not falling into any of the foregoing divisions.

Comments: In Divisions I, II, III, V, VI, and VII there are subclasses, based on color or on the length of the corona. Thus Division

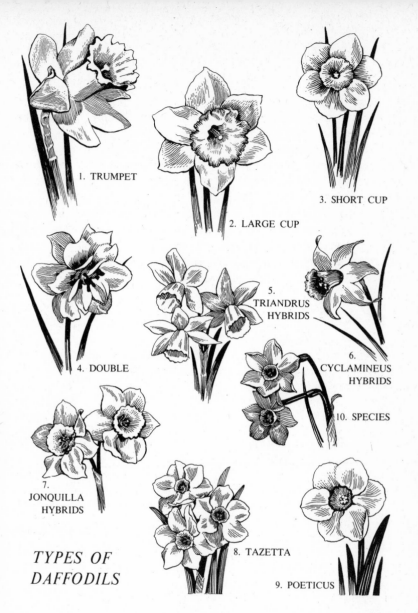

1. TRUMPET

2. LARGE CUP

3. SHORT CUP

4. DOUBLE

5. TRIANDRUS HYBRIDS

6. CYCLAMINEUS HYBRIDS

7. JONQUILLA HYBRIDS

8. TAZETTA

9. POETICUS

10. SPECIES

TYPES OF DAFFODILS

I-a includes the yellow Trumpets; I-b, the bicolor Trumpets; Division V-b, Triandrus hybrids with "the cup not less than two thirds as long as the perianth segments"; etc., etc. These subdivisions are of importance chiefly in classifying varieties for exhibition purposes, where one must "go by the book."

Divisions II and III, it seems to us, might better have been called "Long-cups" and "Short-cups" instead of "Large" and "Small." The classification is based on *length* of the cup, not on its size; and some of the Short-cups (Diana Kasner, for instance) certainly do not have *small* cups.

Division IV (Double) is somewhat ambiguous. Some of the bunch-flowered varieties have double flowers. In the official list of the Royal Horticultural Society, Elvira is put in Division VIII (Tazetta or bunch-flowered), while its double form, the delightful Cheerfulness, is placed in Division IV (Double). Some authoritative catalogues list it in Division VIII, where, it seems to us, it properly belongs. But the argument is immaterial—plant a few, and you'll always be glad you did it. Characteristics of the species and species groups which have lent their names to Divisions V to IX are as follows:

N. triandrus (DIVISION V)—rush-like leaves to 1 foot. Flowers per stem, 1–6, pure white and with cup-like corona half the length of perianth segments.

N. cyclamineus (DIVISION VI)—single flowers, drooping or nodding. Perianth, yellow; segments reflexed. Corona orange-yellow, narrow, wavy-edged, the length of the perianth segments.

N. jonquilla (group) (DIVISION VII)—leaves rush-like to 1½ feet. Yellow, fragrant flowers, 2–6 per stem. Corona less than half the length of the perianth segments, and wavy-edged.

N. Tazetta (group) (DIVISION VIII)—fragrant white flowers, 4–8 per stem, with light yellow coronas much shorter than the obovate perianth segments. Also pure white (Paperwhite Narcissus.)

N. poeticus (DIVISION IX)—flowers usually solitary, white, fragrant, with *red-edged,* flat, waved yellow corona, much shorter than perianth segments.

This brief survey will give you a working idea of the new classification of the various types and how to identify them. Our chief concern, however, is how they fit into the garden.

WHERE AND WHAT TO PLANT

Daffodils are not big plants, nor are they garbed with the brilliant colors which enable many of the other spring bulbs to dominate their surroundings. They offer a challenge to the imagination and craftsman-ship of the gardener: *Here we are; see what you can do with us; if you use us skillfully, we can make your garden a springtime Eden at which every beholder will marvel, taking us for children of the rain and the hoyden wind.*

To accept the challenge successfully, you must use your head. For-tunately you will be working on a canvas where no brush stroke is final, for Daffodils can be shifted about with the greatest of ease and with no danger of loss; and each paint tube will contain more pigment every time you go back to it!

In planning your Daffodil plantings (the plural is used advisedly, for you will want several) keep in mind first of all that they will be for a spring exhibition. So a good way to start is to gaze out of your view window, unless the "view"—as in so many modern houses—is merely the street in front. Looking at your garden from indoors, you can readily pick out spots where, on a drizzly or too windy day in late March or April, there will be emerging from the dreariness of retreat-ing winter the browns and reds and delicate greens of trees and shrubs coming back to life. Among these you can readily visualize settings where a group of Daffodils, large or small, will add just the touch needed to complete a perfect spring picture: perhaps merely a minia-ture to be enjoyed at close range through a window; perhaps a spread-ing vista that invites you to dare inclement weather for a brief stroll where you can observe those day-to-day changes that make even a moderate-sized collection of Daffodils, as one variety after another opens, such an exciting experience.

Daffodils lend themselves, in the various types available, to about every sort of use the gardener can think of. They are *par excellence* the flower for naturalizing—and for informal landscape groups of half a dozen plants or a hundred.

In small groups in the mixed hardy border they "stay put" without crowding in on their neighbors and, after staging their own act, grace-fully retire from the limelight, requiring no further care, except pos-sibly a tucking in of their green skirts, until other plants cover the drying foliage.

For use among rocks, either in the rock garden or more or less haphazardly on a stony bank or about individual boulders, you will seek far and wide indeed to find anything to equal the various Daffodil species and their hybrids. For this type of planting they have

Terrace planting of Daffodils at GrayRock. Tall variety in foreground in Trevithian, a Jonquilla Hybrid.

two advantages: their inherent affinity for rocks and their ability to hold their own with such other rock plants or ground covers as may overrun them. At the same time they do not increase so rapidly as to require constant replanting.

Frequently Daffodils are put to one use for which they are not well suited—narrow border plantings along paths, walls, or driveways. So used, during the few weeks they are in bloom they make a fine show; but following this the foliage, after maturing, gradually dies down, and for the latter part of the season the ground is left bare. If it is desired to make use of them for a planting of this sort, they should be interspersed with a few reliably vigorous perennials so that at least intermittent bloom may be had throughout the season. A good combination is Daffodils for early spring, Irises for late spring, Phlox for midsummer, and low-growing Cushion Chrysanthemums for autumn. Or sufficient space may be left between the Daffodil clumps, even in a narrow ribbon border, to set in pot-grown or seedling plants of such long-flowering annuals as Petunias, Marigolds, Dwarf Nasturtiums, Dwarf Zinnias, Dwarf Dahlias, Portulaca, and *Phlox Drummondi*.

Plan definitely, too, to enjoy Daffodils indoors as well as in the garden. You can, of course, cut them from here and there about the garden, but unless you have many it will be well worth while to have a few short rows tucked away somewhere—the vegetable garden makes a good location—especially for cutting.

To be at their best indoors, blooms should be cut with long stems just as they are about half open. Then, if at once placed in deep water and hardened for several hours in a cool place, they will remain fresh for days. In the garden one hesitates to cut them when first opening; and if open flowers are cut at random, many of the blooms are likely to be several days old and will not keep fresh very long. In the cutting rows, types and varieties may be mixed together indiscriminately, but to assure a long season there should be some extra-early and extra-late varieties. The inexpensive mixtures often sold for naturalizing—for which purpose they are not desirable—do provide good planting stock for flowers for cutting. Surplus bulbs of varieties in the garden which may especially appeal to you for decoration or arrangement indoors are, however, the very best source of bulbs for your cutting rows.

TYPICAL VARIETIES FOR VARIOUS USES

As a starter list for the new gardener, here are some varieties of Narcissi that we have found very satisfactory for the uses indicated.

They should be considered merely as typical examples, as there are many similar ones in each group. The names only are given here; descriptions may be found in any good catalogue.

For naturalizing

POETICUS (fragrant): *Poeticus recurvus;* Horace; Thelma. JON-QUILLA (fragrant): Golden Sceptre; Sierra Gold; Trevithian. CYCLAMINEUS: February Gold. TAZETTA (fragrant): Glorious (semi-shade); Laurens Koster. TRIANDRUS: Pearly Queen; Moonshine (shade). SHORT-CUP: Eclair; Firetail; Nette O'Melveny; Queen of the North; Sunrise; Silver Star; Hera. WHITE TRUMPET: W. P. Milner; LaVestale.

For beds and borders

YELLOW TRUMPETS: King Alfred; Aerolite; Lord Wellington; President LeBrun; Dawson City. WHITE TRUMPETS: Beersheba; President Carnot; Roxane. BICOLOR TRUMPETS: Silvanite; Jefta. LARGE-CUP: John Evelyn; Francisca Drake; Croesus; E. H. Wilson; Fortune; Gertie Millar; Daisy Schaffer; Mrs. R. O. Backhouse; Milford Haven; Scarlet Leader; Scarlet Elegance; Red Cross. SHORT-CUP: Diana Kasner; Mrs. Barclay; Alcida.

For the rock garden

SPECIES: cyclamineus; *Bulbocodium conspicuus; triandrus albus.* TRIANDRUS: Moonshine; Thalia; Agnes Harvey; Shot Silk. JON-QUILLA: Orange Queen; *Jonquilla simplex; Jonquilla flore-pleno.* CYCLAMINEUS: March Sunshine.

For cutting

WHITE TRUMPET: Mrs. E. H. Krelage; Beersheba. YELLOW TRUMPET: Golden Harvest; Alasnam; Dawson City. DOUBLE: Cheerfulness; Mary Copeland; Twink. LARGE-CUP: Bernardino; John Evelyn; Dick Wellband; Havelock; Red Cross; Carlton. TRI-ANDRUS: Pearly Queen; Moonshine. JONQUILLA: Trevithian; Golden Perfection; Golden Pedestal. SHORT-CUP: Diana Kasner; Alcida; Edith.

CULTURE

With a fairly definite picture in mind of the garden effects he can secure with Daffodils, and the purposes for which he wishes to grow them, the gardener's next concern is to handle them in such a way as to get results as perfect as possible under the conditions with which he has to work. The first step in this direction is an understanding of their requirements. Without such knowledge it is of course impossible for him to get the best out of his plant material, no matter how good it may be.

Daffodils have long suffered the fate of all "easy" plants. They will survive with so little care—or perhaps it might be more accurate to say under such extreme neglect—that in the great majority of home gardens, once planted, they are left to shift for themselves like Iris, Phlox, Day-lilies, and a few other stand-bys which will continue to come smilin' through no matter how abandoned to their fates. They get practically no attention from one end of the year to the other, white Roses or Dahlias or some other temperamental sister is cuddled and coddled all season long. But while such neglected Daffodils may continue to bloom spring after spring, they do not give such large flowers nor produce them as freely as they might; nor do they increase in number as rapidly as they are capable of doing, with a resultant extension of the original planting, or the production of surplus bulbs which may be traded with one's gardening friends for other varieties.

To produce really fine Daffodils, the gardener should have some knowledge of how the plant grows—of its growth cycle around the year. This has been covered in a general way in Chapter 5. To be a little more specific, let us take a Daffodil bulb of the type usually delivered to the amateur grower in September or October and follow it through a year's development under garden conditions.

When received from the seed store, the bulb, so far as appearances go, is completely dormant. It should be plump, solid, and heavy if it has been properly handled; and within it already exists, completely formed, the flower or flowers which will appear the following spring. Changes which have taken place within the bulb during the storage or dormant period have prepared it for quick action once it is planted. As soon as it is placed in the soil, new roots begin to push out from

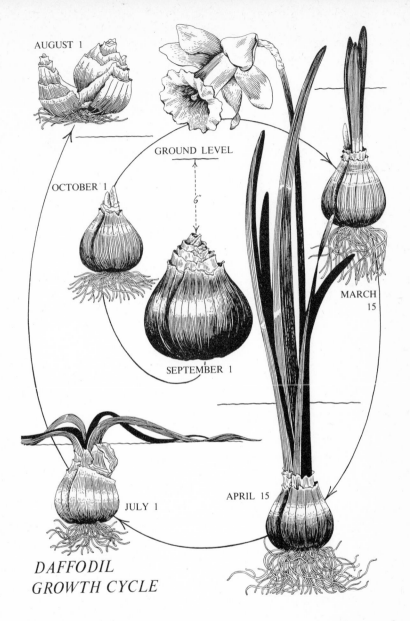

AUGUST 1

GROUND LEVEL

6"

OCTOBER 1

SEPTEMBER 1

MARCH 15

JULY 1

APRIL 15

DAFFODIL GROWTH CYCLE

all around the base. These grow rapidly and within two or three weeks have taken such a firm hold that the bulb cannot be raised without lifting a mass of soil with it. This root development continues until the soil freezes solid for the winter.

In the meantime the new leaves will have pushed up to or slightly through the apex of the bulb. Here, however, under normal conditions, they stop, and do not appear aboveground until the following spring. If autumn is late and unseasonably warm, leaves may push up above the surface of the soil, but this is an abnormal condition. Usually at this time of year, as the nights grow colder, the soil temperature is considerably above that of the atmosphere. This, of course, tends to hold the top growth in check while at the same time giving the roots an opportunity to develop.

During the winter, in cold sections, the bulbs with their mass of new roots freeze solid in the soil, and the processes of growth are suspended. If proper rooting has taken place, the fleshy bulb tissue is in no way injured by such freezing, although unrooted bulbs under the same conditions would be destroyed.

With the return of warmer days and the first thawing of the soil in spring, growth is renewed. The root system, already thoroughly established, supplements the plant food stored within the bulb, making possible an extremely rapid growth of foliage and flower stems.

The flower stems reach full development and the blossoms open and fade long before the foliage reaches maturity. During the period of early spring growth, the energies of the plant are devoted to the production of flowers and of the new bulbs; the old bulbs at this time are flabbier and lighter in weight than when they were planted in the fall.

After flowering, there follows a phase of the cycle of growth, several weeks long, during which the foliage reaches its maximum development. The size, weight, and flowering capacity of the new crop of bulbs, whether they are to be left in the ground or taken up, *are determined by the growth made during this period*. This is the secret of successful Daffodil culture.

The duration of the period of top growth after the flowers fade depends largely upon local conditions. Cool weather, plenty of moisture in the soil, and an adequate supply of plant food tend to prolong the season of top growth to its full, normal extent. Poor soil, dry soil, and high temperatures after flowering tend to cut it short. While it is not true that the biggest and heaviest bulbs (of any particular variety) always produce the best or the most flowers, as a general rule they do. Certain types of soil or an oversupply of nitrogen in the plant-food supply, especially late in the season, may produce heavy, soft bulbs which will not cure properly and are poor in quality. Such conditions are not likely to be encountered under garden culture.

Some varieties seed freely. The majority do not. In either case, the flower stalks and the foliage remain green until, in the bulb's annual cycle of growth, the time for the dormant or resting period arrives. Then the tops gradually wither, dry back to the ground, and eventually slough off at the apex of the bulb under the soil. The roots also shrivel and dry, somewhat more slowly, and are often still firmly attached to the bulb at digging time.

Although the several weeks which follow are usually spoken of as the dormant period, this is—as we have already seen—a decidedly inaccurate use of the term, for growth changes within the bulb continue.

A survey of this annual life cycle shows that there are three periods of active growth: first, immediately after the bulbs are planted, when the root system develops rapidly; second, early in the spring, when the foliage and flowers are being produced; third, a considerable period after flowering, while the foliage is being matured, before it begins to ripen off. Then follows the period when the bulb, *whether left in the soil or kept in storage,* undergoes its rest-period changes. Our system of culture should be built upon these facts.

Soil

In growing Daffodils in the garden, there is not likely to be any very wide choice of soil. Most Daffodils, fortunately, thrive in a wide range of soil types. We have had them do well in extremely light sandy soil within a stone's throw of the seashore and also in heavy clay loam inland. The ideal soil is a deep, rich clay loam containing enough sand to work nicely and be thoroughly friable.

In the matter of drainage, the home gardener is not apt to have much choice. From our own experience it seems that the question of drainage has been rather overemphasized in Daffodil literature in so far as garden culture is concerned. While the roots are active—after planting in the fall and during the spring—most types of Daffodils will in no wise suffer from a high degree of soil moisture. Probably it is for this reason that the Poeticus type—which is the last to cease growth and the first to start it again in the fall, having practically no real rest period—will thrive in low moist ground unsuited to many

Group of Daffodil E. H. Wilson—from six bulbs planted two years previously.

other types. It is drainage during the summer rest period which should cause concern—a point which most writers have consistently overlooked. On several occasions we have known Daffodils to grow normally and flower perfectly on soil quite saturated with water during several weeks in early spring. On two occasions we have had several lots of Daffodils grown in bulb pans for forcing which—owing in one case to an early fall freeze and in the other to a burst water pipe—were literally under 6 inches of water, alternating with solid freezing, in the trenches in which they had been placed for the winter; and they grew and flowered normally after they were brought in. This despite the fact that an undue top growth had been made before they were subjected to this unplanned but convincing experiment.

Where drainage is not good, any of the usual methods of improving it, as suggested in Chapter 6, may be followed. For bulbs in moderate numbers, the simplest plan is to form raised beds 6 or 8 inches above the soil level and held in place by stone or sod borders. Even if this is not done for the entire planting, it may be desirable for the rarer and more difficult varieties, particularly for the light-colored Trumpets.

In selecting an exposure for planting, the gardener may have somewhat more latitude. A slight slope to the south or to the east is to be preferred if it is available. A slope not only assures better drainage, but Daffodils, particularly if they are to be planted in considerable numbers, are infinitely more charming on sloping ground than on a level plot.

Shelter, too, is important. If some of the extra-early varieties, such as certain of the species and species hybrids (February Gold and March Sunshine, for instance), can be placed in a sequestered spot, it may mean a matter of a week or so—in some seasons considerably more—in the time of their first flowering. With many plants, too warm and sheltered a pocket promoting early growth is distinctly a disadvantage, but that is not the case with these dainty but frostproof harbingers of spring.

For the later types, protection from driving winds by a hedge, a shrubbery border, or a wall often preserves the blossoms from being badly battered. Such protection is doubly important when flowers are to be grown for exhibition purposes, or even for cutting for indoor decoration.

Planting

With the ground once thoroughly prepared (see page 70) the work of planting is at least 80 per cent done. Another 10 per cent of the work which remains can be accomplished at one's leisure. It consists of making out labels and setting out the bulbs in the order in which they are to be planted, so that everything will be in readiness for the final rite of actually placing the bulbs in the soil. The rest is not only easy but one of those garden tasks which is almost an unadulterated pleasure.

Just what is the best time to plant Daffodils?

In theory, it is just before the bulbs, having completed ripening and maturing processes which take place during the period of dormancy, are ready to send out new roots. This state will vary somewhat with different types and even with individual varieties, and also with local conditions. On an average, in the Northern United States it would be in late August or very early September.

As a matter of practice, the planting date—at least for bulbs which must be purchased—is determined not by a theoretical ideal time, but by when the bulbs can be procured. But the planter can adopt as a guiding rule the principle of the earlier the better. Daffodil bulbs may be, and frequently are, planted in October or November, and even into December; but late planting is to be avoided if possible. If planting is very late, a heavy mulch, to postpone hard freezing of the ground, will provide a longer period for root development.

Do not let any bulb salesman persuade you that early planting is a matter of no importance. While late planting will by no means spell complete failure—and though it is of course infinitely better than not planting at all!—it does result in giving the bulbs a poorer start, and in all probability less perfect flowers for the first season. Some years ago I had occasion to plant, on a commercial scale, several varieties quite late in the season. They were put in the same field, under exactly the same conditions, as other lots of the same varieties planted some three weeks earlier. The result was certainly convincing proof of the advantage of earlier planting. These late-set bulbs produced barely half the volume of foliage made by those in the earlier planting. The flowers were smaller and the flower stalks little more than half as high. All the bulbs had come from the same source, and if there was any difference in quality, it was in favor of those which had to be planted late.

With many varieties there is another distinct advantage in early planting. Some sorts are decidedly poor keepers and are likely to begin to get soft or even to decay if held long beyond the time when they should be back in the ground. This is especially true of the white and light-flowered Trumpets as a class.

So far as preference in time may be given, Poeticus varieties and extremely early-flowering species and species hybrids should be planted first.

The depth of planting for Daffodil bulbs—like the period during which they may be planted—is a matter of considerable elasticity. For the beginner it would almost be safe to suggest "the deeper the better." The instructions usually given to plant the bulbs deep enough so there will be 4 or 5 inches of soil above the top of the bulb are correct for most varieties and usual conditions. It might be more accurate to say the "shoulder" of the bulb rather than the top, as some bulbs have long tapering necks. The beginner, however, often thinks he has covered the bulb 4 or 5 inches deep, when actual measurement with a ruler would reveal that it was little over half that depth. In light sandy soil it is advisable to increase the depth of planting by an inch or so.

The distance apart at which the bulbs are to be placed depends upon a number of factors. Large bulbs in groups in the border may be placed 6 to 8 inches apart each way. This is close enough to avoid a spotty effect the first season and yet leaves room enough for two or three years' increase before the group will become overcrowded. This is for strong-growing types, such as practically all the Trumpets, and certain vigorous Large-cups and Small-cups. Bulbs of less robust growth—the true Poets, many of the Poeticus-like crosses, the Jonquil and Triandrus hybrids—may well be placed as close as 4 or 5 inches apart.

In naturalized planting, anything like a regular spacing of the bulbs must be studiously avoided or the desired effect will be spoiled. A method often employed is to take a basketful or pailful of bulbs and throw them out on the ground with a swinging motion, so that while the bulk of them fall fairly close together, others will be scattered to a considerable distance, with much more space between the individual bulbs. A few practice attempts usually enable the planter to secure a desirable distribution, and the bulbs may then be planted as they have fallen, with the removal of some where they happen to be too thick.

Even in the border, much more pleasing effects result if straight rows, rectangles, and too regular spacing are avoided in planting. Nothing approaching the abandon of a really naturalized planting can be attempted under garden conditions, but an effect between this extreme on the one hand and studied formality on the other may be obtained. Mark off the soil in the border—after it has been prepared and raked smooth—into somewhat irregular circles and oblongs, each of a size which will accommodate the number of bulbs of the variety to be planted within it. The bulbs are then placed, somewhat irregularly, conforming to the outline which has been made. The effect of such a group, even the first season, will be that of a colony that has developed naturally by itself. If other planting is to be done, either at the same time or the following spring, the location of each group of bulbs can be marked by outlining it with a narrow ribbon of ground limestone or sand applied with a watering can, with sprinkler removed.

Watering immediately after planting, unless nature provides a good soaking, is always desirable. Without plenty of moisture in the soil, the new root growth will be delayed or start slowly and irregularly. In moist soil the roots make a quick strong start and within ten days or so will have taken firm hold and be in condition to forage successfully for themselves even if the soil remains comparatively dry for some time after planting.

As the soil will have become more or less packed down in the process of planting, it is advisable to loosen thoroughly and pulverize it to the depth of a couple of inches after the bulbs have been put in. This is especially important in rather heavy soil with a tendency to pack hard. Unless loosened up comparatively soon after planting, such soil will go through the winter with hard spots that may interfere considerably with the pushing up of the foliage in the spring. If left until spring, it cannot readily be cultivated without danger of cutting or breaking the growing foliage shoots just beneath the surface.

Mulching for the first season after planting is sometimes advisable, but many authorities consider it unnecessary. We have never known varieties of the really hardy types, *if* planted early enough to make strong root growth before the ground froze, to be injured for lack of winter mulching. In severe climates a mulch for new plantings of valuable varieties is worth while as an extra precaution. Varieties of the semi-hardy types, such as Paperwhite and Soleil d'Or, and the hardy Poetaz varieties, like Laurens Koster, Aspasia, and Orange Cup, if planted near the northern limit of where they may safely be grown out of doors, decidedly will be benefited by winter mulching.

In applying a winter mulch, do not put it on until about the time the surface of the soil begins to freeze. Wheat or rye straw and meadow or salt hay are the materials most often employed for mulching. Peat-moss has the advantage, especially for the home garden, of not being unsightly during the winter and in the spring can be worked into the soil instead of having to be removed. Our favorite mulches are pine needles or short evergreen boughs applied just after the soil has frozen, and preferably over snow.

Spring care

The first spring job in the Daffodil border, if a winter mulch has been put on, is to remove this carefully before growth starts. Watch for any foliage which may be pushing up, as some varieties begin growth much earlier than others.

As soon as the sprouts are safely aboveground and the surface soil is dry enough to be worked, give a shallow hoeing or cultivating. This will get rid of any sprouting weed seeds and put the soil in condition to absorb readily spring rains where they fall instead of permitting the runoff resulting from a hard surface.

An application of plant food is also in order at this time. As the annual cycle of growth of the Daffodil plant makes plain (see page 135), there is now renewed activity of the root growth and a very rapid and vigorous development of both foliage and flowers. The fertilizer supplied should contain plenty of available nitrogen. One of the quick-acting, complete chemical plant foods put out under various trade names will answer. If bone meal is used, at least half of it should be in the form of bone flour. A supplementary dressing of nitrate of soda or sulphate of ammonia may be desirable, particularly if the spring is very cold and backward. Needless to say, all fertilizer materials should be applied carefully in accordance with the directions accompanying them. The fertilizers need be only lightly scratched in, as spring rains quickly carry them down to the roots. Fertilizers high in nitrogen should be applied only very early in the season. If used after the buds begin to develop, they are likely to result in soft flowers which stand up poorly, particularly if wanted for exhibition purposes.

For Daffodils being grown in the garden, no further care, except to keep them clear of any weeds which may start, will be required until after flowering. Where flowers are grown for exhibition purposes, protection and support may be required.

After flowering

All too often, as the golden chalices or the gleaming white perianths of the Daffodil blooms fade, the grower's interest fades with them. This is both the most universal and the most serious mistake in the culture of Daffodils in the home garden. While the flowers may be gone, the Daffodil plant is just midway in its most important period of growth. The gardener's aim from this point on should be to keep it growing as long and as vigorously as possible.

A second application of fertilizer, similar to that which was put on when the beds were prepared in the fall, may well be made at this time. In rich soil this may not be needed, but as a rule it is advisable, particularly in the border where the Daffodils must compete with other annuals and perennials for the balance of the season.

A thorough stirring of the soil between the clumps or groups of Daffodils is also important, as the surface about them is likely again to have become packed fairly hard by this time. Some varieties making strong luxuriant foliage growth, such as King Alfred, Lord Wellington, Alasnam, and others of similar habit, may be tied up with green raffia to prevent their sprawling over other nearby plants as the foliage begins to break down, and to facilitate cultivation around them.

Watering, too, must not be neglected during this period of growth if best results for another year are to be expected. Very, often, particularly in the Northeast and the Midwest, an early period of dry weather, even if it does not assume the proportions of a drought, follows close upon the heels of the season of Daffodil bloom. Such weather, especially when supplemented by strong drying winds, will rob the Daffodils of soil moisture just when they need it most. One or two thorough soakings under such conditions greatly benefit the plants. Allow water to run freely from the open end of the hose into the bed until the soil will absorb no more.

Although summer mulches are seldom recommended for Daffodils they are highly desirable in sections where excessive heat and dry weather are likely to be encountered. Not only do they aid in keeping the tops in a growing condition longer, but, where the bulbs are to be left in the soil, the lower soil temperature resulting from the mulch is beneficial, particularly to varieties which make sparse foliage, and in borders where there are not plenty of other plants interspersed with the Daffodils to keep the soil shaded. Where annuals are used to follow the Daffodils, they serve this purpose.

Fall care

The old saying, "Out of sight, out of mind," is nowhere better exemplified in the garden than in the care—or rather the lack of care—provided hardy bulbs which are allowed to remain over from season to season without being disturbed.

In late summer—usually between mid-August and mid-September, but varying with varieties and with conditions—the new crop of roots, put out after the so-called dormant period, will be making vigorous

ABOVE: *Daffodils and Birches go together like peaches and cream. A dozen or two bulbs, in two or three years, will give an effect like this.* BELOW: *Ushering in the season of garden Daffodil varieties is February Gold, a vigorous-growing Cyclamineus × Giant Trumpet hybrid.*

Many of the newer Large Cup and Giant Trumpet Daffodils, such as Music Hall (above) and E. H. Wilson (below), are much more graceful in form than older varieties.

growth. In order to do the job that is expected of them, they must have plenty of moisture and plenty of plant food. Often they lack both. After a dry period it takes more than a few refreshing showers to dampen the soil to a depth of 5 to 8 inches, where these new roots are lying. A little experimental digging in one's own garden will demonstrate this fact.

The gardener, therefore, should make it part of his routine to loosen up the surface of the soil in his Daffodil border or over the Daffodil clumps in the mixed border and, if the soil is dry, to give it at least one thorough soaking to provide more favorable conditions for growth until the usual fall rains take over the job. In order that this important chore may not be forgotten, it is well to fix in mind Labor Day as the approximate date on which it should be attended to.

It is well at this time also to make absolutely sure that there is no lack of plant food. A highly nitrogenous fertilizer is not necessary, but a few pounds of bone meal, supplemented perhaps by wood ashes or a high-potash fertilizer, will provide against any possibility of undernourishment.

A striking illustration of the importance of cultivation and fertilizing came to our attention recently. A large border which had remained undisturbed for several years, made over and refertilized in late summer, produced, the following spring, flowers from bulbs which the owner had thought lost or run out, while others which had been flowering each year were better than they had been since the first season after they were planted.

LIFTING AND REPLANTING

As a rule commercial bulb growers dig or lift Daffodils every year. Occasionally, to provide planting stock (many small bulbs) or because of market conditions, lots of certain stocks may be allowed to remain down for two years, but not longer. The amateur grower will have occasion to lift his bulbs only when he desires to increase some new or choice variety as rapidly as possible; when he may wish to rearrange his planting; and when, as a result of multiplication and consequent overcrowding, the flowers produced are no longer up to par.

The time when lifting may be done covers a considerable period. The ideal time is when the tops have dried sufficiently to fall over and begin to dry up, but while they are still firmly attached to the bulbs, so that the latter may be readily located in the soil.

Commercial growers often dig while the tops are still quite green and before the roots have begun to shrivel. This is particularly true of late-maturing types, such as the Poeticus, and in sections like the Northwest, where in moist spells or in moist seasons the new roots begin to form before the old have entirely disappeared. The only real disadvantage of digging early—this is after the tops have made their full growth but while they are still green—is that the bulbs will not have developed their maximum size. In the home garden this is of little consequence, although with the commercial grower it is, of course, a serious consideration. The chief objection to late digging— after the tops have completely withered and sloughed off of the bulb— is the increased difficulty of locating the bulbs and of getting them out of the ground without mechanical injury in digging.

In most soils a flat-tined digging fork will be found a safer imple- ment to use than a spade and more convenient than a trowel, espe- cially if any considerable number of bulbs are to be taken up. Needless to say, the greatest possible care should be exercised not to cut or spear the bulbs, especially those of choice varieties. This can be ac- complished by digging away the soil on one side to within an inch or two of the clump before attempting to remove it from the soil.

If the bulbs come out clean and fairly dry, with few roots, they will require little or no preliminary drying before being put into storage. This is often the case when the bulbs are dug fairly late. If, however, the tops and the roots are still firmly attached and considerable soil adheres to the bulbs, they should be dried off for a period of from one to several days before being stored. In any case, they should not be exposed to a scorching midsummer sun, as this may result in scalding them on one side. A place in partial shade, such as under a tree where air currents can reach them freely, will usually accomplish such drying as is needed almost as quickly as exposure to full sun. For the home garden ordinary flats with cracks in the bottom make convenient receptacles in which to place the bulbs for drying and stor- ing. Each variety, of course, should be carefully labeled as it is taken up.

Unless there is some special reason for keeping the bulbs in summer storage until autumn, it is best to replant at once. In this event, no pre- liminary drying is necessary. In fact, it is best to have the new locations ready before digging and to shift the bulbs at once as one would growing plants. If there is need to shift a planting without dividing the bulbs, they can be moved at any time after flowering if dug with plenty of soil adhering to the roots and replanted at once.

However, if the grower wishes to obtain "splits" from which to develop new round bulbs, a period of storage is necessary in order that the offsets may be removed readily and without injury to the parent bulb. Or it may be that replanting in a new location cannot readily be done before fall. Then the question of providing the best conditions for summer storage must be considered.

The two most important factors are a reasonably low temperature and ample ventilation. Where only a few flats of bulbs are to be cared for, a shelf arranged near a window or an air duct in a cellar or basement may serve the purpose. A shed or loft, provided ample ventilation may be given, will answer. We once had the ideal setup—a small building under the shade of large trees, previously used for fancy poultry: it was equipped with trap-door openings along the sides, making possible quite complete control of ventilation.

The bulbs should be examined occasionally so that any which show signs of decay or disease may be immediately destroyed. After several weeks, when thoroughly dried and ripened, they may be gone over, cleaned, and graded, the larger bulbs being used for replanting in beds or borders or for forcing indoors, and the smaller ones for growing on.

Replanting

Such home-cured bulbs may be replanted at any time the ground is ready for them. If they can be put in before new varieties from commercial growers or seedsmen begin to come in, so much the better.

Small bulbs and splits are best handled by putting them in rows in a place by themselves, or in the vegetable or cutting garden, where they can be easily and thoroughly cared for. Our method is to open a furrow as deep as possible by running a hand plow in both directions and planting the bulbs in the bottom of this, using a "Slim Jim" trowel to get them well down. They are set 1 to 3 inches apart, according to size and variety. Filling the furrow in level gives a good 4 inches of soil over the tops of the bulbs. A space of a foot or so is left between each variety and the one following it, and stout stake markers which will not be dislodged or broken in cultivating with a wheel hoe are

Group of Moonshine (Triandrus Hybrid) from a stray bulb in soil filled in behind rocks.

used. Well in advance of freezing weather a moderate-sized ridge of soil is thrown over the row by running the hand plow along either side. This is leveled off early in the spring just before the tops begin to come through, leaving a mellow surface free from weeds for the early growth.

Even when one has acquired all the bulbs of a particular variety which can be accommodated in the garden, any surplus may be put to good use by planting in rows in the same way as suggested above, but somewhat deeper if they are full-sized bulbs, to furnish an abundance of bloom for cutting. There are few occasions throughout the year which afford the gardener more pleasure than having plenty of Daffodils, especially if they are of the splendid newer varieties not yet too widely known, to present to appreciative friends. Then, too, full-sized bulbs from the cutting rows may be used for growing indoors for winter bloom. In this case summer storing and curing are not essential. Bulbs may be taken up in early fall, before they have made too much new root growth, and transferred to pots or bulb pans to be taken indoors later on, after they have made the usual preliminary root growth required for flowering indoors. (See page 269.)

DAFFODIL TROUBLES

Having grown Daffodils for well over fifty years and in many types of soil, and having never once had to dust, spray, or fumigate for any disease or insect pest, we do not burst out into goose pimples when we look through bulletins and articles devoted to Narcissus troubles. The full extent of our treatment for these easily grown flowers has consisted in an occasional removal of a plant or the destruction of a bulb that looked "sick." On not more than a half dozen occasions, out of several hundred varieties, we have discarded all the bulbs of a weakgrowing variety.

The Narcissus, nevertheless, does have its troubles. Here are the half dozen or so most commonly encountered.

Diseases

Eelworm (nematode; *Ditylenchus dipsaci*) is commonly listed as a disease, although the eelworm is a worm so minute as to be invisible to the naked eye. Nematodes enter the foliage as it emerges in spring, causing it to become twisted and distorted as it grows, with characteristic swollen pimples ("spikkles") along the edges or at the center of the leaves. Later on the bulbs become affected and gradually rot, with brownish, disintegrating layers between normal firm healthy ones.

Control includes: (1) destroying infected bulbs by burning; (2) treating bulbs which *may* be infected with hot water and formaldehyde added (1 pint to 25 gallons), soaking for 4 hours at a temperature of 110–112 degrees and replanting at once; (3) disinfecting all equipment by dipping in water with formaldehyde added (1 part to 9 of water); (4) sterilizing soil with chloropicrin (tear gas) or DD.

Basal rot attacks basal plate of bulb, causing a chocolate or reddishbrown decay which spreads into the bulb itself. Secondary symptom is a pinkish-white fungus around base of bulb. Spreads through bulbs in storage; most serious in warm climates and on bicolor varieties.

Control: (1) destroy infected bulbs; (2) avoid cutting or bruising bulbs when lifting, and dry off as quickly as possible; (3) just before planting, soak bulbs for 3 hours in Semesan-water solution (13 ounces to 10 gallons), or in New Improved Ceresan (2 ounces to 3 gallons water); (4) store bulbs in thin layers and keep well ventilated, *and examine frequently.*

Mosaic (gray disease), a virus causing stunted plants, with foliage showing grayish, yellowish, or brown stripes, especially in upper two thirds of leaves, and small streaks or blotches on blooms.

Control: (1) as symptoms appear early in growth, begin rogueing when foliage is 6 inches high; (2) keep plants free of aphids, which carry disease.

Narcissus Fire (botrytis) is a disease (similar to the well-known Tulip fire) which affects Narcissus on the Pacific Coast only. The Tazetta species and hybrids, particularly, throw spotted blooms. After withering, these diseased flowers produce spores which cause an infection on the foliage later in the season.

Control: (1) destroy all spotted flowers and blighted leaves as soon as noticed; (2) spray growing plants in spring with Fermate. Similar measures are used against gray mold blight. (See Chapter 10.)

Narcissus Smoulder causes decay of bulbs in storage as well as in garden beds where the flowers and foliage rot. Cold, wet weather conditions foster the disease. Slightly affected bulbs produce malformed shoots which turn yellow and later are covered with gray spore masses. Destroy affected bulbs promptly. For Southern Blight and Leaf Scorch, see Chapter 10.

Insects

The two most commonly encountered insect pests of Daffodils are the large bulb fly (*Merodon equestris*) and the lesser bulb fly (*Eumerus tuberculatus*), the grubs of both of which destroy bulbs in much the same way as the familiar Onion maggot destroys that succulent occupant of the vegetable patch.

The large bulb fly is quite large, in general appearance not unlike a bumblebee, and variously colored, brown, black, or banded. Eggs are deposited singly, usually as foliage is dying down, at the base of the stems. The egg hatches in a few days and the grub spends the rest of the season and the winter eating its way through the bulb, which is completely destroyed.

The lesser bulb fly resembles an ordinary house fly. It lays its eggs in clusters, somewhat earlier than the larger fly, and several larvae find their way into a bulb—two or three to ten times that number. This first brood, leaving the bulb a decaying mass, matures about July, to generate a second brood.

Controls: when planting, never use a soft, "squashy" bulb unless certain it has been given the hot-water treatment or fumigated.

Bulb Mite is the same pest which attacks Lilies. For description and control, see page 115.

If the Daffodil claims as its own that tumultuous season between melting snows and barren boughs, and the time when bursting buds and the green flames of new grass spread through brown meadows, then no less does the Tulip reign supreme when spring has definitely arrived and settled down to stay. The Daffodils have little competition; the season's setting is a perfect foil for their airy and delicate colorings. The Tulips find plenty of competition, but their more massive blooms and brilliant hues make them equal to the task of holding the garden spotlight through the year's most colorful period.

It is difficult to think of a spring garden without visualizing the picture largely in terms of Tulips. Of all flowers, they present the garden maker with the widest range of colors from which to make selections for the effects he may wish to achieve.

If the designer wants strong hues rivaling those of the spectrum in intensity and clarity, they are to be found on the Tulip palette; if he prefers somber shades or the most delicate tints, these, too, are available. Hues in the Tulip world include nearly a full two thirds of the color circle, ranging from violet-blue through reds, oranges, and yellows to green-yellow and white.

Moreover, the gardener can be certain (at least to the extent that one can be certain of anything in gardening) that his colors will come out as he planned them, and when they are needed; for Tulips, if one secures good bulbs, are remarkably dependable in their performance.

While most gardeners think of Tulips as being colorful, comparatively few have any idea of the wide range in form, size, and season of bloom that is to be found among them. Not one gardener in a hundred will name you a *fragrant* Tulip, though there are a fair number of varieties that on this score vie with any Rose.

Or take the matter of season of bloom, which is of the utmost im-

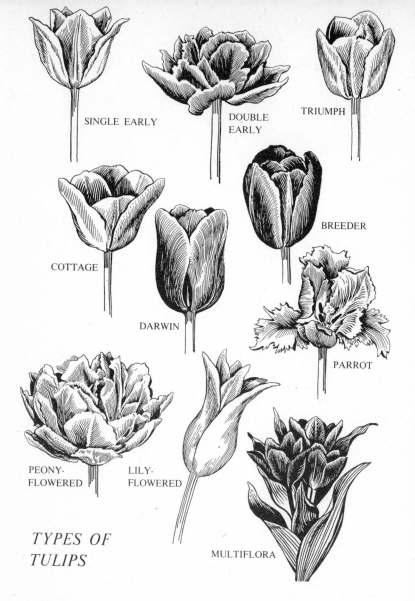

SINGLE EARLY

DOUBLE EARLY

TRIUMPH

COTTAGE

DARWIN

BREEDER

PARROT

PEONY-FLOWERED

LILY-FLOWERED

MULTIFLORA

TYPES OF TULIPS

portance if you wish Tulips to contribute all they are capable of contributing to the beauty of your spring garden.

The three types of Tulips that are best known to gardeners are the Cottage or May-flowering, the Darwins, and the Breeders. All three flower at practically the same period, the Cottage averaging somewhat earlier, and the Breeders possibly a little later. But even with a careful selection of early-, medium-, and late-flowering varieties, you will do well, in a normal season, to get three weeks of bloom. If you are wise enough to include in your plantings some of the species Tulips (and their new hybrids and selections), and some of the really early-flowering garden types, such as the Single and Double Earlies and the Triumphs, you can enjoy an additional three to four weeks of Tulip gaiety.

Nor need you have an estate in order to do this; a few groups of them—a dozen or even a half dozen of a kind tucked in here and there—will give a breath-taking lift and brightness to your spring flower border or foundation planting, to a garden of naturalized bulbs, or to the rock garden.

SIZE AND FORM

While we're rounding up the Tulip picture, let's take a glance at some other differences in this versatile genus that are too little recognized, for the simple reason that the big three (Cottage, Darwin, and Breeder) get all the breaks in color display in most catalogues. Admittedly, a huge 5- or 6-inch cup on a 36-inch stem is more impressive to most people than a much smaller flower held 6 to 20 inches above the ground. But the latter may fit quite as well into a particular garden picture. In fact, these earlier, smaller Tulips are often much easier to use effectively with groups of other flowers than are their giant cousins, with all their regal splendor. There are many shapes and color designs, too, in these little fellows that are not to be found in the more popular types; rounded or star-shaped blooms; tapering, twisted petals that are almost fantastic; others having two, three, or four flowers to a stem; gracefully waved and mottled foliage—in all, a fascinating and intriguing group to discover and a source of such new material as any flower arranger hails with joy.

FOR WEEKS OF BLOOM

To get an idea of how to use the various types to best advantage, let's follow the Tulip trail from one end to the other. We can take them in the order in which they bloom—almost from melting snows to early summer!

Species and Species Hybrids: Here is a whole group of Tulips that bloom ahead of or with your early Daffodils! They are short-stemmed, but so gaily colored, so resistant to injury from storms or cold, and so long-lasting that they are quite as rewarding as the larger ones that flower a month later. Moreover, they remain much longer without "running out," and therefore are really valuable for naturalizing.

A few of the species bloom late, but the group of *Kaufmanniana* varieties and hybrids are the earliest of all generally available Tulips, and most of the species bloom well in advance of the popular garden sorts. As if to make certain of giving the gardener his money's worth, many of them put on a double-feature billing, with brilliantly striped, pointed, closed flowers in the morning and evening and on cloudy days, and entirely different, widely expanded blooms when a few sunny hours cause them to open.

The uses to which the various Tulip species can be put are manifold. They will thrive in soil less well supplied with plant foods than that required for the large garden varieties, and they rather like a pretty thorough baking during the summer. They are ideal for planting among or around rocks or along a path with a stone edging. In selecting a location, keep in mind the height of the particular kind being planted, as they vary from 6 to 10 inches, with a few going to 15 or more. The bulbs of most of the species are quite small, but do not overcrowd them when planting; a spacing of 5 to 6 inches is none too much.

The Single Early Tulips come next in time of flowering. In this group there have been few new varieties introduced recently, and in most catalogues they receive scant attention. Don't overlook them, however, when making up your bulb order. For growing indoors, too, they rank at the top of the list, especially as many of them are delightfully fragrant.

The Single Earlies, formerly used extensively for bedding, should not be discarded because that particular type of planting has gone out of favor. Of moderate height—10 to 16 inches—they withstand more hard weather than the Darwins and Breeders and hence are better for exposed positions. In the mixed border they should be toward the front.

The Double Earlies are similar to the single forms, but the flowers are much longer-lasting, both in the garden and when cut. They are equally desirable for forcing.

Triumphs and Mendels: These two new groups fill in the gap, in time of flowering, that formerly existed between the Single Earlies and the Cottage, Darwin, and Breeder groups. They were developed by crossing Single Early with Darwin varieties, with the result that they are about ten days earlier than the latter and much larger-flowered and taller than the former, averaging in height from 20 to 24 inches. They are excellent for forcing, having the advantage over the Single Early of stiffer, more upright stems and longer-lasting blooms.

Peony-flowered: These would be more accurately listed as Double Triumphs, but their large, Peony-like blooms have won for them the more popular name. They come into bloom with the earlier Darwins. While making very effective and long-lasting color groups in the border, they are likely to be bowed down in rainy weather.

Late-flowering

The species and early sorts take us through three to four weeks of Tulip enchantment, but we still have ahead of us the really big show: the May-flowering Cottage, Darwin, and Breeder groups, which completely dominate the garden scene during their season of bloom. As these are so well known, we give them little space here, except to point out a few differences that still exist to some degree, although interbreeding has been carried on to such an extent that the lines of distinction are rapidly disappearing. Few May-flowering Tulips are adapted to forcing.

Cottage: These are characterized by long, flexible stems; flowers with rather long, pointed petals and clear, brilliant colors, often blending. Many tones and tints of yellow and orange, but no purples, lavenders, or bronzes are found in this group. They are easier to manage in arrangements than Darwins or Breeders.

Darwin: Long, slender stems support huge, globular flowers in a wide range of color from pure white through deep shades to near black; often with strongly contrasting centers.

Breeder: Very upright, stout, stiff stems bear substantial cup-shaped flowers, usually bi-colored, in rich Rembrandt tones of terra cotta, brown, bronze, and purple, often with a decided "bloom."

Parrots and Lily-flowered: These two interesting groups are really strays, with distinctive flower forms, from other classes. Most of the Parrots are sports from well-known garden varieties (Fantasy from

Clara Butt; Therese from Farncombe Sanders, etc.), which have lacini-
ated and more or less twisted petals, often with green markings. Even
the stems tend to assume informal curves. The Lily-flowered Tulips
have long, pointed, recurving petals. Mrs. Moon, clear yellow, and
Picotee, white-edged with pink, are known to many.

Both the Parrots and the Lily-flowered Tulips are exceptionally
useful as cut flowers, alone or with other plant material.

While bulb catalogues give a good idea of the Tulips available for
your garden, especially the May-flowering sorts, the only sure-fire way
of getting precisely what will please you best is to make selections
where you can actually see them in bloom. Extensive collections are
to be found at botanic gardens, many public parks, and at the trial
grounds of nurserymen and seedsmen. Why not treat yourself to a
"Tulip Day" so you'll know exactly what you'll want to order for
next fall's planting?

USES

Despite their brilliant and varied coloring, Tulips are much more
limited than Daffodils in the uses to which they can be put in garden
making. The horticultural varieties require rich soil and careful culture
if they are to be kept flowering for more than a season or two; hence
they are of little use for naturalizing or for landscape groupings, even
quite aside from the fact that in Northern latitudes they just do not fit
into naturalistic settings.

Some of the species, such as *Kaufmanniana, dasystemon,* and *Marjoletti,* self-seed freely and in congenial surroundings form spreading
colonies. Even the species, however, are by no means as sure-fire as
Daffodils for naturalizing, nor adaptable to so wide a range of soils
and drainage conditions. Most of them should have particularly good
drainage and like rather sandy soil and a real sun baking during the
summer months. Their ideal home is a rocky slope or bank, or in the
rock garden.

The large-flowered horticultural varieties of Tulips, from the Single
Earlies to the latest Breeders, are at their best in mixed borders or in
a special Tulip border. In either case, height, color, and flowering time
should be carefully considered in ordering bulbs and in making up the

*Mixed Tulip border—third year flowering, without lifting—edged with
Creeping Phlox and other low rock plants, such as Cerastium.*

planting plan; otherwise there will be gaps in season of bloom and jarring notes in the color scheme. In making out an order list for Tulips, it is advisable to put down first the types you would like to grow and then to select varieties under these headings. By so doing you can keep your plantings balanced and be assured of a long season of bloom.

In former days Tulips were considered the ideal flower for "design" beds, or for uniform blocks of color in large, formal landscape designs. They are still occasionally so used, but with the passing of big estates (and the imported-professional-gardener school of landscaping that accompanied them), and with the more informal treatment of public buildings and grounds now in vogue, this type of Tulip planting has almost disappeared. Even in flower-show gardens, where it clung to the bitter end, one now looks for it—with a thankful heart—in vain.

As a general rule Tulips should not be planted in mixtures. (This does not apply to the cutting garden, to which odds and ends and surplus bulbs from replantings may well be consigned.) Like all general rules, however, this one is sometimes broken to advantage. We recall one place where, each fall, the gardener placed a few stray bulbs of tall Tulips in the edge of a planting of broad-leaved evergreens. Coming out a few at a time, their unexpected appearance in such a setting carried with it a certain elfin charm, as though the pixies had been at work when the gardener's back was turned.

We once had a somewhat similar result. We used a truckload of soil from an old Tulip border in mixing compost for a new rock garden. Some of the bulbs that came along with this soil must have been covered at least 18 inches deep, but they all found their way up the following spring, from under stones and through spreading rock plants, to provide bursting stars of color over a period of several weeks. The flowers were much smaller than normal for the varieties—a fact that contributed largely to the artistic effect. Our clients were highly pleased and free with compliments, but in all honesty we had to confess that the whole thing was purely an accident.

CULTURE

The need of securing top-quality bulbs has already been emphasized, but with Tulips special care in this respect is of vital importance.

Tulips grouped against stone wall. Use of white makes interesting contrast.

With Daffodils and most of the other hardy spring bloomers, a small bulb or even an injured one may improve during the following season or two. Unless you can provide them with exceptionally good care and have a soil to their liking, *the flowers from your Tulips will be better the first spring after planting than they will ever be again.*

When to plant

It has long been taken for granted that Tulips should not be planted until October or early November. The argument is advanced that earlier planting is likely to result in premature top growth, especially during a late, mild fall. A considerable amount of research through Tulip literature has failed to reveal an account of any experiments or tests to prove or disprove this assumption. It seems to be another of those taken-for-granted statements handed down, without being challenged, from one generation of gardeners to the next.

In England, where in many sections there is little or no deep freezing of the soil, and in our own Southern states, late planting may be desirable, but for the rest of the country there doesn't seem to be any advantage in it. In plantings we have made in various types of soil from Massachusetts as far south as the District of Columbia, we have never had any injury from early planting; nor have we ever heard of an authentic case of such injury. In southern New Jersey, where for several years we had charge of commercial plantings of forty acres or more, we had to begin planting—to get them all in—as soon as the bulbs were received (earlier than they usually can be obtained from seed stores); and even in that comparatively mild climate there was never any serious premature fall growth.

Again, what happens to Tulips that remain in the ground from one season to the next? Surely these have every opportunity to make premature top growth. But they decline to do so and, while making vigorous roots, keep their tightly rolled little white caps safely underground until spring. Today, January 20, we dug one up from a sheltered spot, mulched by nature with fallen leaves so the ground had not frozen. The top growth was still three inches below the surface. Bulbs, like seeds, have built-in automatic controls that usually work under normal conditions. (Ever have a cluster of self-sown Tomato or Squash seed come up in your garden? Didn't they wait until danger of late frosts was over, no matter how warm the weather had been earlier in spring?)

The most substantial argument we have found against early planting is given by Sir Daniel Hall in his *Book of the Tulip*. There he makes the point that early-planted bulbs may emerge in January or early February, and that "the tips of the shoots may easily be damaged by frost following wet, and so afford entrance for the botrytis spores. The later the development of the shoot, the safer it is from attack." But this is not at all the same thing as premature fall growth. And in sections where there is any danger of growth starting too early in the spring, winter mulching *after* the soil has frozen is a more reliable method of delaying spring top growth. In our experience, the date of planting makes very little difference in the date of emergence.

Many varieties of Tulips, held long after being received before being planted, are likely to deteriorate, especially under such makeshift storage conditions (far from an even 40 degrees temperature, which is the ideal) as the amateur is likely to be able to provide. In addition to

ABOVE: *With Tulips, as with Daffodils, differences in size and form are much greater than most gardeners realize. Shown are Red Emperor and diminutive* Tulipa biflora. BELOW: *Fantastic in form, and now available in many dramatic color combinations, are the fringed and feathered Parrot Tulips.*

ABOVE: *Thumbing their chilled noses at frosty nights and late snows, gaily colored Tulip species (Gaiety, right, and Gluck, left) last an incredibly long time.* BELOW: *An orange flame against evergreens or a rock, the species Tulip Praestans Fusilier brings brilliant color to the early garden.*

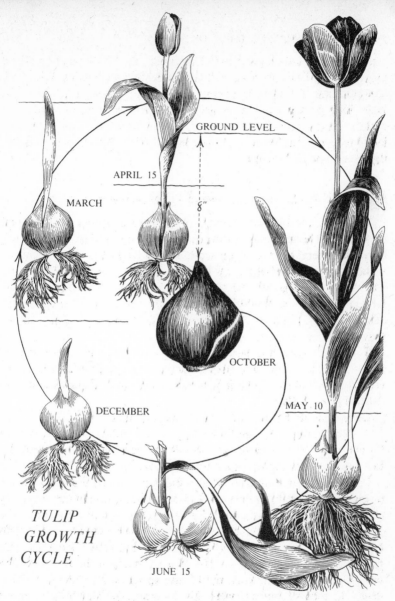

GROUND LEVEL

APRIL 15

MARCH

8"

OCTOBER

DECEMBER

MAY 10

TULIP
GROWTH
CYCLE

JUNE 15

drying out, bruises invite infection, dry rots, and molds. We consider *the dangers from long-delayed home storage much greater than those from early planting.*

On the other hand, if bulbs are not received until late, or if for any other reason planting must be delayed, the grower has nothing to worry about. If still in good sound condition, the bulbs may be planted as late as mid-December and still give perfectly good results. With such late plantings, however, mulching is desirable. (Pages 78, 82.) J. D. Islee, long manager of the Henry A. Dreer Company, once told me that the most successful outdoor exhibition planting of Tulips that firm ever made was put in, owing to late arrival of the bulbs from Holland, during a thaw in January.

Depth of planting. How deep should Tulips be planted?

That is a question concerning which there is a deal of discussion these days. The tendency is toward deeper planting than has formerly been the general practice. The depth usually advised is 4 to 5 inches— without specifying whether this is to the top or the bottom of the bulb. The depth given should be to the *top* of the bulb, as otherwise the largest bulbs (some of which will be 2 inches or more in vertical diameter) will have the least covering, whereas, if any distinction is made, they should go deepest.

Tulips will grow and flower perfectly well, however, when planted 10 or 12 inches deep, and such deep planting, as often as not, is advisable. The Tulips will be happy either way: it all depends upon the gardener's objectives.

Deep planting has several very definite advantages:

1. It discourages the multiplication of new bulbs; and as fewer are formed, they have a better opportunity to develop and consequently to produce better blooms the following year.

2. With a limited number of new bulbs produced, the necessity for lifting and separating is delayed. Under favorable conditions they may continue flowering satisfactorily for five years or more instead of the usual two or three. Many instances of continuous good bloom for eight to ten years have been reliably reported. Individual varieties vary greatly in their capacity to survive. In a test made at the Brooklyn Botanic Garden, the following, out of fifty varieties, all planted 6 inches deep (to tops of bulbs), were still blooming satisfactorily after six years: Anton Mauve, Arethusa, Eclipse, Faust, Fiancee, Jeanne Desor, King George V, Louis IV, Mayflower, Martha, Monica, Persimmon, Prince of Wales, Zwanenburg. With us, Clara Butt, Kathleen Parlow, Rev. H. Ewbank, Inglescombe Yellow, Dom Pedro, Indian Chief, Picotee, and Fantasy have appeared to be good survivors.

Clusiana, the Candy-stick Tulip; dainty, striking, and a great favorite for cutting.

3. Deep planting lessens the danger of injury from "fire" or botrytis blight (see page 167). In one set of experiments made in England, two beds planted 14 inches deep showed 4 to 12 per cent infection; two planted 12 inches deep, 10 to 15 per cent; and those planted at the regulation depth of 5 inches, 50 to 65 per cent. The record was taken when the flowers were ready to cut, by which time the disease, starting with the shallow-planted beds, had had an opportunity to begin to spread to the others. One test doesn't prove a case, but other experiments have seemed to substantiate the assumption that deep planting definitely lessens the danger of botrytis. Deep planting also gets the bulbs down below the level of mole runs and the accompanying danger of fall injury from mice and/or moles, and also out of reach of chipmunks.

4. Deep planting makes it possible to cultivate and to grow annuals or tender bulbs near or even directly over the Tulips without danger of injuring them. This is especially important where Tulips are used in groups in a mixed flower border. Dwarf Dahlias, Cannas, Montbretias, started in pots, or late-planted Gladiolus are but a few of the

many fill-in plants that make attractive succession plantings to conceal the maturing foliage of Tulips and provide masses of late-season color in their place.

Despite all advantages, however, the gardener should be careful about going off the deep end on deep planting. It may well result in failure *if:* (a) drainage is poor, so that the bulbs would have soil water standing about them; (b) the soil is not prepared to a depth of 15 to 18 inches to provide congenial conditions for root growth below the bulbs; (c) or the soil is heavy clay, shutting out air and offering mechanical obstruction to emergence.

Again, if you wish to increase your stock of a favorite variety, if you wish to rearrange the planting of your border after a year or two, or if you are not certain that you have found exactly the right location for a group planting or for a particular variety, then you will do better to plant not more than 5 or 6 inches deep. In any event, it is advisable to try deep planting first on a small scale, to see if *your* conditions favor it. If the bulbs give satisfactory bloom the second year, you can feel safe in proceeding on a larger scale.

Planting

The general procedure for planting outlined in Chapter 7 applies to Tulips. Extra precautions to protect them from injury from rodents may be necessary. The most effective protection from moles is to plant in wire baskets, bought ready-made or constructed from ½-inch mesh wire. Such baskets have a secondary use when it comes to taking up the bulbs—they can be "lifted" quite literally. Baskets are practical for a few groups but involve more expense and work than most gardeners will wish to assume when any considerable number of bulbs are being planted. Some gardeners claim successful protection by using naphthalene flakes generously in the soil about the bulbs. Chopped-up tobacco stems are recommended by others; we have never tried them, but most animals dislike them, and at least they would add some organic matter and potash to the soil. Another control that has proven effective in some cases is powdered red lead—one pound to 50 bulbs. Place a few bulbs at a time in a tight container, and "powder" with the lead as a housewife sugars doughnuts; wear gloves to protect hands. (For mole controls and protection from rabbits, see pages 116, 167.)

ABOVE: *Parrot Tulip Fantasy, old-rose pink, and light blue* Phlox diva-ricata *make a pleasing combination.* BELOW: *Light and dark Peony-flowered Tulips against a protective background of evergreens.*

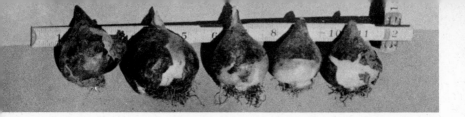

Home-grown Tulip bulbs, cured and ready for replanting.

In the deep south, where the soil does not freeze after planting, many growers have had best success by pre-cooling the bulbs for three to five weeks, at a temperature of 35° to 40°, before placing them in the ground, which is done in December.

Cultivation

Tulips, more than most hardy bulbs, must be kept free from the competition of grass and weeds if they are to do well. When they first come up in the spring, the leaves are rolled together in tight spikes. At this season it is easy to work between them and loosen the surface soil with a hand weeder or small-bladed hoe, such as the "all-purpose." Later—often only a few days later—the broad, brittle leaves will have spread out, and any working about them is almost certain to result in cracks or bruises which invite the attack of botrytis blight and other diseases. If large weeds come in later, they should be removed by hand.

Fertilizing

The best time to apply fertilizers is also very early in the spring. Garden Tulips (those of horticultural origin), more than any other hardy spring bulbs, are dependent upon a generous, well-balanced diet. Quick-acting, high-nitrogen fertilizers should be avoided, for there is no purpose in hastening early growth. In fact, it is better to hold it back. If only a complete fertilizer—such as 5–10–5—is available, it is well to supplement it with wood ashes and superphosphate.

Mulching

Where the bulbs are to be left in the ground, weeding during summer and autumn can be much reduced by the use of a mulch. It should be a material that will not remain wet and soggy after rains, and is best not applied until after the foliage has begun to ripen. We have found buckwheat hulls and tobacco stems satisfactory.

DISEASES

Only one Tulip disease is likely to prove troublesome in the garden, and you may grow them for years without encountering it.

TULIP FIRE (*Botrytis tulipae*). Its appearance and spread depend largely upon weather conditions; it usually appears during a warm, wet, or muggy spell in spring, when the foliage is growing rapidly, up until the time flower petals are dropping. The first symptom is usually a yellowing and shriveling of the leaf tips, followed by spots near the edges which increase and run together. White spots appear on dark flowers and brown spots on white, followed by rotting and the development of a mushy gray mold. Under favorable conditions the disease spreads so rapidly as to have earned it the common name of "fire."

If detected early enough, the disease can be checked to some extent by removing affected leaves, buds or flowers, and especially fallen petals, and spraying thoroughly with Bordeaux mixture or preferably with Fermate (2 pounds to 100 gallons of water). Precautionary measures are: plant in soil where Tulips have not been grown for three or four years or where there is free circulation of air and full sun; examine bulbs at planting time and discard any which show tiny hard black specks—the sclerotia that carry the disease over the winter—on or under the brown skins or on the basal plates.

PESTS

The most serious insect and animal pests of Tulips are aphids, bulb flies, mites, nematodes, moles, mice, and slugs, for all of which see Chapter 10.

Frequently injury from moles or mice is not noticed until the flower buds are well developed or even beginning to open. Then a sudden withering of a plant shows that something is wrong, and the slightest pull will remove the stem from the ground, revealing that it has been eaten through just above the bulb, which will be found intact. *Immediate* action with the Cyanogas pump will usually save the remaining bulbs—but the italics must be heeded.

CHAPTER *13. Crocuses*

Of all very early spring bulbs, Crocuses are the most colorful and most widely grown. Often, despite extreme neglect, they persist for years, increasing by natural multiplication of the corms and by self-seeding.

Despite the popularity of the horticultural or garden varieties—the "Dutch" Crocuses displayed in color in most catalogues—comparatively few gardeners know, and still fewer grow, any of the species and species varieties. These are immensely more interesting, and most of them are considerably earlier and remain longer in bloom.

To enjoy these intriguing, more graceful "wild" Crocuses, it is by no means necessary to possess a rock garden, although they are ideal subjects for such a setting. Despite their small stature—they range in height from 3 to 6 inches—they will make a fine showing if they are planted where they will not be overcrowded by other plants, or overlooked. In the lee of individual rocks, around the bases of trees, at the edge of a small pool (but where the ground is not wet), they will make a brave showing.

Crocuses are often naturalized in lawns or other grass areas. No other flower defiantly thumbs its nose at the biting winds of March with quite the same irrepressible pertness. But if you want Crocuses in a neatly kept lawn that must be cut early in the spring, it is best to figure on planting additional bulbs each fall. Unless the foliage can be left for several weeks after the flowers fade—even if it does not reach full maturity—the succeeding corms will be severely injured. Often, however, there are spots in corners, around trees, and fronting shrubbery where they can be naturalized without any necessity for shearing off the foliage too soon in the spring. We have a group of them in a semi-kempt terrace under Birches that has been in for ten years and is still going strong. In fact, these Crocuses seem to have a

Crocus Remembrance, a light lavender blue, naturalized by a pool.

taste for adventuring and occasionally pop up in unexpected places—and with parental records that would not stand too close questioning.

While in most home gardens Crocuses are thought of as supplying a two to three weeks' show in spring, they may be enjoyed during three or four months of the year if one will take the trouble to include both the spring- *and* autumn-flowering species. And if you want to do a little specializing in Crocuses and the Crocus-like but not closely related Colchicums (often catalogued as Giant Autumn-flowering Crocuses), you can add another month or two to that! With very few exceptions, all of the Crocuses ordinarily obtainable are very inexpensive, and a few dollars will provide quite a collection of them to start off with.

CULTURE

Crocuses are exceptionally easy to grow and are seldom troubled by any insects or diseases. Unfortunately, however, the corms seem to be considered choice tidbits by mice, squirrels, and chipmunks, and rabbits are equally delighted with the young foliage. Keep this in mind when making your plantings. We lost completely a very nice collection by planting them too far from the house, with no protection. Of recent years, with a cat and a dog, which serve as deterrents, and the trusty gas gun (page 116) to take care of underground enemies, we have experienced little trouble.

Crocuses, more particularly the species, have a liking for soil a bit on the sandy side. In heavy soil it is advisable to dig in a shovelful or two of sand or cinders where each group is to go. (If hard, sharp coal cinders can be obtained, they will tend to dampen the enthusiasm of burrowing mice.) The garden varieties take to a well-fertilized soil, but the species will do on a rather meager diet; if fertilizer is used, apply only about half the usual amount.

As to exposure, Crocuses like full sun—the more the merrier. Light high shade, after the flowering season, will do no harm. *Effective shelter from prevailing spring winds will often make a difference of two weeks or more in the, opening of the first flowers.* The bloom period can readily be nearly doubled by making two plantings of a variety in different exposures.

Planting

Plant as soon as you can secure the corms—early in September if they are available. *This is especially important with autumn-flowering kinds.* If they are planted late, after growth starts—which it will, even if the corms are stored dry in paper bags!—your first crop of flowers may be curtailed or sacrificed entirely. In ordering, it is advisable to request that autumn Crocuses (and Colchicums) be shipped in advance of the rest of your other bulbs.

For planting Crocus corms, the depth given in most articles and bulb-planting charts is 2 inches. We plant them considerably deeper— a good 4 inches to the tops of the corms, which are spaced 2 to 4 inches apart. For this deeper planting there are three reasons: they come up just as well and, apparently, just as early; they are less likely to be found by mice or squirrels; and the corms are in less danger of working up close to the surface. It is possible, too, that they multiply less rapidly, though we have no evidence of our own—nor have we found it elsewhere—to prove this.

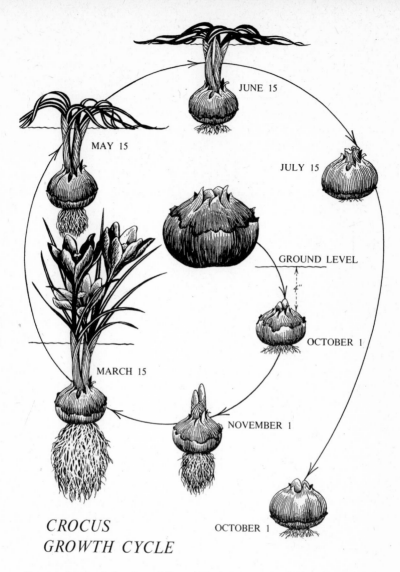

JUNE 15

MAY 15

JULY 15

GROUND LEVEL

4"

OCTOBER 1

MARCH 15

NOVEMBER 1

OCTOBER 1

CROCUS
GROWTH CYCLE

In speaking of the "working up" of the corms, we touch upon one of the interesting points in the Crocus growth cycle. As with the Gladiolus, new corms are formed on top of the old one, which withers away. When Crocus corms get too near the surface, long fleshy roots penetrate deep into the ground and, after becoming firmly established, exert a contractile force which, unless the soil is unduly dry and hard, will pull the corms deeper down into it.

Any ground cover used over Crocuses should be low-growing and not too dense. Creeping Phlox (*Phlox subulata*), Arenaria, Dianthus, *Vinca minor* (which has not become too dense) and Primulas are a few that do nicely. Started seedlings of the lighter growing annuals, such as Candytuft or Pansies, may be set in among groups of Crocuses to provide a flowering cover for the dying foliage. Crocuses may be used, too, as an edging for beds of later spring bulbs, such as Daffodils or Tulips, their curving foliage—which Mrs. Louise Beebee Wilder has described as the most graceful line in nature—making a pleasing finish. (See illustration, page 176.)

Like most other hardy bulbs, the Crocuses will eventually become too crowded to continue a good display of flowers. When that point is reached, they should be taken up as the foliage begins to die down, sorted, and immediately replanted. The very small corms can be saved for growing on, or placed in new colonies where, after a year or two, they will reach full flowering stage.

For indoor bloom

No bulbs are more easily grown for flowering indoors than the Crocuses, nor more charming in the peculiarly cheerful uplift they can give to a room during the frequently dull and dark days of January, February, and early March. For window-sill culture, their dwarf stature, as compared with that of many other bulbs used for forcing, is a distinct advantage. We have found, too, that they may be transplanted with the greatest of ease even when the buds are well developed, and therefore are ideal material for use in dish gardens or for inserting in pots of taller-growing bulbs; the foliage remains attractive even after the blooms have faded and been cut off.

The term "forcing," which we have elsewhere referred to in its connection with spring-flowering bulbs (page 267), is even less applicable to Crocuses than to Daffodils, Tulips, and others. The Crocuses should not be forced in the slightest degree. After they have made root growth in bulb pans or flats, any temperature above freezing, combined with plenty of sunshine, will bring them into bloom. This makes possible a "have your cake and eat it too" proposition in so far as Crocuses are concerned. If the foliage is kept growing until they can be planted out in open ground, they will usually give a full crop of flowers the succeeding spring, without skipping a season as is the case with many forced bulbs.

Planting for indoor bloom should be done early. A 5-inch pot or bulb pan will accommodate eight to ten corms of average size; a 6-inch pot, however, requires little more space and will make considerably more of a showing owing to the increased number of blooms obtainable. An ordinary flat with the corms spaced 2 to 2½ inches each way will provide four or five dozen plants for transplanting as suggested above.

Except for the advisability of extra-early planting and the necessity of keeping them very cold—frozen if possible—after the roots have formed until it is desirable to bring them indoors for February or March bloom, the details of planting are the same as those suggested in Chapter 20.

THE MORE IMPORTANT CROCUS SPECIES

The spring-flowering Crocus species are very different from the popular horticultural or "Dutch" varieties, for they bloom earlier and are more persistent. Leading the procession is the dull lilac Crocus *Imperati* in early March, followed by blue *Sieberi* and golden *susianus* (Cloth-of-gold). *Tomasinianus,* pale lavender, is especially free-flowering and good for naturalizing, as is *biflorus,* the old favorite Scotch Crocus. *Korolkowi,* golden orange, is popular for rock gardens, together with *susianus minor,* a dwarf form; *aureus* (*moesicus*) is orange-yellow; *aureus sulphureus concolor,* a pale yellow.

There are autumn-blooming Crocus species, too, which give a peculiar charm to the fall garden. Dutch catalogues list many species and varieties, and in garden books you can find mention of still more. Of the half dozen to a dozen generally listed in American catalogues, the best known are *zonatus, speciosus,* and *sativus,* though the latter is sometimes unreliable and may well be omitted if only a few kinds are to be planted. Its red-violet flowers are less attractive to most persons than those of other species. *C. speciosus,* with light blue flowers and brilliant orange stigmas, is one of the most reliable as well as one of the most beautiful; normally it begins flowering in late September. Of this there are some half dozen sub-species and varieties. *Aitchinsoni* is a very pale blue and the largest of the wild forms; and *albus* is

ABOVE: *Autumn-flowering Crocus,* speciosus Aitschisoni. BELOW: *Colchicum or Meadow Saffron (sometimes listed as Autumn Crocus) brings a sudden and unexpected renaissance of spring to the late garden.*

white with a rose tint on the outer petals. *C. zonatus* blooms a little later than *speciosus,* its pale lilac, yellow-throated flowers usually carrying into October.

C. medius is perhaps the showiest of all the species, with scarlet stigmas contrasting with its deep lilac petals. It is also very free-flowering and a vigorous propagator. *C. asturicus* produces dark violet blooms in mid-October; *cancellatus albus,* late September, is a pure white that contrasts nicely with the other varieties and has fragrance to add to its charm. Other whites are *pulchellus* Zephyr and *ochroleucus,* small-flowered and exceptionally dainty. Latest to flower—often into December—is *laevigatus,* white flushed with pearl, and fragrant.

There is a group of spring-flowering bulbous plants usually referred to in the trade and in garden literature as the "minor bulbs." The gardener thinks of them as minor because most of them are diminutive in stature; the dealer, perhaps because of the small part they play in the total of his bulb sales—and certainly in most instances he gives them a very minor display in making up his catalogue.

But in the pleasure they afford and in the touches of exquisite, delicate beauty they can bring to the garden, these less well-known bulbs are by no means minor! Of all the plants we grow, there are none to whose reappearance each spring we look forward with keener anticipation. And there are none with which visitors are more delightfully surprised, or concerning which they seem more amazed when informed that most of them could be enjoyed about their own grounds with little or no more care—and in many instances with less—than they bestow on the things they do grow.

The species to be discussed in this chapter, because they merit somewhat more extended treatment than others listed in Part Three of this book, include the following:

Early spring

Chionodoxa (Glory-of-the-snow) Hyacinth
Eranthis (Winter-aconite) Leucojum (Snowflake)
Fritillaria (Guinea-hen Flower) Muscari (Grape-hyacinth)
Galanthus (Snowdrop) Scilla (Squill)

EARLY SPRING GROUP

Always, in late July or early August, there comes a day when, walking about the garden at dusk, we become conscious of that touch of sudden, peculiar coolness in the air which so definitely presages autumn. That first unkind foreboding of impending change usually projects on the screen of imagination the melancholy picture in Bridges' lines:

> *The wood is bare; a river mist is steeping*
> *The trees that winter's chill of life bereaves;*
> *Only the stiffened boughs break silence, weeping*
> *Over their fallen leaves,*
> *That lie upon the dank earth, brown and rotten*
> *Miry and matted in the soaking wet,*
> *Forgotten with the spring that is forgotten*
> *By them that can forget.*

But even this rather dismal preview of onrushing darker days and driving rains leaves us, we confess, with no sense of sadness. Our thoughts turn, rather, to what will be happening then down in the ground, deep under the matted and miring leaves. For there, we know, will be stirring into life the hundreds of tiny bulbs that have been sleeping comfortably all summer long—the little fellows that give us a full extra month of amazing and vibrant color just at the season when we feel most in need of it and when other gardens about us are still brown and barren.

In the mixed borders, against clumps of Birches, with their backs against great boulders acting as warming pans for their cold beds, and especially in the nooks and crannies and along the twisting narrow footways in the rock garden, they will be drinking in the autumn rains, pushing out greedy roots, and thrusting their pointed noses up—but not too far!—getting ready to respond to the magic of March sunshine with a burst of pre-spring glory.

Natives of many climes, these little fellows—from the high Alps and low Mediterranean shores and the forbidding vasts of Russia—as yet little "improved" by the hand of man; immigrants gathered together here in a happy band, asking little but the opportunity to find a foothold, and welcome the first staggering, half-frozen bees to the gaily decked feasts they spread in such abundance.

Do you know them? Do you *grow* them? If not, we can think of no greater garden service we can perform for you than to urge that you make their acquaintance. By all means give them an invitation to *your* garden and enjoy a real pre-spring show.

ABOVE: *The perfect setting for a colony of Crocus: the blooms are protected from spattering soil and the foliage may be left undisturbed to mature.* BELOW: *Crocuses make an ideal succession planting with Early Tulips. Blooming just ahead of the Tulips, they leave their attractive foliage as an edging. (See page 49.)*

ABOVE: *Grape-hyacinths, inexpensive and sure-fire, are the most striking of the few blue flowers of early spring. They self-seed freely.* BELOW: *Exotic but not difficult to grow is the Blood-lily or Haemanthus. (The variety shown is H. Katherinae.) Bulbs are stored over winter. Also excellent for the greenhouse.*

Major roles for minors

Quite as intriguing as the many and varied forms and colors to be found in the little spring bulbs are the things one can do with them in the way of getting unusual garden pictures. Used in quantity—the "drifts" that landscape architects like to write about—they produce spreading, low masses of color in early spring that are most charming. Such results, where one has conditions suitable for this type of planting, are not beyond the means of the average home owner. Bought by the hundred, many of them can be had for from 3 to 10 cents apiece. Even without this much of an investment, however, one can get extremely satisfactory results. A dozen or two bulbs, costing from 50 cents to $2.00, will provide a delightful spot picture.

Fortunate is the gardener who possesses a stony bank, a rock ledge, or the means of creating even the most elementary sort of rock garden. For then he can give these small-scale beauties just the kind of setting that suits them best. But let him by no means be discouraged if such an ideal setting cannot readily be provided. Unusual indeed is the place where some nook or corner cannot be found that will serve to accommodate at least a moderate number of these enchanting couriers of spring, ready to bring glad tidings that her green and golden legions are on the march, forcing winter's white-raimented regiments back, slowly but surely, northward.

The smallest of the minor bulbs are best placed where they are elevated somewhat above the general ground level. Such a location makes it possible to see them in detail. It also provides protection from chance accidents, and assures that extra-thorough drainage which, with few exceptions, is an essential factor in their continued happiness. Permanent labels are extremely important. Even if you can trust to memory for names, or just don't give a darn what they are so long as you have the flowers, the labels serve as added protection, for these little fellows spend much of their lives underground and in the course of the year's operations are quite likely to be dug up, overplanted, or otherwise maltreated or lost track of unless their locations are plainly marked. Such labels need not be conspicuous, but they should be sufficiently substantial to resist heaving and chance dislocation.

One thing to keep in mind in planting these little bulbs is that, with a few exceptions, the flowers are borne on comparatively short stems. This, combined with the fact that they bloom in early spring, when frequent driving rains occur, results in their becoming so mud-spattered that much of their beauty is lost unless they are so placed that this cannot happen. Do *not* plant in such locations as the front of a bare-soil perennial border or in rows or groups in any open soil.

Both for artistic effect and for their comfort and good growth, the little bulbs are best planted in sheltered nooks and crannies. They associate particularly well with rocks, where they get good drainage, protection from wind, and the full benefit of the earliest spring sunshine. They are good for naturalizing, either in quantity or in "spots" under deciduous trees, because they are through blooming by the time the shade becomes dense. Another desirable planting place is the southern side of evergreens, where the spring sun can reach them under the lower branches.

The common characteristic of all these little fellows is their informality. Give them a setting where this will be enhanced by their surroundings. Above all, they should never be used in a mixed planting of the several species.

The range of colors in the early spring group includes a wide spread of blues, from deep grape-purples to delicate azures and lavenders, and some good pure yellows. Reds are lacking, and the pink varieties, on the whole, are not too pleasing. The pure and glistening whites, however, at this season of the year are quite as effective as strong colors.

CHIONODOXA. If we had to be restricted to one of the half dozen species mentioned at the beginning of this chapter, our choice would be the Chionodoxas. Best known, perhaps, is *C. luciliae,* with informal starry flowers of Delphinium blue shading to white centers, borne eight or more on a stem. There are white and pink varieties of this. *C. sardensis* has deeper, gentian-blue flowers. *C. gigantea* has larger flowers of light blue. Chionodoxas and the widely naturalized Coltsfoot (*Tussilago farfara*), with its golden Dandelion-like flowers, make a charming combination. Chionodoxas are especially lovely, too, as cut flowers.

CROCUS. Though all the choice types and varieties of this well-known harbinger of spring are discussed at length in Chapter 13, they rightfully belong among the minor bulbs. They have so much to offer the gardener that we have devoted a separate chapter to them.

Winter-aconite—first gold in the spring garden. Variety is Eranthis Tubergeni; *photographed March 30, Hyde Park, N.Y.*

ERANTHIS HYEMALIS. The Winter-aconite appeals to gardeners in Northern sections because it is usually the first bulbous flower to put in an appearance, running neck and neck with the Snowdrop. Its bright yellow blossoms, like miniature Marsh-marigolds, are borne on 2- or 3-inch stems above decorative foliage reminiscent of that of an Anemone. Plant the little shriveled-up-looking tubers as soon as they are delivered. If they seem very dried out, plump them up in moist peatmoss before planting. Place them in a raised bed in the rock garden or at the top of a wall where they can be seen readily without stooping. Semi-shade during midsummer is desirable.

FRITILLARIA. There are some seventy species of Fritillaria hailing from temperate zones in all parts of the world, but only a few of these are generally available. Most appealing is *F. meleagris,* the so-called Guinea-hen Flower, which takes its name from the mixed reddish-brown and purple coloring of its nodding bells. There is also a white form.

Blooming early in April on 12-inch wiry stems, this modest little bulb has an appeal all its own. Plant the bulbs as soon as they are received, 3 inches deep in light shade in a spot in the rock garden which

The quaint and decorative Checkered-lily or Guinea-hen-flower—Fritillaria meleagris.

will not dry out completely during hot weather. The Fritillarias native to our own West are commonly called Mission Bells. They are somewhat taller than the Guinea-hen Flower, except for *F. pudica,* a dwarf of 6 inches, each short stem bearing a single, clear yellow, bell-like bloom. This species likes full sun and a typical well-drained, sandy rock-garden soil; as does also *F. pluriflora,* another low-growing sort with racemes of pink-purple flowers of four to a dozen blooms in each cluster, each 1¼ inches long. For naturalizing in open, rather dry woods, try *F. lanceolata,* 18 to 24 inches, flowers mottled brown and green, and *F. recurva,* of similar height but with bright orange-scarlet flowers resembling a true Lily.

GALANTHUS. The Snowdrops are beloved of all gardeners because of their quaint nodding blooms that, despite their frail appearance, defy the last desperate onslaughts of frost, snow, and ice. Outside our kitchen window is a clump that frequently is snowed under for one to three weeks *after the flowers have opened,* yet they always come out smiling to provide their good cheer for a long period.

The Snowdrop most commonly grown is *G. nivalis. G. Elwesi* has larger flowers. Snowdrops prefer a rather heavy soil and do well in considerable shade, spreading slowly by self-seeding.

HYACINTH. Here is another good flower which has suffered from association of ideas. The Hyacinth has so long been used for mass bedding effects, especially when "design" flower beds were in vogue, that few persons ever stop to consider the possibility of planting it in any other way. The giant exhibition Hyacinths displayed at flower shows, with their huge, stiff, almost club-like stalks of bloom, certainly do not tend to suggest that the Hyacinth should be given a place in modern informal home-garden landscaping.

Discard your prejudices and try a few Hyacinths, either in small, irregular groups at the front of the mixed border, against shrubs, or in a grassy spot in sun or semi-shade that does not have to be cut close in spring; or a few groups at the edge of the foundation planting if your house is on a small plot. And they are especially charming near a small pool.

Many gardeners, we find, have a feeling that Hyacinths are not reliably hardy. With the exception of the French Roman Hyacinths, we have found them fully so. We have a large group of the pale yellow City of Haarlem planted on a semi-shaded terrace twelve years ago that is still a spot of beauty each returning spring. Other varieties, after having been grown indoors for winter bloom and then transferred to the open, have readily established themselves and gone on for years.

Grades of bulbs: Bulbs of Hyacinths, which are comparatively expensive, are listed in catalogues as top size (exhibition), 19 cm. or over; first size, 18–19 cm.; second size, 17–18 cm.; third size (bedding), 15–16 cm.; and Miniature (Dutch Roman or Cynthella), 14–15 cm. There are also "prepared" or "treated" Hyacinths—higher-priced and used especially for early forcing. The *varieties* in all these grades are identical, but the smaller sizes throw up rather loose graceful spikes, very different in appearance from the formal, stiff blooms from big bulbs. The French Roman Hyacinths, however, are quite distinct

One that really blooms in the snow—and continues in bloom for a month or more: the common Snowdrop, Galanthis nivalis.

from the Dutch Hyacinths. They flower earlier and are not as hardy. The individual florets are smaller, and several spikes are produced in succession. If attempted out of doors, they should be well mulched.

Culture: Extra-good drainage is probably the most important requirement in Hyacinth culture, for they cannot stand wet feet. In heavy soil or on low ground it is best to use a raised bed with gravel, small stones, or other drainage material under it. Hyacinths also demand full sun, but for perfect blooms a sunny location should be provided, with natural shelter against storms, as in an exposed position the heavy heads of bloom are easily beaten down.

A rather light soil is best for Hyacinths. Clay or heavy loam should be lightened with sand or sifted coal ashes. At the same time add humus in the form of peatmoss to help hold the moisture. If large bulbs are being planted in a formal bed where masses of bloom are desired, the bed should be well enriched with cow manure, either well rotted or the commercially dried. For a formal bed dig out a foot of soil where the bed is being made, and then mix the manure and bone meal into the soil below, which should be thoroughly turned and broken up. Now cover this bottom layer of the "cake" with a layer of sand, set the bulbs in place on this, and fill in with the soil which you removed, well pulverized and mixed with peatmoss. Cover the bulbs 4, 5, or 6 inches deep, depending on the size. After planting—which should be in late September or early October—give a good watering if the weather is dry. Moisture is needed all through the late autumn to help the bulbs develop a strong root system before hard freezing. After the soil freezes during the year of planting, mulch with leaves or salt hay. Thereafter no winter mulch will be necessary.

When planted in formal beds, Hyacinths are usually lifted after bloom to make room for other flowers. They are carefully heeled in to ripen, or lifted with a fork *after the foliage has turned yellow,* and stored like other hardy bulbs, or covered with *dry* soil in a frame with the sash on but partly open for ventilation, until they have cured. If Hyacinths are informally planted in groups or in the mixed border, there is no need whatever to lift them until they become so crowded that bloom ceases. We have found that this does not occur for from six to eight years when the bulbs are planted deep and far enough apart—6 to 8 inches—to allow for increase.

Varieties: There are many varieties, in good clear colors, from which to select. It is also possible to choose varieties with blooming heads of different shapes. All are not heavy and club-like. Recommended varieties are: *Early:* L'Innocence, white; Moreno, Pink Pearl, pink; Jan Bos, Tubergen's Scarlet, red; Delft's Blue, Dr. Lieber, light blue; Zulu King, dark blue; Prince Henry, Yellow Hammer, yellow and orange. *Medium:* Albatros, Edelweiss, white; Gertrude, Lady Derby, Marconi, pink; Garibaldi, La Victoire, red; Myosotis, Perle Brillante, light blue; Mary, dark blue; Orange Boven, orange. *Late:* Queen of Whites, white; Queen of Pinks, pink; Cyclops, red; Queen of the Blues, light blue; Ivanhoe, King of Blues, dark blue; City of Haarlem, yellow.

LEUCOJUM. To follow the Snowdrops in bloom there should be a planting of Snowflakes (Leucojum), which are somewhat similar but later-flowering, larger, and taller. The Spring Snowflake (*L. vernum*) has drooping, bell-like flowers tipped with green. The variety Gravetye Giant is even more robust. The Summer Snowflake (*L. aestivum*), attaining a height of 12 to 18 inches, blooms in May.

MUSCARI. Grape-hyacinths are the most commonly encountered of the little bulbs, probably because of their extreme long-lastingness and the freedom with which they self-sow. We have come across their upstanding, tapering little spires of cobalt-blue bells around old home-sites where no gardener's foot had trod for years. *M. azureum* (strictly, *Hyacinthus ciliatus*), in a sheltered spot, will flower in February or early March. *M. armeniacum* (Early Giant) is the variety to get if you want but one. It is larger and a clearer blue than Heavenly Blue, and fragrant; an excellent companion for Daffodils. *M. armeniacum* Cantab is a new variety of lighter blue and considerably later. *M. botryoides caeruleum* and its variety *album* both have more compact foliage and are good for small rock gardens. The Grape-hyacinths thrive in almost any well-drained soil, in sun or light shade. Don't be alarmed if some of them form clumps of foliage in the fall!

SCILLA. Earliest of the Squills to flower are *Scilla sibirica* and its white form, *alba*. Spring Beauty is a more robust form, growing to 6 inches or so, nearly twice as high as *sibirica*. The color is a real singing blue—we know of no other flower that can add quite so much cheer to a dull spring day. *S. bifolia* is also early, but of a Gentian-blue color. *S. pratensis,* deep blue, flowers in May. The broad, spreading foliage of the Scillas affords some protection from mud spattering and makes them more suitable for use in borders or for edging, especially if allowed to form thick groups.

FOR LATE SPRING

Entirely different from the early-flowering Scillas are the varieties of *Scilla hispanica* (usually catalogued as *campanulata*), the Wood-hyacinth, and of *S. nonscripta* (*nutans*), the English Bluebell. These bloom much later—about the same time as the late Tulips—and are much taller, often up to 18 inches. Unlike most of the early spring bulbs, they prefer partial shade (though they will take full sun) and are therefore good for naturalizing in open woods or planting under trees—even Pine and Hemlock—and under shrubs. The foliage is heavy and coarse and should be left uncut—a fact to be considered when selecting a location for planting. The several varieties of *S. hispanica* include light and dark blue-purples, pink, and white.

The so-called Feather-hyacinth or Plume-hyacinth (*muscari como-sum monstrosum* or *plumosum*) is a very interesting frilled or lanci-nated, almost freakish, violet-flowered species which blooms in late May. Lasting unusually long, it is good for cutting and will prove to be arresting in an arrangement at your local flower show.

A May-blooming member of the Fritillaria family which is as showy as the Guinea-hen Flower is modest is *Fritillaria imperialis,* or Crown Imperial. This traditional bulbous flower may be seen blooming in many old-fashioned gardens, where it throws up 3- to 4-foot blossom stems which bear red, yellow, or orange umbels of drooping bell-shaped flowers in a crown-like cluster under a whorl of leaves. Once established, it should not be disturbed. Plant 4 inches deep in rich, partly shaded ground as soon as the bulbs are delivered. Its one un-desirable feature is a characteristic Skunk-cabbage-like smell.

CAMASSIA: Lovely flowers, far too little known, that are easily satisfied and hardy without protection. Their first delicate racemes of tall, lacy florets appear with the Daffodils, while other species bloom one to three weeks later. Unlike some other natives of our West, Camassias are of easy culture and seem to acclimate themselves readily to Northeastern conditions. Some species indeed are native to Pennsylvania, Minnesota, Georgia, and Texas. They are showy enough to be a very real addition to the border or large rock garden. In our own rock garden they have thrived for several years in considerable shade, among rocks where their delicately colored, starry, deep or

China-blue spikes of bloom attract attention from a considerable distance.

Well-worth growing are these Camassia species:

Cusicki, to 3 feet, with pale blue flowers
esculenta, 2 feet tall, flowers a rich purple
Leichtlini, also 2 feet in height, varying in the color of individual
    plants from dark blue through China-blue to creamy white
Howelli, 1½ feet, with pale blue flowers

Planted in rich, loamy soil in sun or semi-shade, 9 inches apart and 4 inches deep, the bulbs of this member of the Lily family should thrive untended for years. (Though most authorities stipulate 3 to 4 inches between bulbs, having grown Camassias for some years, we know that the basal foliage soon covers almost a foot of soil.) If you are lucky, they will increase slowly by self-sown seeds.

CULTURE

In general the culture required by these less well-known bulbs is the same as that suggested for Crocus.

As few of the minor bulbs have been developed into horticultural varieties far removed from the original species (many of them are untamed species or selections from them), there is little to be gained by intense feeding; in fact, it is more likely to be harmful than beneficial. Most of them we plant with no additional fertilizer, in fairly good soil that has had a considerable amount of sand or gravel or fine crushed stone dug into it. Sharp crushed stone—pieces ¼ to 1 inch—seems to discourage the foraging of mice and chipmunks, two of the worst enemies of most small bulbs.

Many of the minor bulbs are quickies, as far as their vegetative growth aboveground is concerned. Their flowers appear almost as soon as the foliage starts growth; and from the time the foliage dies down, they are out of sight until the following spring. Seedling plants of shallow-rooted annuals—Petunias, Ageratum, dwarf spreading Zinnias such as *Z. linearis,* or the Zinnia-like Sanvitalia—may be transplanted to take their place. Our favorite succession crops are Sweetalyssum and Portulaca, the seed being sown as the bulb foliage withers. Both of these self-sow but never become really troublesome.

CHAPTER *15. Lilies*

With the fading of the last of the Tulips there is a temporary lull in the show made by hardy bulbs in the garden. Oriental Poppies, Irises, and Peonies take over; but before these have passed, the bulbs are staging a comeback, with Lilies playing the leading role.

We have had the earlier Umbellatums, such as Golden Chalice and Rainbow Hybrids, open their spreading cups by the first week in June, with Candidum and Bellingham Hybrids following in close succession; and from then on they supply a series of garden high lights until late in summer. No other group of plants is followed with greater interest or for so long a period.

In two respects the Lilies stand quite apart and distinct from other hardy bulbs: they have, as a group, a very much longer period of bloom, and they are tall, upright growers. The Lily enthusiast with twenty-five or more species and varieties can enjoy a practically un-interrupted succession of flowers from mid-May until mid-September or later, and even the half dozen or so kinds which any small garden can accommodate will, if selected with regard to their flowering dates, provide a very satisfactory all-season effect.

Owing to their height, habit of growth, and the distinct form of the flowers, almost any variety of Lily, even if there be but a single stalk of it, is pretty sure to dominate its surroundings. This, coupled with the fact that some species or variety may be had in flower at any time except spring, makes them almost indispensable in the design of at-tractive gardens.

THE NEW OUTLOOK

Several things have happened recently to give impetus to the use of Lilies in American gardens. There is the success achieved by our hybridizers in finally breaking through the traditional reluctance of Lilium species to intercross, and thus providing a whole new race of hybrid strains and species that have made headline news in garden publications and even in the leading national magazines. There is the fact that American-grown bulbs, reaching the gardener earlier and in better condition than imported bulbs, have greatly decreased failures that were formerly due to unseasonable planting, to dried-out, withered roots and bruised scales, and to diseased bulbs. And there is the increasing knowledge on the part of amateur gardeners as to the proper culture of Lilies. The recently organized American Lily Society, which held its first national show in 1950, will undoubtedly exert a tremendous influence in increasing still further the appreciation and use of this most important of summer-flowering bulbs.

The development of Lily hybridizing and the commercial production of bulbs in America provide one of the most interesting chapters in our horticultural history, but we can here give it only a passing paragraph. While there were some American Lily hobbyists in the early days, the credit for serious work, both in hybridizing and the commercial production of bulbs, belongs to the late Dr. David Griffiths, who, while internationally esteemed among professional horticulturists, was little known to the public. It is not generally recognized, for instance, that while E. H. Wilson brought us the Regal Lily from western China, it was Griffiths who interested American growers in its propagation and dissemination.

While American hybridizers achieved some success in developing new varieties, it was not until World War II practically terminated the importation of bulbs from Japan and Europe that commercial production of bulbs in this country was undertaken on a large scale. On a trip we made in 1947 up the West Coast, the atmosphere in every bulb-growing center reminded one of accounts of the Tulip mania in Holland. Small fortunes had been made in a season or two on a few acres devoted to growing new strains of the Easter Lily, such as Croft, Estate, and Ace.

Of greater interest to gardeners is the fact that in the last couple of decades American hybridizers have not only produced more than those of all other countries together, but have succeeded in cross-breeding original species never before successfully mated. The progeny of these crosses, for the most part, hybridize readily, so that now the doors are wide open for innumerable new creations. Doubtless many of these will be "improvements" in name only. One shudders to think, for instance, of a flaming orange Madonna Lily—by no means an impossibility in the not-distant future. But there are definite indications that many of these new Lilies, with the usual character, vigor, and adaptability of hybrids, will undoubtedly be more amenable to garden culture than are most of the species. This quality, in fact, is already apparent, and if we should gain nothing more than this from the hybridizers' efforts, it will be an improvement well worth while.

Until recently the commercial production of Lily bulbs has been almost entirely by asexual propagation—bulblets and scales. As to the best procedure in the further development of Lilies, there are two schools of thought. The older one, which has been followed for a long time, is that of establishing clones, or stocks developed from a single plant.

The original plant used to establish a clone is a "selection"—that is, one picked as having the most desirable qualities from a group of plants of the same kind; a sub-species that differs in some way from its normal type; a sport (a natural mutation that differs from the normal type in some characteristic, such as color, size, or habit of growth); or a new variety resulting from a seed cross. Whatever the source of the individual plant that becomes the foundation of a clone, the process of propagation from it is, as compared with growing from seed, slow and expensive. The result is that bulbs so produced become available but slowly, and long remain quite high in price. Many of these are worth the cost, it is true, but the number of gardens to which they can find their way is limited.

Quite different from this method is the newer one of mass production from seed. Some species are very prolific seed producers and are readily grown from seed. Notable examples are the Regal Lily (*Lilium regale*) and *L. formosanum*. Bulbs of these have long been commercially grown from seed; that is why they have become so universally available at moderate prices.

There is some variation in the plants from such seed-grown bulbs but not enough to make them less desirable for garden use. In fact, in the garden, some range in height and time of flowering is often desirable. (For florists' use for forcing, it is a different story, since here it is very important to have a crop that is uniform, especially in the matter of date of flowering.)

In addition to this speedier and more economical production, an-

VERMICULITE FOR
STARTING SEEDLINGS.
1. BASE MEDIUM – GRAVEL IN PAPER INSERT
2. COARSE VERMICULITE.
3. SEED BED MEDIUM – FINE VERMICULITE.
4. POT IN CENTER – FOR WATERING.

Flat prepared for starting Lily seeds. Three layers are placed as indicated. (Courtesy U.S.D.A.)

other important advantage of seed-grown stock is that bulbs so produced are more vigorous and free from diseases, especially the dread mosaic (related to the Cucumber virus disease), which is the one greatest scourge of amateur Lily growers.

By growing from seed and transplanting the seedling stocks to fresh soil, in areas thoroughly isolated from old stocks, it is possible to produce bulbs that are 100 per cent free from mosaic, whereas bulbs produced from scales or offsets are sure to carry it if the parent stock is infected; and no Lily plant once suffering from mosaic can ever be cured by any control yet discovered.

Those who favor propagation from seed feel that supplying vigorous disease-free bulbs is, from the amateur gardener's point of view, more important than obtaining such uniformity in flower form, color, or habit as may result from clone bulbs produced asexually. Fortunately most Lily species, and many varieties, come reasonably true from

Lily seedlings from a single lot of seeds, showing variation in germination and development. (Courtesy U.S.D.A.)

seed. Seed-grown hybrids, of course, show more variation, but by continued selection and reselection they are developed into strains that are sufficiently uniform.

Not only new Lilies but new methods of producing the bulbs commercially are being developed in the Northwest. At the Oregon Bulb Farms we saw the almost incredible sight of a block of Lily seedlings that had been sown in the open in January and by mid-May (when the photograph on page 193 was taken) looked like an experiment-station test plot of small grains and grasses. It was estimated that these beds would produce some 600,000 small bulbs by transplanting time, when they would go into field rows for two years. Experimental work on the development of a machine that will speed up transplanting was well under way.

Another method for increasing production opens up intriguing possibilities. It now seems probable, with the newer achievements accomplished in crossing varieties, that the characteristic of forming stem bulbils (possessed by a few species, such as *L. tigrinum*) can be transmitted to many Lilies, or their offspring, that previously have not produced them. An example of this is the new variety *L. Maxwilli,* var. *bulbiferum,* which produces bulbils almost as freely as *L. tigrinum.* The propagation of desirable clones will, of course, be tremendously speeded up if this characteristic proves to be one that can be transmitted to many species.

IN THE GARDEN

There are three purposes for which Lilies are especially suited: as accent plants in the mixed border, for landscape groups, and for naturalizing. In the rock garden they play a very minor role, and that, unless the landscaping is on a fairly grand scale, is limited to two or three species.

Because of their height, size, and form Lilies have the power to dominate any group of plants in which they appear. For this reason, as well as for their cultural requirements, the gardener should exercise particular care in placing them. They are not plants to be purchased in a moment of enthusiasm and then stuck into any corner that happens to be available. Like most tall and slender flowers, Lilies are seen at their best when silhouetted against a suitable background,

ABOVE: *Lilies are best planted against a protecting background of evergreens or shrubs and kept heavily mulched rather than cultivated.* BELOW: *Lilium centifolium, attaining a vigorous height of 6 to 8 feet, is unsurpassed for a tall accent in the mixed border or for cutting.*

Typical of several new groups of Lilies are the Mid-century Hybrids
(L. tigrinum *crossed with various hybrids) varying somewhat in color*
and form.

Beds of Lily seedlings grown in open at Oregon Bulb Farms. Sown in March; photographed in June; to be transplanted later in season.

such as evergreens, shrubs, a wall, or the shadowy depths of open woodland.

Two other points to bear in mind are that Lilies make much more beautiful displays when grown in groups or colonies, and also that they are *effective at a distance,* and therefore can well be used, especially in white or light-colored varieties, near the termini of vistas viewed from either indoors or outdoors.

When you have decided to add Lilies to your garden, a good practical plan is to start out with an armful of bamboo stakes or other markers and place one or more in each location that seems particularly suitable for a group of Lilies. If some of these spots are already occupied by other plants, don't be deterred by the necessity of transplanting them, for there are few indeed which will merit priority over the Lily.

With your markers in place, check each location:

First, for good drainage; the primary requirement for their successful growth.

Second, for background—and with it, protection from strong winds.

Third, for garden effect as points of interest in the landscape scheme, or for their relation to surrounding plants if in a border.

Fourth, for sun and shade, a matter of much less import than commonly believed, because most species, and practically all the horticultural varieties, will tolerate either full sun or partial shade, provided other conditions—such as adequate mulch or moisture if they are in full sun—are favorable.

So far, each stake or group of stakes represents an X variety—one not yet decided upon. With the planting positions once determined—and not until then—you can make the most intelligent selection of varieties that will give you what you want, for some Lilies grow only 2 or 3 feet tall, others 5 to 7; some flower in June, others during July or August (when possibly you are away for the summer), or as late as October.

But before we attempt to select individual species and varieties, let's consider conditions which Lilies prefer, and their general culture.

CULTURE

We have already emphasized that *good drainage* is the primary requisite in growing Lilies. At peril of becoming boresome, we reiterate it again here—annoyance sometimes becomes a successful barb in making a point stick in one's memory. Aside from drainage, the matter of soil is not nearly so vital a factor as many writers have indicated. Don't take our word for it. Dr. George Slate, a Lily authority with extensive experience in growing many species under home-garden conditions, says, "Cultural requirements are easily met. Any good garden soil that is well drained and has demonstrated its suitability for a general assortment of vegetables and common annual and perennial flowers will do very well for Lilies. If neutral or slightly acid in reaction, and well supplied with organic matter or humus, it will serve satisfactorily."

In the far-flung acres of Mr. de Graaff's Oregon Bulb Farms almost every species of Lily available for gardens can be found growing and flowering vigorously in cultivated rows in the full sun.

The above quotation from Dr. Slate mentions soil "neutral or slightly acid," and "well supplied with humus." The directions in Chapter 6 tell you how to provide these requirements. In soil that is likely to be too wet, drainage can be assured by one of the methods described on page 68. Most Lilies have their roots well below the surface, so a *deep* soil—at least 12 inches and preferably 18—is desirable. Extra depth can often be provided more easily by making a raised bed than by excavating, and this method at the same time improves the drainage.

As Lily bulbs often are not received until after hard frosts, *assure easy planting by preparing the soil well in advance and then covering it.* A layer of peatmoss, straw, or leaves 4 or 5 inches deep, covered with scrap boards or pieces of old roofing paper, will keep ground open through December even in a severe climate.

Care on receipt

The ideal time to plant a Lily bulb is within fifteen minutes after it has been dug! Such planting, of course, is impossible except with bulbs dug in your own garden. So the best we can do in buying bulbs is to get those which have been out of the ground as short a time as possible. In this respect American- and Canadian-grown bulbs have a decided advantage over imported ones, though as air freight becomes more general, this advantage will be diminished.

Much of the food for the new growth of a Lily bulb, with most species, is stored in the persistent fleshy roots. The less these have become desiccated or bruised during the period they are out of the ground, the better. If they shrivel completely, the bulb is severely injured even though it may grow.

The scales of a bulb in good condition are plump, firm, and securely attached to the basal plate. If soft, fleshy, and easily dislodged, they indicate that the bulb has suffered in transit. Bruised scales invite disease, rots, and molds that eventually destroy the bulb. Bulbs only moderately shriveled and otherwise in good condition can be plumped up by placing them, for a fortnight or so *only,* in moist peatmoss or sand before planting. Injured bulbs can be salvaged by using them as a source of bulblets. (See Scaling, pages 107–9.)

Bulbs that must be held for a considerable period or kept over winter for spring planting are best stored in peatmoss or sand. We use a mixture of both, as it is less likely either to dry out or to stay too moist. The mixture should be kept barely moist enough to prevent shriveling. Even better, however, if one has the facilities, is to pot the bulbs individually, keep them in a dark, cool, frostproof place until they can safely be transferred to a cold frame in spring, and plant them out after danger of severe frosts. We once carried through an assortment of late-arriving bulbs in this way without the loss of a single one, and with much better first-season results than if they had been kept in dormant storage.

Spring planting

Many Lilies, however, especially stem-rooting kinds, make a good showing the first season from bulbs planted in spring *if* the bulbs have been properly stored. If bulbs must be planted in spring, get them in as early as possible and, above all, plant immediately upon receiving them.

We have often wondered why nurserymen and seedsmen do not make a practice of planting Lilies in late fall in large paper pots—such as those used for Roses—so that they can be sold in the spring *in growth*. Our own experience would indicate that such a practice would be entirely feasible.

Planting

As a general rule for depth of planting, two to three times the thickness of the bulb (vertical diameter) will answer. The important point is that the roots should have moisture, but not be in wet soil. In light, sandy soil they may go 50 to 75 per cent deeper than in heavy soil. These depths are to the *top* of the bulb when planted.

Some Lilies throw out roots from the stem growth just above the bulbs as well as from the bases of the bulbs. These are termed "stem-rooting" and are planted considerably deeper than those which root only at the base. Usually, base-rooting sorts should go 4 to 6 inches (to top of bulb) and stem-rooting kinds 8 to 10. It is better to plant too deep than too shallow. Planting depths for individual species and hybrids are given in the catalogues of some specialists.

American and English authorities seem to differ as to the advisability of placing sand under and around the bulbs when planting. Evidence in

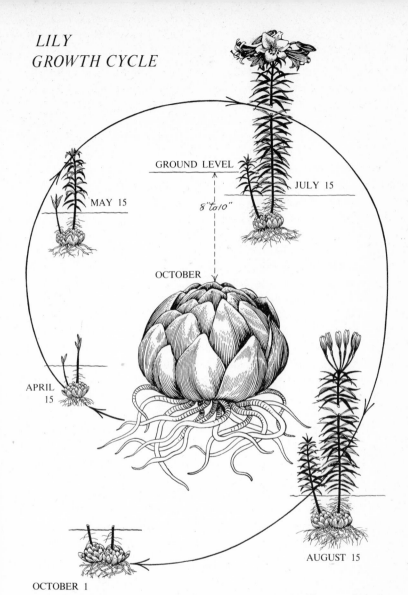

LILY
GROWTH CYCLE

GROUND LEVEL

JULY 15

8" to 10"

MAY 15

OCTOBER

APRIL
15

AUGUST 15

OCTOBER 1

the form of direct comparative tests seems to be lacking, as it is in so many gardening rules that are handed down from one writer to another. Certainly sand is not needed where drainage is as good as it should be. We have used sand (or fine gravel) when planting in heavy soil in wet weather—on the theory that it might help and could do no harm. But ordinarily we never use it. Most American authorities agree that sand planting is wasted effort. The same holds true for setting bulbs over inverted flowerpots. Some growers plant thick-scaled bulbs (such as Regal and Martagon) on their sides, the theory being that surplus moisture will drain out. With bulbs taken up after a heavy rain, we have failed to find any difference resulting from this method of planting.

Two things that are helpful can be done in preparing the bulbs for planting. The first is to cut back the withered tips of fleshy roots and in general give them a trimming that will make them easier to handle in planting; the second is to dust them with Arasan or dip them in Tersan or Fermate, 2 ounces to a gallon of water. (Do *not* use any of the root-inducing powders. Experiments have shown that these may encourage, rather than ward off, disease.)

In planting, make a hole sufficiently large so that the bulb can be placed in it with the roots spread out and down, as they naturally grow. Holding the bulb with one hand, work fine soil under and around it to secure it in this position. We have seen so-called gardeners force the bulbs into small holes in such a way that the roots were actually turned up around them, crowded together and pointing skyward.

As the first year's performance, and to some extent the future life of a Lily, will depend largely on vigorous new root growth before the soil freezes deep, the following precautions may be taken to attain this end. First: if the soil is really dry, water the bottoms of planting holes, repeating until the soil will not readily absorb more, then fill in a little dry soil and plant. Second: if planting must be done just before frosts, mulch to keep ground frost-free as long as possible. Third: make sure that surface soil does freeze later (removing mulch if necessary), and when it has frozen, mulch thoroughly (*over snow if possible*) to prevent the early emergence and consequent injury from late frosts, especially if the planting has a sunny southern exposure.

The location of each bulb or group should be marked with a substantial, permanent label. Where there is a group planting, it may well be outlined for the first season with a barrel hoop or a ribbon of lime or white sand.

Spring care

The sprouting stalks of Lilies are about the most brittle things in the garden. Roots of the stem-rooting kinds grow quite close to the surface.

For both these reasons, early spring cultivation about any Lilies should be undertaken only with great care.

Lilies, more than most plants, insist on open, well-aerated soil; a hard-packed surface means poor growth, if not eventual death. The surface soil should be kept loose by shallow cultivation with a prong hoe held at an angle preventing the teeth from digging deep into the ground. After the first spring, cover plants or mulches will practically eliminate hoeing and weeding.

Feeding

Many Lily species in their native habitats are found growing in meager soil. Most of them, however, respond readily to a rather generous diet in the garden. As the period of growth before blooming is a long one, we make two applications of plant food, the first after they are 6 to 10 inches high, the second as flower buds develop. We use our regular bulb mixture (page 57) supplemented by wood ashes to assure a plentiful supply of potash. In soils tending to be alkaline, it would be better to secure the potash in some other form, such as a high-potash (2–8–10 or 0–10–10 formula) fertilizer. An ample supply of potash, it has been fairly well established, tends to increase resistance to diseases. *Excess nitrogen is to be avoided.* It results in soft growth and weak stems. The usual 5–10–5 garden fertilizer will provide ample nitrogen but is low in potash.

As the plants use much more food during their later growth, when two applications are made we use about one third in spring and the balance later. In terms of a 5–10–5 formula, this would mean 1 to 2 pounds per 100 square feet in spring, and 2 to 4 pounds later on.

Mulches and ground covers

The use of mulches, which is so rapidly increasing in connection with all kinds of plants, has proved particularly beneficial to Lilies. We have already spoken of it in connection with late planting; reference is made now to mulching as part of the year-round culture.

Lilies do not like bare ground. An all-season mulch applied in spring, after the winter-protection mulch has been removed, conserves moisture, keeps the ground cooler, and does away with most weeding. Whatever the material used, it should be such as to remain open and

Early varieties of Lilies in bloom in late June garden, with later sorts ready to take over in July and August.

porous to admit air and water freely. Real leafmold is excellent. Dr. Slate uses coarse hardwood sawdust. We have found both pine needles and buckwheat hulls satisfactory. Peatmoss, unless mixed into the soil surface, may become too packed and more or less impervious to rain or watering. In some sections, chopped straw, chopped cornstalks, or ground corncobs are available. Lawn trimmings, half-rotted leaves, and other materials that may form a sodden mat should not be used.

By fall, most of these mulches will have partly decayed and settled to a thinner layer. As soon as the soil has frozen an inch or two beneath them, the winter mulch—marsh or bog hay, clean straw or evergreen boughs—is applied over varieties whose winter-hardiness may be questionable.

Ground-cover plants to be grown in combination with Lilies are often recommended. Japanese Spurge (*Pachysandra terminalis*) and Periwinkle (*Vinca minor*) are two favorites. While serviceable in areas where Lilies and other bulbs are naturalized, we have found them, under other conditions, not too practical. Pachysandra, especially, makes rather too thick a mat of foliage for any but the stronger-growing Lilies, and it is an insatiable moisture-robber—a particularly serious objection with stem-rooting Lilies.

For Lilies grown in landscape groups and in the mixed border, there are some spreading or light-foliaged perennials and many annuals which make desirable companions for them. Among our favorites are *Phlox subulata,* Iberis, Arabis, Aquilegia, Heuchera, among the former, and *Phlox Drummondi,* Petunia, Pansy, Sweet Alyssum, among the latter.

Watering

Despite the best of care in providing ample humus in the soil, and in mulching, in prolonged periods of dry weather Lilies will suffer. Even if they have bloomed, this lack of moisture will take its toll in preventing normal development of the bulbs.

To be of much use, watering must be copious enough to moisten the soil to a depth of a foot or more. Begin watering when the soil has dried out to a depth of 3 or 4 inches, and thus conserve the water lower down. We use a soil-soaker hose, laid on top of the mulch, and let it run for several hours. A good method for landscape groups is to sink a 4- or 5-inch drain tile about a foot into the ground, with a couple of shovelfuls of small stones supporting the lower end. A hose stuck into this and allowed to run slowly will give a thorough subirrigation. In either of these methods, the foliage is kept dry and the watering can be done in the evening. If a sprinkler must be used, water in the early morning.

Cutting

Lilies are as beautiful and desirable in the house as they are in the garden, but he who wishes to enjoy them both ways finds himself in a dilemma. Unless most of the stem is taken with the flower, its decorative value is lost. If most of the stem is taken, the bulb—having lost its lungs—will be severely injured. The only satisfactory compromise is to grow some bulbs just for cutting, and then to leave as much foliage as possible, and not to cut every year from the same bulbs. Having this supply for cutting is not difficult if one is careful to save the natural increase from offsets or to grow some from scales. Many kinds, including some of the very best for indoor decoration, increase rapidly.

In the border the flowers should be removed as they fade and no seed pods allowed to form unless they are wanted for propagation. First-year plants which for any reason seem to be weak will be helped by pinching out the flower buds and thus saving a certain amount of food for the development of the bulb.

The stalks should be cut only after the foliage has withered and begun to dry up. We leave 4 or 5 inches of stem, to mark the location of the bulb, removing this in spring as new growth emerges.

Replanting

While some Lilies increase slowly and may be left undisturbed for years, others will need replanting after three or four years. It is not entirely a matter of variety—congenial conditions are quite as great a factor.

Need for replanting will be evidenced by a close-crowded group of flower stalks with few or inferior blooms. The best time to replant is during the period when the bulbs are nearest to being dormant—when the seed pods are ripening, several weeks after the flowers fade.

Cascade strain of Madonna Lily (L. candidum)—*the oldest and still one of the most popular of all garden Lilies.*

TYPES

The reader will recall that some pages back we took a little journey about his garden for the purpose of selecting locations where Lilies might best be placed, and got as far as leaving a lot of bamboo stakes stuck in the ground. Now let's survey the field of available Lily material and see which ones to select.

Types

The true Lilies include four distinct types:

I. TRUMPET OR FUNNEL-SHAPED FLOWERS: Examples: Madonna (*L. candidum*); Regal (*L. regale*); Easter Lily (L. *longiflorum* varieties).

II. BOWL OR SAUCER-SHAPED BLOOMS: Examples: Gold-banded Lily (*L. auratum*); speciosum Lily; and the Tiger Lily (*L. tigrinum*), which the botanists have now shifted to Group IV, despite the shape of its flowers.

III. ERECT FLOWERS, WIDE OPEN: Examples: our native Wood Lily (*L. philadelphicum*); *L. concolor; L. umbellatum.*

IV. PENDULOUS OR NODDING FLOWERS, WITH PETALS RECURVING AS FLOWERS OPEN FULLY; USUALLY REFERRED TO AS MAR-TAGON TYPE: Examples: *L. martagon;* our native field Lilies (*L. canadense* and *L. superbum*); *L. amabile; L. pumilum.*

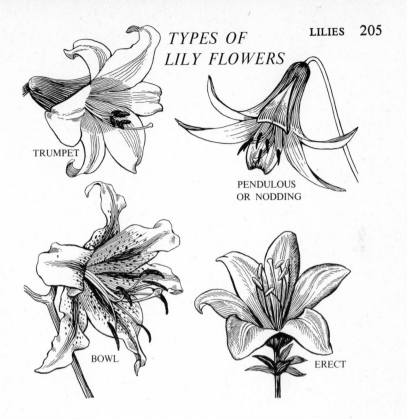

TYPES OF
LILY FLOWERS

TRUMPET

PENDULOUS
OR NODDING

BOWL

ERECT

For lists of recommended varieties, see pages 327, 328, 330, 331.

PROPAGATION—see pages 104, 107–9.

LILY TROUBLES

(*The figures in parenthesis refer to the page on which further information and controls are given.*)

Few insects are troublesome to Lilies. Aphids (208) sometimes molest them but are more dangerous in that they carry the Lily mosaic. In some sections, slugs (116) become a nuisance. More devastating is likely to be an attack by moles and/or mice (116). Thrips (208) and mites (208) attack the bulbs, chiefly in storage.

Diseases, however, are another matter and by far the greatest hazard to success in growing Lilies. The "big three" are mosaic (206), botrytis blight (207), and basal rot (207). There are others which cause rot in bulbs in transit or storage, but the home gardener is not likely to encounter these.

The beginner with Lilies should not be discouraged by the existence of these diseases. He may grow Lilies for years without encountering any of them, or he may even have them and still have Lilies, for many varieties are sufficiently resistant to keep on growing and flowering. A conspicuous example is the popular Madonna. Other resistant Lilies are listed below.

Diseases

In the past there has been no important group of garden flowers more seriously plagued by disease than the Lilies. They are still so bedeviled, but, happily, improved methods of control by bulb growers and the fact that the bulbs, where formerly imported, are now largely American-grown (and therefore less subject to mechanical injury and the development of disease in transit) make it possible for the gardener to get off to a much more favorable start when he begins his adventure in Lily growing.

As previously mentioned, three diseases account for most of the trouble with Lilies in gardens. They are mosaic, botrytis blight, and basal rot.

Lily mosaic is a virus disease which affects all parts of the plant. A few species, even though attacked, continue to grow and bloom year after year; others survive in a weakened, abnormal condition; but a great many species perish completely after a year or two.

Symptoms of mosaic include premature dying of the leaves, beginning at the base, usually accompanied by dwarfed growth; also by striping or mottling of the leaves. This occurs most commonly as circular blotches distributed over the leaf surface; in other species, as light-colored irregular spots which ultimately dry out; in others, as narrow streaks running from base to top of the leaves, which are abnormally small but not distorted. These symptoms are more discernible in spring than later in the season. Infected plants should be removed and burned.

Control measures for mosaic are not easy. Fortunately it is possible to have some Lilies without complete control. The following are resistant or immune: *amabile; candidum; elegans; Hansoni; martagon;*

Maxwilli; *pardalinum;* Preston Hybrids; *speciosum;* T. A. Havemeyer; *testaceum; tigrinum; umbellatum.*

Lilies *grown from seed* are seldom infected. If such bulbs can be planted 300 or 400 feet from any infected bulbs, they will be comparatively safe. The following Lilies are easily grown from seed: *amabile; concolor; Davidi; formosanum; Henryi; pumilum (tenuifolium);* *regale; Wilmottiae.*

Botrytis blight (Botrytis elliptica), a fungous disease, is much less destructive than mosaic because it seldom injures the bulb. Most gardeners who have grown the Madonna Lily (*L. candidum*), its most common victim, know the characteristic "bare stems" of one season contrasted to normal leafage in others.

First symptoms of this botrytis are orangey-brown spots, circular or oval in shape, which may spread and coalesce. These are followed in about ten days by spores which develop in the form of a grayish mold. Form and coloring of the spots vary somewhat in different species. If the disease spreads to the flowers, it develops very rapidly, resulting in a messy decay similar to the familiar botrytis of Tulips. The infection starts on the lower leaves and ascends. The fungus lives over the winter in diseased leaves, stems, and flowers.

The standard control for botrytis blight is Bordeaux mixture, 4–2–50. This can be home-mixed, or purchased ready for use by adding water. It must be applied frequently enough—beginning when spring temperatures get up around 60 degrees—*to keep all new growth covered.* The Bordeaux spray will adhere better and longer if a "sticker," such as Penetrol, is used with it. Bordeaux dust may be used, but is generally considered less effective. Micronized copper has been claimed to be a successful preventative, but many authorities question its effectiveness. As with black spot of Roses, there is no *cure;* it can only be prevented. Plant where there is good circulation of air, with plenty of space between plants, and destroy affected parts as soon as noticed.

Basal rot. The third serious Lily disease, basal rot, is responsible for the death of many Lilies which simply disappear, as it attacks roots and bulbs before affecting foliage.

Aboveground symptoms are delayed emergence in spring, stunted growth, and foliage that turns yellow and dies down prematurely.

Control consists in digging up any bulbs apparently affected. If examination shows that the basal plate is unaffected, remove decayed roots and tissue and sterilize by immersing bulb for thirty minutes in a solution of 1 part 40 per cent formaldehyde to 100 parts water, and replant in another place. As a precaution against loss of the bulb, it may be well to use a few scales for propagation. (See pages 107–9.)

For gray mold blight, Fusarium rot, stem rot, see Chapter 10.

INSECT PESTS

Unlike the diseases, insect pests give the Lily grower little trouble in the garden. It is in storage and transit that they work havoc. The three most harmful of these are mites (related to spiders, so not strictly an insect), thrips, and aphids.

The bulb mite (*Rhizoglyphus hyacinthi*), most serious Lily "insect" pest, is minute, pale yellow, and almost transparent. It breeds between the scales, develops rapidly under favorable conditions, and may cause severe losses. The gardener should examine newly purchased bulbs, *especially if they are bruised or otherwise injured,* with a magnifying glass to make sure that they are not infested. If there is much decay, it is best to destroy them after reporting their condition to the shipper. If injury does not appear severe, they can be cleaned up by fumigating with paridichlorobenzene (obtainable from most seed stores) at the rate of 3 ounces of crystals to each cubic foot of an airtight container. Use burlap or fine mesh wire to keep bulbs from direct contact with crystals, and leave for four days, keeping at a temperature as near 60 degrees as possible. Expose to sun for a day before planting.

The Lily thrips, like the mite, completes its life cycle between the bulb scales. It is large—for a thrips—and glossy black, with wings which it does not use. Fumigate with paridichlorobenzene crystals, 3 ounces to 1 cubic foot of airtight space, for 96 hours, or dust with DDT.

Aphids. The Lily and Melon aphids, most dangerous because they distribute the mosaic disease, sometimes do direct injury to new growth. Black Leaf 40, rotenone, or pyrethrum applied *promptly* will clean them out. One form, *Macrosiphum lili,* is found only on under sides of leaves. Another, *Myzus circumflexus,* attacks terminal buds and shoots.

Other insects which sometimes attack Lilies are the Narcissus bulb flies, Lily-bulb thrips, and stalk borer. For these, see Chapter 10.

CHAPTER *16. Dahlias*

It is regrettable that so much prejudice against the Dahlia still exists. In many garden circles it has for a long time been considered smart to look upon the Dahlia as a coarse and plebeian thing not worthy of admittance into the society of graceful and tastefully gowned members of the sisterhood of desirable garden flowers.

Anyone who assumes this attitude is denying himself—or more often herself—the pleasure of growing one of the most accommodating, colorful, and long-seasoned of all tender bulb-like plants. The fault lies largely with Dahlia growers, the fanatical fans of the decade or two just past who had no use for any flower but the Dahlia—the "man's flower"—and who derided as a sissy any male who took interest in growing other flowers. I was once secretary of a local Dahlia society—our meetings were held in the back room of a barbershop—which expelled those of us who insisted on having flowers other than Dahlias at our fall show!

The attitudes of the pro- and the anti-Dahlia growers of those days is illustrated by another experience. Following a talk on bulbs, two intensely earnest ladies sought me out. One said, "I did enjoy your talk so much. But I must say I think you were not very fair to Dahlias. I'm glad my husband wasn't here—he might have created a scene. They are the only flowers he takes any interest in. Our garden is full of them—some blooms a foot across, and such *gorgeous* colors! I like to hear about the other flowers, too, although we don't have room for any."

As soon as she had turned away a fellow club member said: "I just wished to ask if you were really serious when you suggested planting Dahlias in our gardens—right in with other flowers. I think they are all *awful!* I'd no more think of planting them in my garden than I would Cabbages!"

The Dahlia today is an accepted flower. The hybridizers finally awoke to the fact that there is a demand for Dahlias other than the huge, ungainly "exhibition" varieties. Any modern Dahlia show has well-filled classes of small-flowered and single-flowered varieties and the tiny pompons that can be cut in graceful sprays. The arrangement classes give ample evidence that Dahlias are attractive autumn flowers for indoor decoration.

INDOORS AND IN THE GARDEN

Without question it is as cut flowers that Dahlias have their greatest value. But some types have their place in the garden; and as they are so prolific of flowers and continue in bloom for so many weeks, they are among the few bulbous or tuberous plants that can be gathered freely without having a supply in a separate cutting garden. From two or three dozen plants in our borders, we have Dahlias to gather literally by the basketful from late July until frost cuts them down. They are, incidentally, one of the most satisfactory of flowers to use as a follow-upper among or near deep-planted Tulips. Potted plants set out late in May attain good size about the time the Tulip foliage is mature enough to be removed.

There are many places about the garden where a small group of Dahlias, *or even a single plant,* may be used to good effect. Few shrubs flower after midsummer. And even the species that have colorful foliage or berries in the fall go through a period when they are but masses of leaves, attractive but without color. Borders or groups of such shrubs, and also broad-leaved evergreens, make excellent backgrounds for Dahlias, especially those of the lovely autumn hues in which the Dahlia is unequaled by any other flower except the Chrysanthemum.

The use of Dahlias in this way is a challenge to the gardener's skill. Very large-flowered, heavy-headed varieties are not suitable, and the use of too many plants or of too many colors will produce effects that are grotesque or ridiculous rather than artistic. Plants can be staked if necessary, for Dahlias planted in this way will usually be seen from a distance, and stakes will not show. Staking will seldom be needed, however, as the shrubs themselves support and protect the Dahlias.

Another use for Dahlias is to grow them as an inexpensive, temporary hedge. For this purpose the dwarf-growing sorts, such as the English bedding types and the Pompons, are best. The former, grown from seed started under glass, will provide a hedge for as little as one penny a running foot. When purchasing tubers or plants, it is desirable to stick to one variety so the row will be uniform. Bishop of Llandaff, with its dark maroon foliage and brilliant scarlet, golden-stamened single flowers, is especially good for this purpose.

DAHLIA TYPES

The Dahlia is an American flower, hailing from Mexico. The Mexicans used it as a garden flower before the coming of the Spaniards and probably had developed garden varieties. The original name of the species, *Dahlia variabilis* (later changed to *Dahlia rosea*), was indeed appropriate. Although the Dahlia is comparatively a Johnny-come-lately among garden flowers—the types we know having been developed since 1800—it boasts a range in size and form of bloom, in habit of growth, and in coloring that has few equals in the plant world. It provides blossoms a foot and a half across, on stems like broom handles, for the exhibitor who wants the "best" flower in the show, and dainty nodding little Pompons an inch in diameter.

Indeed, so rapidly do the types of the Dahlia change and intermingle that the American Dahlia Society has been hard put to provide suitable classifications. Those which are "official" at the moment are as follows:

Definitions

INVOLUTE: turned inward, forward, or toward face of ray.

REVOLUTE: turned outward, toward back of ray. When fully revolute, margins of rays overlap or approximate each other.

CLASS IA. SINGLE DAHLIAS: Open-center flowers, with only one row of ray florets, with the margins flat or nearly so, regardless of the number of florets. Examples: Pequot Yellow; Purity.

CLASS IB. MIGNON: Plants do not exceed about 18 inches in height. Examples: Coltness Gem; Torquay Gem.

CLASS II. ORCHID-FLOWERING: Flowers as in Singles, except that the rays are more or less tubular by the involution of the margins. Examples: Dahliadel Twinkle; Imp.

CLASS III. ANEMONE: Open-centered flowers, with only one row of florets, regardless of form or number of florets, with the tubular-disk florets elongated, forming a pincushion effect. Examples: Croix du Sud; Vera Higgins.

CLASS IV. COLLARETTE: Open-centered flowers, with only one row of ray florets, with the addition of one or more rows of petaloids, usually of a different color, forming collar around disk. Examples: Sparkle; Tribune.

CLASS V. PEONY: Open-centered flowers with two to five rows of ray florets, with or without the addition of smaller curled or twisted floral rays around the disk. Examples: Susan Coe; The U.S.A.

CLASS VI. INCURVED CACTUS: Fully double flowers, with the margins of the majority of floral rays fully revolute for one half their length or more, tips of rays curving toward center of flowers. Examples: Ohio; Nightfall.

CLASS VII. STRAIGHT CACTUS: Fully double flowers, with margins of the majority of floral rays fully revolute for one half their length or more, rays straight, slightly incurved or recurved. Examples: Miss Belgium; Zenith.

CLASS VIII. SEMI-CACTUS: Fully double flowers with margins of majority of floral rays fully revolute for less than half their length; rays broad below. Examples: Amelia Earhart; Edith Wilkie.

CLASS IX. FORMAL DECORATIVE: Fully double flowers, with margins of floral rays slightly or not at all revolute; rays generally broad, either pointed or rounded at tips, with outer rays tending to recurve and central rays tending to be cupped; all floral rays in a somewhat regular arrangement to the extent of having four or more recognizable rows of rays surrounding center. Examples: Commando; Five Star General.

CLASS X. INFORMAL DECORATIVE: Fully double flowers, with margins of floral rays slightly or not at all revolute, rays generally long, twisted, or pointed and usually irregular in arrangement. Examples: Jane Cowl; Murphy's Masterpiece.

CLASS XI. BALL: Fully double flowers, ball-shaped or slightly flattened, floral rays blunt or rounded at tips and quilled or with markedly involute margins in spiral arrangement, the flowers 3½ inches or more in diameter. Examples: Mary Helen; Rosy Dawn.

CLASS XII. MINIATURE: All Dahlias which normally produce flowers that do not exceed 4 inches in diameter, Pompons excluded, to be classified according to the foregoing descriptions. Miniature Single: Fugi San; Prince of Bulgaria. Miniature Peony: Bishop of Llandaff; Pink Lassie. Miniature Cactus: Betsy T. Kay. Miniature Semi-Cactus: Little Diamond; Snowsprite. Miniature Formal Decorative: Buckeye Baby; Little Lemon Drop. Miniature Informal Decorative: Chico; Rapture. Miniature Ball: Dusky.

CLASS XIII. POMPON: Same characteristics as Ball Dahlias but, for show purposes, not more than 2 inches in diameter. Examples: Atom; Johnny.

The little Dahlias

If you are familiar only with the big show Dahlias in the "gardens" of Dahlia enthusiasts that contain small forests of 6-foot stakes to which they are chained until show time, don't turn thumbs down on all Dahlias before you have given some of the little fellows at least a trial.

First, there are the Miniatures. These are merely smaller editions of the big fellows, with flowers 2 to 4 inches across, on bushy plants 2 to 4 feet tall. No need for staking or for disbudding unless you prefer to have somewhat larger and more perfect flowers. They produce blooms by the dozen over a long period, and can well be given a place in a large border or against a hedge or shrubbery.

Our favorite among the Miniatures is still Bishop of Llandaff—or one of its descendants. The Bishop is a semi-double (officially classified as Peony-flowered) of bright scarlet with golden stamens and distinctly bronze-maroon foliage; it is one of the most satisfactory of all flowers for cutting. Andre's Orange, unusual in color, is another extragood one. Tea Rose, light buff and cream; Baby Hale, salmon; Blue Bell, violet; and White Fawn provide a good range of attractive colors.

Pompons

While often confused by beginners with the Miniatures, Pompon Dahlias are entirely different. They are characterized by small, almost globular, honeycomb-like flowers, 1 to 2 inches in diameter, borne on thin, wiry stems, and produced, under favorable conditions, literally by the score. Often they can be cut in sprays that in themselves make attractive bouquets. The plants are spreading, usually not over 30 inches or so high. The colors are clear and bright and blend nicely.

Among the popular varieties are: Amber Queen; Yellow Gem; Dee Dee, lavender; Tip Top, fiery red; Bobby, plum-purple; Rosa Wilmoth, rose-pink; and Joe Fette, white.

Bedding or dwarf

The so-called bedding Dahlias got their name from the fact that they are used extensively in England for mass plantings where large-flowered, slower-growing types were not suited to the climate. They come into flower so quickly that seed sown in the open around Bean-planting time will give several weeks of bloom in late summer and fall. Started in a cold frame or indoors, they transplant readily, being no more difficult to handle than Marigolds or Zinnias.

Of the three types most readily available, Mignon, with single flowers, is the tallest—about 2 feet. Coltness Single has less formal flowers on somewhat dwarfer plants; and Unwin Hybrids have semi-double blooms. If you select but one of these, we would suggest the Unwin Hybrids. We have recommended them to many gardeners and have never known one to be disappointed with the results. The range of colors is all that could be desired; any that you particularly like can be saved for another season by storing the tuberous roots over winter.

PLANTING

The first rule in Dahlia growing is to give them full sun. They are among the least tolerant of shade of all bulbous or tuberous plants.

The second is to keep them well supplied with water. The native Mexican name for Dahlia was Acocotti, which means "water pipe." In its natural habitat, the "water pipes" grew on volcanic soils in areas that never lacked for moisture during the season of active growth.

The third is to supply an abundance of plant food. The amounts suggested for bulbs in general (page 72) may safely be increased by 50 per cent. Fertilizers are best provided in several applications—about a third at planting time and the balance at intervals of two to four weeks, the last being made soon after the first flowers are open. Well-rotted manure can be used at planting time, placed a few inches below the tubers.

Roots vs. plants

When you are starting with Dahlias you will have the choice of pro-curing "tubers" (actually tuberous roots) or "green plants," which are

Growing Dahlias from seed is no trick at all. Space seeds evenly; cover ⅛ inch deep. Keep in full sun and evenly moist until ready to transplant. Seedling plant, a few weeks old, shows "tuber" already forming at base of stem.

cuttings that have been potted up just long enough to form a fairly good root ball.

A Dahlia root, being literally a root and not a bulb, is much more likely to become dried out or otherwise injured in transit and handling, and the gardener therefore should make doubly sure that his purchases are in good condition.

Equally satisfactory results can be had from roots and from green plants. The latter are less expensive—usually about half for new, high-priced varieties. Once you have a supply of Dahlias, it is a very easy matter to start your own plants from cuttings if the root divisions do not supply a sufficient number.

As Dahlias are extremely frost-sensitive, plants should not be set out until after any danger of late frost—a week or so later than usual Tomato-planting time. Tubers can be planted a week or so earlier. Plants grown for exhibition are often set out somewhat later—up to mid-June—as this brings the flowers on during cooler nights, which the Dahlia likes, and in time for the shows.

If plants are to be supported, it is advisable to set the stakes *before* planting. For large-flowered varieties, regulation Dahlia stakes 6 to 7 feet long are generally used. In our garden—we do not grow show Dahlias—we prefer the less conspicuous wire stakes (page 86) if it is necessary to use any. Plants grown for show purposes are usually spaced 3 to 4 feet each way, to allow room for pruning, disbudding, and cutting. Miniatures and Pompons should be allowed at least 24 inches, and the dwarf bedding kinds 18 to 20 inches.

For prize blooms, it is advisable to prepare a planting hole for each root or plant. Remove soil 10 to 12 inches deep, add compost, manure, or fertilizer, incorporate thoroughly with the soil, and then fill back enough plain soil so that the root—which is placed horizontally—will be 5 or 6 inches below the surface level.

In early planting, the roots are at first covered only an inch or so, and the remaining hole is gradually filled in as the top grows. In late planting—when the soil is thoroughly warmed up—the soil is all filled in at once.

Green plants from pots are set about 3 inches deep, to the top of the root ball, the lower leaves being removed if necessary. For green plants —and for sprouted plants from tubers—Hotkaps or, better, the newer plastic domes can be used to ward off injury from late frosts: this makes it safe to plant a week or ten days earlier. Plants which have

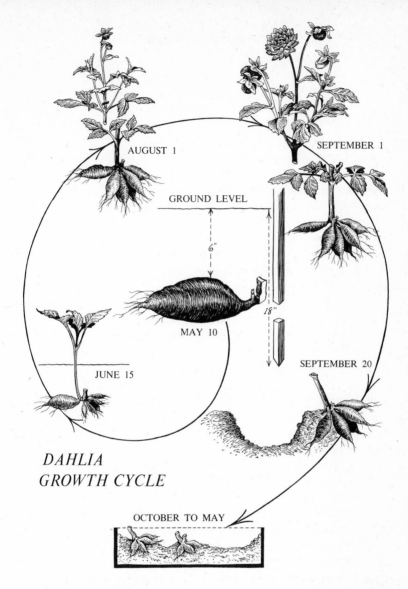

AUGUST 1

SEPTEMBER 1

GROUND LEVEL

6"

18"

MAY 10

JUNE 15

SEPTEMBER 20

DAHLIA
GROWTH CYCLE

OCTOBER TO MAY

been grown in a greenhouse or a hotbed should be well hardened off before being transferred to the open. Purchased plants received by mail may be too tender to be set out at once. A good practice is to pot them and grow them on for a couple of weeks in a cold frame or a sheltered spot before planting; you will get your first blooms just as soon, or sooner.

CULTURE

The one outstanding necessity in the culture of Dahlias is to *keep them growing*. The character of the structure of the plant is such that any serious check, from whatever source, will *cause the wood to harden*. Once that happens, they are through flowering for the season. Sometimes early-planted Dahlias bloom themselves out long before frost. Plants that have gone on strike during July or early August can often be rejuvenated by cutting back the main stem, just above a new shoot at the base of the plant, or else a few inches above the lowest branches. Such a beheading—plus plenty of water if the soil is dry—may result in new growth that will give late blooms.

It is much more satisfactory, however, to prevent the check that throws the plant into semi-dormancy. Lack of moisture in the soil is the most frequent cause of premature hardening of the arteries in Dahlias. Frequent but shallow stirring of the soil around plants, especially after heavy rains or packing of the soil from tying, disbudding, etc., helps to conserve moisture. Clean cultivation also eliminates weeds, insidious robbers of soil moisture.

Mulching is especially desirable for Dahlias because of their need of moisture, their near-the-surface roots, and the frequent treading on the soil between the rows in the care they require when grown for big blooms. Peatmoss is a satisfactory material when water is available; if one must depend on rains, a more open substance, such as pine needles, buckwheat hulls, or clean straw, is better.

Pruning and disbudding are two operations in Dahlia culture which often confuse the beginner. The former is used for controlling the shape or growth of the *plant;* the latter, for control of the *flowers*—to get larger blooms or to time them for a definite date.

A Dahlia plant left to itself is likely to form a tangle of branches and foliage, with small flowers on stems but a few inches long. Or it may send up one bean-pole-like cane, subject to breakage in the wind, and bearing flowers only at the top. Those who grow Dahlias for exhibition figure on supporting them by stout stakes; those who wish to use them as garden flowers want lower-growing, self-supporting, and more floriferous plants.

To get specimens of the latter type, with several branching stems low down, cut or pinch out the tip of the main stem as soon as three or four pairs of leaves have developed. Plants so grown will support themselves. They should be allowed room for horizontal growth. Cutting the flowers or removing faded ones will usually give all the additional pruning required.

To get specimen flowers, a single vertical main stem is left. When the first cluster of three buds appears at the tip, the two side ones are pinched (or "rubbed") out. This is *disbudding*. It takes from 20 to 40 days from bud formation to the opening of the flower, the average being 30.

The small shoots starting in the axils of the pairs of leaves below the terminal flower bud are also removed from several sets to provide a long, unbranched stem for the big flower—which may look like a Cabbage on a broomstick but still win you a coveted blue ribbon. The axillary buds *below* the point where the stem is to be cut are left—or *one* of each alternate pairs may be removed. The lateral stems growing from these axillary buds are then treated in the same way as was the original main stem. Thus a succession of large, long-stemmed flowers is produced.

For Pompons and bedding types, the original pinching back of the main stem is all the pruning likely to be required, and disbudding is not needed.

Cutting: There are few points in connection with Dahlia culture on which the experts are more completely at variance than on the simple matter of cutting and keeping the blooms. A series of careful experiments made by Alex Laurie of the Ohio Experiment Station showed pretty conclusively that the much-advocated singeing of the stem in a flame or plunging in hot water does *not* result in the blooms keeping longer after cutting. One of the country's largest commercial growers cuts blooms at any time of day, prefers to have them wilt considerably, and then places them in cold water up to their necks. After they have revived, he advises, only the bases of the stems should be kept in water. This system, plus the usual precaution of changing the water daily, recutting the stems, and avoiding drafts, gives him the best results.

Protection: The first touch of Jack Frost's chilly fingers will finish off the Dahlias—if you let it. They are, however, readily protected against a few degrees of frost; and no flower—with the possible exception of Chrysanthemums—will give greater rewards for a few minutes spent in this effort, for they frequently go on producing blooms for two or three weeks if one gets them past that first hit-and-run attack of the enemy—usually made in the full o' the moon on a starry night with no breeze stirring. We keep a supply of plant-protecting cloth (treated muslin) on hand, supplemented by old bags, curtains, and sheets. It's the work of but a few moments to throw these over the plants—from which newly opened or half-opened flowers have hastily been cut. Such protection can be left on two or three days if the temperature remains low, but usually it comes off the next morning.

STORING FOR WINTER

As the Dahlia "bulb" is merely an enlarged fleshy root—not even a tuber—it is subject to drying out, or drying *up,* much more rapidly than the general run of bulbs. We have known a whole collection of valuable varieties to be completely lost in ten days' time from being stored, immediately after digging, near a heater to "dry them off."

The dual objective in winter storage of Dahlias is to keep them just sufficiently moist to prevent shriveling, and just cool enough to prevent sprouting. Many different methods are employed to achieve these ends. The one which will work best *under your conditions* you will have to determine for yourself. This will mean inspecting the roots carefully at least once a month for the first winter or two. After that you can probably establish a routine that you know you can depend on, with nothing more than a look-see around New Year's just to be sure that all is well.

We use vegetable baskets lined with roofing paper or newspapers, and either medium-coarse peatmoss or sphagnum moss to pack under, around, and on top of them. Some growers prefer sand, despite its greater inconvenience and the fact that it is more difficult to prevent it's becoming too dry unless the storage space itself is very moist. The temperature should be 35 to 45 degrees. Don't just guess at storage temperatures; keep a thermometer handy.

Dahlias, in their native habitats, are not—as Hamlet's father was— cut down "grossly, full of bread"; they come to a dormant period through a *gradual* drying off at the close of the rainy season. Don't dig, then, immediately after the plants have been killed by frost. Allow a few days for the roots to absorb what they can from the fleshy stalks and to ripen. Then—on a dry sunny day if possible—cut the stalks about 4 inches above the crowns and fasten a wired label *through* each stalk to keep varieties from getting mixed. With a spading fork, dig up a clump and let it drop, bottom down, just hard enough to jar off most of the soil, allowing what will to adhere to the roots. Clumps with large, hollow stem stubs are placed on their sides, or inverted, to prevent moisture from collecting in them.

After digging, store the clumps loosely in deep flats, allow them to dry off for a few hours, and put them in a dark, cool, moist place until they can be gone over and packed for winter storage. Some varieties, especially the first season from seed or from cuttings, make long, stringy roots which dry out quickly. These should be given special attention, even to the extent, if they are valued, of wrapping in sphagnum held with rubber bands. Another method of protecting valuable roots is to coat them with paraffin wax. To do this, wash roots clean with a hose; fill a large pail two-thirds full of hot (about 80 degrees) water; pour in a pound of melted wax; dip tubers into water and remove slowly so the floating wax will coat them thoroughly. After wax coating hardens, pack in sawdust or peatmoss. In any event, all thin or stringy roots should be examined frequently.

As planting time approaches, the roots are removed from storage and either started to provide cuttings for green plants or cut up to make single-eye divisions for growing in pots or setting out directly where they are to grow. For green plants, allow 60 to 70 days to setting-out time. Placing roots in moist peatmoss two or three weeks before planting will give the buds at the base of the old stem a chance to start sufficiently so that they can be divided to the best advantage—one strong eye to each root. (See page 217.)

DAHLIA TROUBLES

The most baffling of the many ills that may plague the grower of Dahlias is the one commonly called "stunt." The term is used rather loosely—often applied to a plant of abnormal, undersized growth from any cause, such as insufficient plant food or insect injury. Such plants usually recover if the cause of poor growth is remedied or removed.

True stunt, caused by the Dahlia-mosaic virus, is characterized by the typical mosaic mottling of the leaves, with yellowish stripes along the veins and curling, malformed foliage. Roots and stems are also dwarfed. There is no cure. Immediate destruction of all sick plants may keep it under control. Growing plants under cheesecloth prevents infection by green Peach aphids which carry the virus. Plants being propagated under glass can be protected by fumigation. Mosaic is *not* carried in the soil, nor transmitted by handling or tools, or through seeds; but divisions or cuttings of affected plants are almost certain to continue the infection.

Diseases

Wilt diseases, causing ring spots on foliage or rotting or browning of stems of growing plants, and decay of roots in storage are serious troubles for which there is no real cure. Dig up plants with soil about them if severely infected and destroy with quicklime. Dust roots in storage with Arasan or Floral Dust at first sign of any decaying spots. For spotted wilt and stem rot or wilt, see Chapter 10.

Powdery mildew sometimes attacks Dahlias in late summer, when a powdery gray deposit appears on the foliage. Control by dusting with sulphur.

Insects

Among the insect pests which may attack Dahlias is the Potato leaf-hopper, a wedge-shaped sucking insect which jumps or hops when disturbed. Symptoms are the burning or browning of leaf margins, followed by stunting of the plants. Stunted plants should be destroyed, but spraying or dusting with DDT will kill the leafhoppers if applied in time.

Other possible Dahlia pests include aphids, Corn borer, Stalk borer, Cyclamen mite, root-knot nematodes, red spider, tarnished plant bug, and thrips. For any of these, refer to Chapter 10.

CHAPTER *17. Gladiolus*

Much that was said in the previous chapter about Dahlias, and why many persons are prejudiced against them, applies equally to the Gladiolus. As flowers go, the Gladiolus is, like the Dahlia, comparatively a newcomer to gardens; and like the Dahlia, also, under cultivation it has shown a surprising facility in responding to the touch of the hybridizer, crossing and crisscrossing until its devotees have finally thrown up their hands in despair at any attempt to keep the original horticultural types distinguished from each other.

The prejudice against "Glads" is largely unjustified. They do have a place in the garden; they are—usually—easily grown; they provide the possibility of having bloom for three months or more by the simple expedient of making succession plantings from early April to early July, thus assuring color where and when you may want it. And they propagate so readily that from a half dozen corms of a variety one will have in a few years more than he knows what to do with.

For accent plantings in mixed borders or about the grounds, Gladiolus possess the advantage that they grow vertically. A clump of six to a dozen can be tucked in between other plants with little trouble and removed at the end of the season with very little disturbance of the roots of other plants near them. As with Dahlias, the largest-flowered show varieties of Gladiolus are least suited to general garden use; those more moderate in size of individual florets and in height of stalk give more pleasing results. Varieties of the Primulinus type and the Miniature Glads, now becoming popular, are better for this purpose.

At this point it may be helpful to clear up the confusion which has existed in regard to the terms "Miniature" and "Baby" as applied to Gladiolus. The Miniatures are small-flowered varieties of the ordinary garden type. The Babies, on the contrary, have been developed from

Elizabeth the Queen, typical of the modern type of Gladiolus with evenly spaced, wide-open florets, facing one way.

the Nanus and Colvillei strains and formerly were used almost exclusively for greenhouse forcing. They are now, however, becoming popular as garden flowers in warmer sections of the country. Typical varieties are Blushing Bride, Nymph, Peach Blossom, Amanda Mahy, in the Nanus group; and The Bride and Red Bride in the Colvillei group.

All the Baby Gladiolus are tender, withstanding temperatures not below 10 degrees above zero. Being winter-flowering, *they must be planted in the fall*—October to December. In warm climates they may be left for two or three years, to form attractive groups, before being lifted and replanted. In the North they must be grown in a greenhouse or in a deep, tight frame.

CULTURE

Soil

While commercial growers usually prefer a deep loam, slightly on the sandy side, for the growing of Gladiolus, either for cut flowers or for corms, the home gardener gets wholly satisfactory results in soils ranging from almost pure sand (as near the seashore) to heavy loams. Again, while they do best with soil acidity between pH 5.5 and 6.5, another .5 point either way is not serious.

The matter of providing extremely good drainage is less important with Gladiolus than with most hardy bulbs, because they do not remain in the ground over winter. If only soil that remains fairly wet is available, however, raised beds (see page 69) are advisable.

Fertilizers

While the plant-food requirements of Gladiolus are in general similar to those already recommended in Chapter 6, special attention should be given to the time at which they are applied.

Recent experiments have demonstrated that, in soil already in fairly good tilth, better results will be had in using all plant foods in the form of side dressings during growth, rather than applying them in the furrow at planting time as was formerly the practice. The reason for this is that the plants' greatest need for nutrition is during the flowering period, *and afterward,* while the new corms and cormels are forming. (See growth cycle, page 227.)

The results of these experiments emphasize again what we have re-iterated throughout these pages: *the grower of bulbous plants should concentrate on producing good fat, strong bulbs, corms, or tubers; then the flowers will follow as the day the night.*

Of course if the soil is new or poor, it should be improved and fer-tilized before planting, with special emphasis on the addition of hu-mus. Then, about the time the flower spike is developing, apply a 5–10–5 fertilizer, or its equivalent, at the rate of 1 to 2 pounds per 100 square feet, and follow this with 2 to 3 pounds more when the flowers have been cut. Flower heads left for garden display should be removed above the top leaf as soon as they fade.

Planting

As Gladiolus are semi-hardy (I have had corms come through the winter out of doors without protection in mild winters in Northern Connecticut), they may be planted as early as the ground can be worked—and from then on until the first week in July. In Northern latitudes, *early* varieties (maturing in 60 to 75 days) should, of course, be used for the latest plantings.

If you do not already have corms from previous plantings, it is best to order all you will want early in the season; the chances are that you can keep them in better condition than you are likely to obtain if making late purchases from a store. Or you can order them to be shipped at different dates; their arrival will then serve as a reminder for making each succession planting.

A word on purchasing Gladiolus corms may be helpful to the beginner. No. 1 size is 2 inches or more in diameter. Very large, flat bulbs with a concave upper surface are generally inferior to much smaller ones with a greater vertical diameter. These are termed "high-crowned." Corms grown from cormels are of this type, and to be preferred to those grown from old corms.

Beware of extreme bargain offers. Size Nos. 1 and 2 (1½ and 1¼ inches, respectively) will produce satisfactory flower spikes; No. 4 (1 inch) or smaller in most varieties will require another season's growth before flowering. (See illustration page 230.)

Gladiolus grown for cutting are planted in rows, 24 to 36 inches

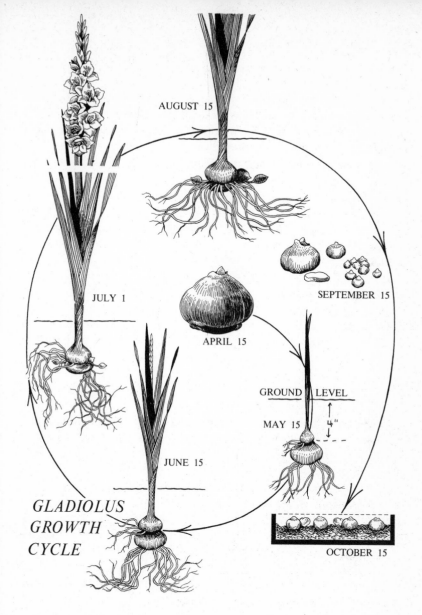

AUGUST 15

JULY 1

SEPTEMBER 15

APRIL 15

GROUND LEVEL

MAY 15   4"

JUNE 15

OCTOBER 15

*GLADIOLUS
GROWTH
CYCLE*

apart, according to the method of cultivation to be used; or, where space is at a premium, in double rows, 6 or 8 inches apart, with a 2-foot walk between. The corms are spaced 3 to 6 inches apart, the wider spacing in rich soil and for extra-fine individual spikes. Cover 3 to 4 inches deep in fairly heavy soil, an inch more in lighter soil.

The first planting will start growth somewhat more quickly with an initial covering of 2 inches. Fill the trench in as growth progresses.

In flower borders and for landscape use, individual planting holes are readily made with a "Slim Jim" trowel. At least half a dozen bulbs of a variety should be placed in a group. As Gladiolus grow straight up, with little spread of the lower leaves, they can be used for interplanting where subjects of spreading habit would not fit in.

Cultivation

Gladiolus thrive best in a soil kept open by fairly frequent cultivation and free from weeds. These conditions are particularly important during the first few weeks of growth.

If they are being grown in rows, cultivate deeply soon after planting (before they break ground) between the rows to loosen thoroughly the soil, which will have become more or less packed down in planting. Subsequent tillage, with cultivator or hoe, should be shallow (1 to 2 inches), but frequent enough to prevent formation of a hard surface crust.

Watering; mulching

Gladiolus will come through dry seasons, even drought conditions, with relatively little damage except somewhat smaller growth. Experiments have indicated that the critical need for an ample moisture supply is during the first six to eight weeks—the period until the new corm has formed and put out its own vigorous roots. In poor soil an occasional application of liquid fertilizer, just before watering, is decidedly beneficial. Any watering should be sufficiently heavy to penetrate to a depth of 6 inches or more.

As Gladiolus throw comparatively little shade, mulching is particularly beneficial. Often it is not applied until fairly late in the season, but both weeding and watering will be greatly curtailed if mulch is applied as soon as the plants are well up.

Supports

Reasonably deep planting supplemented, if necessary, by moderate hilling—such as is often used for Sweet Corn—will usually keep

Gladiolus growing in an upright position. Tall-growing varieties, especially if in very rich soil or in exposed positions, may require support. Spikes being grown for show purposes are much safer if supported, for here a crooked stem, which might well be a positive asset in using the spike in an arrangement, will practically eliminate any chance of its winning a ribbon.

Posts made of two-by-fours, driven in at intervals of 15 feet or so along the row, will serve to support wires or stout cords run along both sides of the row at the proper height. The first strand should be placed as the flower spike begins to emerge, and another, if needed, a foot or so above it.

For exhibition

In growing especially for exhibition, ascertain (from growers' catalogues) the number of days to flowering, and make three plantings at intervals of five days, the middle date being fixed by counting back from the date, fixed or probable, of the show. (Time from planting to flowering ranges from 55 to 90 days, with the average around 80 to 85.)

Give individual plants more space than ordinarily, and support carefully. *Do not try to force by overfeeding;* this is likely to result in soft, flabby growth and failure of the florets to remain in good condition when cut. Spikes should be shown with the first three or four florets wide open. Cutting two or three days before the show and keeping in a cool or a warm temperature will help to some extent in delaying or hastening the opening.

STORING OVER WINTER

After flower spikes have been cut or faded blooms removed, the last application of fertilizer should be made, cultivated or hoed in, and the ground thoroughly watered if the weather is dry. No further care will be required until the foliage begins to turn brown—a period of 30 to 50 days, according to variety and seasonal conditions. If normal ripening is cut short by a hard frost, dig as soon as possible thereafter. It always is desirable to dig while the stems are still firmly attached to the corms.

Gladiolus cleaned and separated after curing yields two first-size corms, the shriveled remains of the original corm planted in the spring, and dozens of pea-sized cormels.

The first thing to decide when digging is whether the cormels are to be saved. Usually the increased number of corms will provide the home gardener with all the stock he wishes. In case of a favorite variety or a new high-priced one, the grower may wish to multiply his stock as rapidly as possible by growing the cormels on to flowering size.

If the cormels are not to be saved, digging is a very easy matter. A fork thrust into the soil near the base of the plant, with downward pressure applied to the handle, will loosen it sufficiently so that the stem, with its corms adhering, can readily be lifted out by the foliage. Then all loose soil is shaken off.

Have available a sufficient number of containers—flats, boxes, or splint baskets—so that each variety, with a substantial label, can be kept by itself. To economize on space, the tops can be cut off an inch or less above the corms immediately after lifting. The practice of twisting the tops off is not recommended; it often results in injury to corms.

The dug corms are dried for a few hours in the sun and then removed to a frostproof shed or garage to cure for a few weeks before being cleaned up for winter storage. They should have free circulation of air; a high temperature (unless the humidity is excessively low) will not be harmful.

When the corms have dried and cured sufficiently so that the stems, old corms, and husks may be removed readily, they are cleaned, sorted, and labeled. Each lot may be placed in a stout paper bag, a small box, or a section of a flat. The temperature for winter storage should be as near 40 degrees as possible, but 10 degrees or so higher will answer. Packing in sand, sawdust, peatmoss, or vermiculite will help if storage conditions are poor, but usually it is not necessary.

Immediately after cleaning is the proper time to apply any dust-control measure to combat thrips. (See pages 117, 234.)

PROPAGATION

Cormels

If it is decided to save the cormels, the corms should be lifted very carefully and placed in tight boxes, with some soil adhering. As the cormels—some of which may be little larger than buckshot—dry out much more rapidly than the corms, it is advisable to separate them as soon as possible. They may then be stored in *slightly* moist sand or peatmoss. They should be examined from time to time during the winter to make sure they are in plump condition, but not starting to sprout.

As early in spring as the ground can be worked, the cormels can be planted. If dry and hard, we soak them in tepid water for two to five days until, as one of my helpers once put it, "they're just ready to bust." They are planted about 2 inches deep in rows 18 inches apart. If in quantity, they can be sown like peas; in smaller numbers, spaced 1 to 2 inches apart.

Careful weeding is essential until the grass-like foliage has attained a good start.

Cultivation, feeding, and watering when necessary should be maintained during the growing season. Adequate soil moisture is especially important during the first two months. The cormel does not grow larger, but after about six weeks' growth is replaced by a corm forming just above it, at the base of the stem.

To facilitate harvesting, which is done just when the tops begin to die down, remove soil with a hoe or wheel hoe along both sides of the row and then lift the corms out carefully.

The crop of corms (known as virgin corms) will vary considerably in size. Commercial growers grade corms into six sizes, ranging from no. 1, 1½ inches or over, down to No. 6, ½ inch or smaller. Each grade is ¼ inch smaller than the one preceding it. Many of the new corms will be of flowering size—No. 3 (1 to 1¼ inches) or larger; others will require growing on for a second season before reaching flowering size.

Large Corms

Large old corms often show two or more "eyes" (growth points) —readily discernible on peeling back the husk—on the upper, concave surface. They can be cut with a sharp knife, dusted with Semesan, a disinfectant, or Rootone, a root-inducing hormone, and planted in the usual way. Each cut segment, of course, must contain an eye.

Seed

Growing Gladiolus from seed is not difficult, but as garden varieties will not come true there is little point in it unless one wishes to develop new varieties of his own. The seeds are fairly large and in appearance much like Parsnip seed, with a fleshy "germ" near the center. They are gathered as the pods *begin* to open and stored in tight containers in a cool, dry place.

Seeds may be sown in greenhouse or hotbed in February or early March, in a cold frame in March or early April, or in the open ground in April or May. Early-sown seeds often produce some flower spikes the first season. The general care of the seedlings is the same as given in Chapter 9.

Gladiolus were formerly classified by the shape of the individual florets, such as large-flowered, hooded (Primulinus), ruffled, orchid-flowered. With the multiplication of varieties, this system had to be abandoned, and for show purposes the classes are arranged according to size and color. Here is the present classification:

OFFICIAL CLASSIFICATION OF GLADIOLUS

Formal Type—paired arrangement of florets
Informal Type—alternate arrangement of florets

Sizes

Giant	500 series	5½ inches and up (floret size)
Large	400 series	4½ to 5½ inches
Medium	300 series	above 3¼ to 4½ inches

Sizes

Small	200 series	2½ through 3¼ inches
Miniature	100 series	under 2½ inches

Color separations

White	Salmon	Lavender
Cream	Scarlet	Purple
Yellow	Pink	Violet
Buff	Red	Smoky
Orange	Rose	Any other color

GLADIOLUS TROUBLES

The Gladiolus provides an interesting example of the ups and downs which a flower may undergo in popularity as a result of the ease or the difficulty of growing it. Until a couple of decades ago it was considered the easiest of all summer-flowering bulbs. Then suddenly along came the thrips and several diseases, and gardeners by the thousands just crossed it off their lists. Fortunately, effective—and not too difficult—controls have been found for most of these ills, and the stately Gladiolus has won its way back.

Diseases

Fusarium dry rot or *brown rot* of Gladiolus is a serious menace in some sections. Infection starts in the ground when small, reddish-brown lesions occur on the lower parts of corms. During the storage period the lesions enlarge and become uneven or circular brown spots, the whole corm sometimes becoming brown and hard. At digging time, corms should be inspected and any showing lesions destroyed at once. Unaffected or but slightly affected corms taken from a planting where dry rot is present should be cured as quickly and thoroughly as possible. In spring, *just* before planting, treat with New Improved Ceresan, 1 ounce to 3 gallons of water, soaking the corms for 15 minutes. Or corms may be soaked for 3 hours in a mixture of 4 tablespoons of Lysol to 3 gallons of water.

Fusarium yellows, the commonest of Gladiolus diseases, is most likely to occur in warm climates and sandy soils. First symptom is a yellowing or browning of the tips of the leaves, which gradually die back until the plant perishes. The old corm, if dug, will be found badly rotted, and the new corm forming above it will show a dark area at the base. This disease flourishes in dry weather and at high temperatures. Dig suspected corms at once and destroy. When storing for the winter, and again at planting time, carefully examine corms and destroy any with spots on their basal plates.

Botrytis shows symptoms similar to the above, but may affect any part of the plant, eventually reaching and rotting the corm, converting it to a soft, spongy mass. Its spread is favored by wet weather. Spraying foliage with Dithane D-14 and zinc sulphate has given some control if repeated every five days in wet weather. Burn all refuse. Diseased plants should be destroyed, as for fusarium rots. Dry harvested bulbs quickly at high temperatures if botrytis is present.

Scab, sometimes called neck-rot, as it causes the decay of several inches of the stem just above the ground, is indicated on dry corms by dark spots on the husks and circular, hard depressions on the tissue beneath. Remove the husks, cut out scabs, and treat corms with Semesan; or soak corms for 2 hours in a 1–1000 solution of mercuric chloride (deadly poison); or for 1 minute in 1 pound calomel to 5 gallons of water. Destroy badly infected corms.

For blue mold rot, see Chapter 10.

Insects

Thrips, by far the most prevalent of all Gladiolus troubles, attacks the foliage, buds, and flowers of growing plants, and even injures the corms in winter storage. First evidence in the garden is whitish streaks on the foliage and brownish, malformed buds. For effective control, begin spraying (or dusting) when plants are 6 inches high, and repeat every week or ten days (4 tablespoons of 50 per cent DDT powder to 3 gallons of water) until plants, especially in the leaf sheaths, are clean under examination with a magnifying glass. Thrips on corms in storage is controlled by sifting 5 per cent DDT dust over the corms soon after digging them, a teaspoonful of powder to 100 or 150 corms. The dust is left on indefinitely.

For aphids, Corn borer, mites, cutworms, wireworms and tarnished plant bugs, see Chapter 10.

My first encounter with Tuberous-rooted Begonias occurred many years ago when, as a youngster, I took to our county fair some handsome specimens of *Begonia semperflorens* (the ordinary garden Begonia known to everyone) which I was confident would carry off a first prize. They didn't. In the Begonia section was a collection of a dozen or so plants which I didn't know, with flowers so breath-takingly beautiful that they completely stole the show. Upon inquiry, I found that they were Tuberous-rooted Begonias and that the old couple exhibiting them had grown these same plants annually for fifteen years and still had the original tubers. Fascinated by the size, forms, and colors of these exotic blooms, I immediately ordered a small collection of them. They have been one of my favorite flower hobbies ever since.

For many years Tuberous-rooted Begonias—which might more accurately be called simply Tuberous Begonias—were not grown in this country, despite their popularity in Europe and in England, as generally as they deserved to be. It was a case of "give a dog a bad name"; many gardeners got the impression that they were extremely difficult and unreliable. It is true that in many sections of the United States climatic conditions are not ideal for them, but there are few areas in which they cannot be grown. They are different rather than difficult.

Gradually this fact came to be realized. No other bulbous plant during recent years has increased in favor quite so rapidly as the Tuberous Begonia. Back in the early twenties, when at Seabrook Farms in southern New Jersey, we grew some 300,000 of them, I staged an exhibit in the Dahlia Show in New York. Not one person in a hundred of the visitors to that show knew what they were. They attracted so much attention that the show management seriously considered asking that the exhibit be withdrawn as unfair competition to the Dahlias. Today Tuberous Begonias are shown in gorgeous color plates in almost every seed catalogue, and such national magazines as The *Saturday Evening Post* and *Life* have run stories on them, illustrated in full color. American gardeners are growing them in ever-increasing numbers.

What have Tuberous Begonias to offer the home gardener? First of all, they produce flowers more varied in form and color and over a longer season than any other bulbous plant. The range of blossom forms is almost unbelievable; and for purity and delicacy their coloring, especially in the lighter tints, is unsurpassed. The colors range through the entire scales of reds, pinks, yellows, and oranges, with pure crystalline whites thrown in for good measure. Blue and its associated hues are absent.

Second, Tuberous Begonias are incomparably the most colorful of all plants which, in Northern latitudes, can be grown in the shade. At least moderate shade in most sections they demand; and they will tolerate a lot of it if it is "high" shade, as from overhead trees. Around our own house we have a great deal of shade in summer; it is part of our plan of living, and we like to be able to enjoy shade and nearby flowers at the same time. Tuberous Begonias have played a big part in providing an answer to this problem.

Finally—and here we expect some gardeners will take issue with us—we grow Tuberous Begonias in quantity because they are easy to grow. Perhaps having tried them and failed, you are among those who will say this statement is inaccurate; but, like Bret Harte's Truthful James, "the same I arise to maintain." I have grown them for some forty-odd years in several states and under widely varied conditions, in quantities ranging from a dozen or so to commercial production on a large scale; it would take a lot of evidence to convince me that I am wrong.

No matter what kind of soil you have, you can grow Tuberous Begonias. The range of shade they will tolerate is wide. Starting the tubers, to get good bushy plants, is the simplest thing in the world. Growing from seed is much more difficult, but that, too, can be done.

As to pests and diseases, the only troubles I have ever encountered in over forty years of growing these Begonias were one infestation of Cyclamen mite and occasional malformation or dropping of the buds in extremely hot, muggy weather.

Overfeeding, especially after midsummer, is likely to cause soft growth that may result in stem rot. Testers in the Men's Garden Club of America's Tuberous Begonia program have been unanimous in reporting no trouble from insect pests or diseases.

All this adds up to a substantiation of the statement that Tuberous Begonias are easy to grow. Compared to many other flowers—such as Roses or Dahlias, for instance—they are a pushover. The one most likely source of trouble in some sections is the hot, humid weather of midsummer. This they do not like. But even this handicap can be overcome to a large degree by the proper cultural conditions—with less effort than that required for combating the usual troubles of many other flowers.

How about expense? It isn't great. First-class tubers (1½ to 2½ inches in diameter) can be purchased for 25 to 50 cents each. Even small ones, at a lower price, will flower generously the first year, as will also seedling plants shipped by mail to customers within range of the nurseries which grow them. As the tubers are readily kept over winter for growing again year after year, this initial cost is distributed over many seasons.

IN THE GARDEN PICTURE

No matter what your garden scheme is, you can count on these glamorous flowers to provide additional beauty and interest. There are any number of ways in which they can be used, the several types adapting themselves admirably to one purpose or another. You can try them in mass plantings to provide exceptionally colorful beds or borders; in small groups as an interesting edging-down for broad-leaved evergreens which are often grown under overhead shade; along the front of a foundation planting on a shaded side of the house. Groups of three or four—or even individual plants—will brighten up small shady spots such as may be found in the general planting, around house corners, or in the rock garden. One of our favorite uses for them is along the front of the area devoted to summering house plants which, though most of them are not in bloom at this season, provide foliage that makes an attractive background.

They are ideal, too, for a shaded porch, and the pendent or hanging types, alone or in combination with upright forms—or with other plants which tolerate some shade, such as Fuchsias—for porch boxes or hanging baskets.

As house plants they are less useful; their normal flowering season is from midsummer to frost, when—if one has a garden—plants for indoors are not especially sought after, while during early winter the lack of humidity indoors is likely to prove too great a handicap. All in all, however, Tuberous Begonias are adapted to quite as many different uses as the most obliging of other garden flowers.

The type or types of Tuberous Begonias you grow will depend on the purpose for which they are to be used. For bedding or a mass-color effect to cover a considerable area, the single-flowered forms are on the whole the more satisfactory. The flowers, being much lighter than those of the doubles, stand up better against wind and rain and make a quicker comeback if storm damage occurs. Where the beauty of individual blossoms is the prime consideration, the double-flowered forms are of course more glamorous and intriguing. One waits for each new plant to open its first bud, never knowing exactly what will be forthcoming.

Both the singles and doubles have a number of fairly distinct flower forms. These are remarkable, especially among the doubles, for their resemblance to other flowers—so much so that the Tuberous Begonia may well be called the mockingbird of the floral kingdom.

Flower types among the singles include *gigantea,* with huge flat opening flowers often 6 to 8 inches across; *crispa,* with ruffled-edged petals; *cristata,* with the petals peculiarly crested like a cockscomb; and *narcissiflora,* with tubular centers quite suggestive of a Giant Trumpet Daffodil.

The doubles come in such flower forms as *camelliaflora,* with flowers startlingly like those of a Camellia; Rose, a fairly recent development from the foregoing; *fimbriata,* densely fringed, giving a carnation-like effect; *tabulata,* with overlapping flat petals similar to those of a Zinnia.

In addition to these types or forms, there are two others which differ from them in habit of growth and in the uses to which they can be put.

The hanging or basket type (*Begonia tuberhybrida pendula*), listed in most catalogues as *Lloydi,* is the one to use for porch or window boxes, hanging baskets, atop low walls, or in any shaded position where a flowering plant is desired and where there is fair protection from wind. The hanging type can be had in both double and single forms, in a good range of colors. Named varieties, much used in Europe, are becoming more available here. All have much smaller flowers than the singles and doubles previously described.

Multiflora, which also has comparatively small leaves and flowers, long popular abroad, is becoming better known here. Plants of *multiflora* are branching and compact in habit, and the blooms—as the name implies—are produced much more freely. They will stand considerably more sun than the large-flowered sorts and are much the best for use as a pot plant indoors. Here again named varieties are becoming available in this country. Frau Helene Harms, a double golden yellow, is one of the best. We venture the prediction that many American gardeners will discover this little-known type during the next few years—and be delighted with it.

GROWING METHODS

In general, there are two methods of growing Tuberous Begonias: planting them in ground beds or borders in the open, or carrying them through the season in pots. In either case they may be given a running start by bringing the tubers into early growth under glass. They may, however, be planted in the open. The advantage of starting them under glass is that flowering will begin four to eight weeks earlier. Being tender plants, they cannot be set in the open until after danger of frosts—Tomato-planting time in your vicinity. Unstarted tubers can be set out a week or ten days earlier than growing plants.

The tubers, as received from your seedsman, are rough, hairy, and saucer-shaped. They may be purchased from January to May—unless the supply is exhausted before then, as frequently happens. If you do not have facilities for starting tubers under glass and want early bloom, you can purchase growing plants from a local florist, but of course these cost considerably more than dormant tubers.

Starting the tubers yourself is a very simple matter, especially as they do not require full sunshine. While a greenhouse furnishes the ideal conditions, any fairly light space in a room where the atmosphere is not too dry will anwer. The ideal temperature for starting the tubers into growth is 55 degrees at night, with 10 to 15 degrees more during the day. However, a night temperature of 45 to 50 degrees

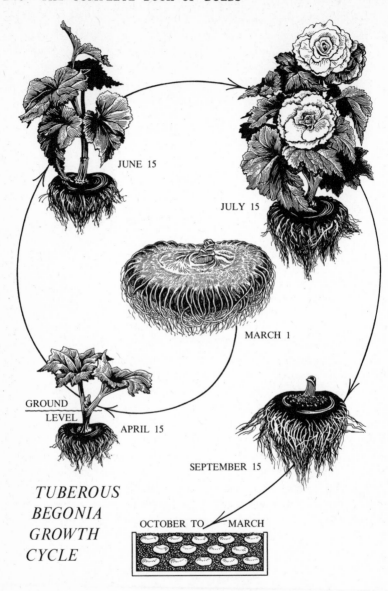

JUNE 15

JULY 15

MARCH 1

GROUND
LEVEL
APRIL 15

SEPTEMBER 15

*TUBEROUS
BEGONIA
GROWTH
CYCLE*

OCTOBER TO — MARCH

will serve; growth will be considerably slower, but the plants as good. A hotbed or cold frame will do for starting them a month or so in advance of outdoor planting.

The first step is to fill a box or flat, about 3 inches deep, with peatmoss that has been thoroughly moistened. The tubers are pushed down into this until the tops are slightly below the surface. Place them 2 to 3 inches apart each way, *concave side up.* (Usually pink sprout buds will be showing in the hollow of the tuber.) An ordinary flat, 13 x 21 inches, will hold from 18 to 36 tubers, according to their size.

An occasional watering, to keep the peatmoss moist *but not wet,* is all the care required until the plants attain a height of 3 to 5 inches. Then they should be transplanted to other flats, or to pots or bulb pans sufficiently large to take the mass of roots without crowding. For this transplanting use a compost of ½ peatmoss, ½ well-rotted manure (or leafmold), plus 10 to 15 per cent coarse sand or sandy loam. *A light, porous, and rapidly draining compost is essential for good results.* To one half of this compost add bone meal or cottonseed

ABOVE: *Tuberous Begonias are started into growth by placing the tubers in moist peatmoss, concave sides up.* BELOW: *When several leaves have formed they are transplanted to pots or bulb pans; shaded from full sun.*

After further growth they are removed to outdoor beds, or shifted to large pots for flowering.

meal (we prefer a mixture of both) at the rate of one quart per bushel, and use this in the *bottoms* of flats or pots when transplanting; this is to avoid the mold that may otherwise form on the surface. Water moderately at first, increasing as growth develops.

Plants to be grown to maturity in pots should be shifted again to 6-, 7-, or even 8-inch size. We prefer bulb pans to standard pots, as they are much less likely to be tipped over. Some specimens of double-flowered sorts will require twigs or light bamboo sticks to hold them upright, as the heavy blooms may drag them over. Pinching out the tips of tall stalks about the time first buds show will produce stockier plants.

OUTDOOR CULTURE

The four essentials for satisfactory growth with Tuberous Begonias out of doors are: shade; a porous, fibrous, rich soil; perfect drainage; abundant moisture. *The soil need not be deep,* for they are surface rooters. It makes little difference what the original soil is, so long as it will drain. If it won't, you can build up a bed 6 to 8 inches deep right on the surface. In any case, the soil in which tubers are to be placed or plants set should be similar to that recommended for potting; most soils can be made so by digging in several inches of peatmoss and manure and adding sand if necessary. Plants in pots may be plunged to the rims in a bed of peatmoss.

As warm weather approaches, the critical point in culture is maintaining the moisture supply. Here the "seldom-but-thorough" formula for watering should be changed to "moderate-but-frequent"—for Tuberous Begonia roots require moisture in the surface soil. During excessively hot dry spells *spraying the foliage* is almost as important as watering the roots. Use a fine mistlike spray, applying it late in the afternoon.

Plants that have been flowering for several weeks will be benefited by an occasional application of liquid fertilizer—preferably made from manure, though a chemical solution will do.

Winter care

With the approach of freezing weather, all watering is stopped. If plants are in pots, they can be brought indoors to finish flowering, but under no circumstances should they be subjected to a hard freeze. A *light* frost, blackening the foliage, will not harm the tubers. Plants set in the ground are taken up, *with all adhering soil,* and with the tops left on, and spread out under cover to dry off for a week or two. The tops are then cut back, leaving 3 or 4 inches of the fleshy main stems and the roots, to dry up gradually. This will take several weeks. When the stem stubs will come off at a touch, remove them, shake the tubers out of the dry soil, and pack them for winter storage in peatmoss, vermiculite, or sand, and store in a temperature of 45 to 60 degrees. With plants grown in pots, we remove the tops and store the pots, on their sides, until they have thoroughly dried out, then remove and store tubers as above.

SEED

The growing of Tuberous Begonias from seed is a ticklish proposition, but a patient and painstaking amateur can do it. (Choice plants can also be propagated from stem cuttings and by division of old tubers.)

Growing Tuberous Begonias from seed requires patience and expert care. Give seed pan plenty of drainage, water from bottom, and keep surface covered with glass until seedlings are well up. Transplant when second or third leaf has formed.

If you are not averse to testing your skill as a gardener, try the seed method. Sow not more than a packet or two for the first attempt. If a greenhouse is available, sow the seed in February, and you'll have —*if* you succeed—blooms during late summer and a supply of small tubers to carry over until next year.

A night temperature of 65 to 70 degrees is desirable—almost essential, in fact, for lower temperatures mean slower and poorer germination. Even in a greenhouse the seed is best started in a propagating frame, where humidity (as well as temperature) can be closely controlled.

Bulb pans or small seed flats are prepared for receiving the seed by placing a 2- or 3-inch layer of gravel or sifted cinders in the bottom and covering this with about 1½ inches (*not more*) of fairly coarse, loose compost. This can be made up of 2 parts leafmold and 1 part peatmoss, with a pint of pulverized charcoal added to a peck of compost. Smooth over, *but do not pack down*. On top of this sift (through ⅛-inch mesh) a thin (not over ¼-inch) layer of the same mixture, leaving it loose. Then place in a pan or dish of water and let it soak up from below until the surface *begins* to show moisture.

The seed is extremely small—almost dust. Distribute it thinly and evenly. Cover loosely with moist blotting paper and (unless in a propagating frame) also with glass. After a few days watch carefully for germination and, at first sign of sprouting, remove paper. In a few days more, remove glass. If temperature and moisture are kept uniform, growth will be fairly rapid. *Never let the surface dry out;* syringe with fine spray if necessary. Gradually give more ventilation, but *no* direct sunshine. In six to ten weeks seedlings will be ready for transplanting. (See illustration on page 244.) The earlier the transplanting is done, the better.

For transplanting, use the same mixture, placed not over 2 inches deep on top of ample drainage material. No fertilizer is needed. As they crowd again they will be ready to set outdoors (after hardening off) or transferred to pots—the same as for plants started from tubers.

The first transplanting is a very delicate operation; the seedlings are both tiny and brittle. Have soil in seed pans, and in flats also, moderately moist. Lift seedlings gently, a few at a time, and spread out on a flat surface. Lower roots into planting holes and press in gently; do *not* press surface of soil down hard. Syringe daily for several days.

CUTTINGS

Growing plants from cuttings is much easier and has the advantage of making it possible to increase the supply of plants which you particularly like. The general routine to be followed is the same as that which has already been described (pages 109–10).

Tuberous Begonias are grown from soft cuttings, secured by removing the tops of sprouts from tubers started in flats or pots—somewhat more developed than those shown in the illustration on page 241. At least two, preferably three or four, leaves should be left below the cut, which should be made with a very sharp knife (we use a razor blade) so as not to bruise the brittle, fleshy stems. The "wings" (or leaf bracts) are removed from the lower part of the stem, and the lower leaves may be cut back a third to a half.

For a rooting medium use peatmoss, or two parts peat and one of sand. Slight bottom heat is desirable but not essential. A propagating case is, however, most helpful, as humid atmosphere is even more necessary with these Begonias than with most house or garden plants. Once rooted, the cuttings are transferred to 3- or 4-inch pots and shifted later to larger ones.

DIVIDING TUBERS

Begonia tubers gradually increase in size for several years, but never split up or form offsets. They do, however, send up sprouts from two or more points in the "cup" of the tuber, instead of from one point only, as is the case with younger tubers. Old tubers can be cut into two or more pieces, each with one or more "eyes" or growth points.

To do this, place the tubers in moist peatmoss in February, March, or April, and when the sprouts have started sufficiently to be readily distinguished, cut the bulbs—with a sharp, thin blade, to avoid bruising—and dust the cut surfaces with Rootone. Then reset the pieces in peatmoss, to continue root and top growth, until they are ready for potting up or setting out of doors.

BEGONIA TROUBLES

Leaf spot (*Begonia bacteriosis*) is a disease which attacks both tuberous and fibrous Begonias throughout the United States. Roundish dead spots, brown with yellow translucent margins, appear on the foliage, followed by premature falling of the leaves. Sometimes the stems soften and rot. Transmitted by a yellow ooze on the infected leaves, leaf spot rapidly spreads, especially under greenhouse conditions. Control consists in watering from below to keep the foliage dry, and keeping pots widely spaced to give good circulation of air and to avoid contact. If the disease is present, spray with Bordeaux mixture.

Gray mold blight—a form of botrytis—may also attack Tuberous Begonias. For description and control, see Chapter 10.

Pests

The only insects likely to be encountered are mealy bugs and Cyclamen mites, for which see Chapter 10.

CHAPTER *19. Other Summer and Autumn-Flowering Bulbs*

In addition to the summer-flowering bulbs discussed in the preceding four chapters, there are others, some tender and some hardy, which carry on the garden's display of bulbous flowers through the summer and well into autumn.

The more important of these are described here, as they merit somewhat fuller treatment than those included only in the general catalogue of bulbs in Part Three. So here we will take up:

Summer-flowering

Galtonia   (Summer-hyacinth)
Hymenocallis   (Ismene; Peruvian-daffodil or Basket Flower)
Polianthes   (Tuberose)
Tigridia   (Tiger-flower; Shell-flower)
Tritonia   (Montbretia)

Autumn-flowering

Colchicum   (Meadow Saffron)
Lycoris squamigera   (Wonder-lily; Magic-lily-of-Japan)
Sternbergia lutea
Zephyranthes   (Fairy-lily; Zephyr-lily)

(The many lovely little autumn-flowering Crocuses which add so much color and personality to the fall garden are discussed in Chapter 13.)

One of the intriguing things about growing these less well-known subjects is, of course, that they are out of the ordinary; another is that they make such excellent material for arrangements. None of them is troublesome so far as its culture is concerned.

Galtonia (Cape- or Summer-hyacinth), 3 to 4 feet or more in height and flowering in midsummer, is easily grown.

SUMMER-FLOWERING

Galtonia

Perhaps the most graceful and dignified of this group is tall *Galtonia candicans,* the common name of which is Cape- or Summer-hyacinth. The flower scape, rising to 3 or 4 feet in height above a group of long, pointed basal leaves, is set with large, nodding, bell-shaped white flowers borne in a loose raceme.

Coming late in July in the vicinity of New York City, they are a welcome touch of white in the back of the summer border. We place ours behind the Ismenes and Acidantheras with Haemanthus in the foreground, thus creating an impressive bed of tender, summer-flower-

Acidanthera bicolor, *midsummer-flowering bulbs meriting much wider use. The butterfly-like flowers are fragrant and excellent for cutting.*

ing bulbs. The flowering scapes of the Galtonia rise well above the Ismene blooms and handsome, persistent foliage, the latter hiding the less decorative leaves of the Galtonia.

Galtonia bulbs should not be planted out of doors until the soil is thoroughly warm. Set 3 inches deep in rich, well-worked soil which can be kept watered in case of drought. The plants shoot up with remarkable speed after planting.

Before frost, lift the bulbs, dry, and store at approximately 60 degrees.

Ismene (Hymenocallis) or Peruvian-daffodil has dramatic, slightly fragrant flowers which last well when cut. Blooms in early summer. Also easily forced. Shown are festalis (top) *and* calathina.

Hymenocallis

This satisfactory and showy tender summer-flowering bulb has long been popular. *H. calathina,* the species usually grown, was formerly known as *Ismene calathina* and is sold commercially as Ismene, sometimes as Peruvian-daffodil.

The large, fragrant white flowers have tubular crowns 4 inches long, surrounded by fringed perianth segments 2 inches long, the large trumpet-like tube giving it the common name of Peruvian-"daffodil." The other common name of Spider-lily is suggested by the narrow, fringed perianth segments. *H. hybrida* Sulphur Queen is a yellow hybrid, while Festalis, another hybrid, has extravagantly curved perianth petals. *H. speciosa* and the hybrid Daphne are desirable for their larger flowers.

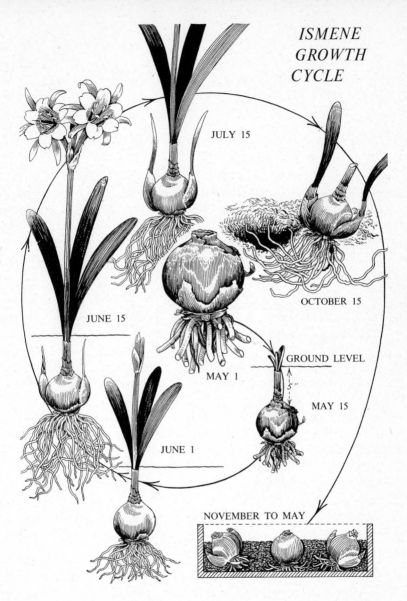

ISMENE
GROWTH
CYCLE

JULY 15

OCTOBER 15

JUNE 15

MAY 1

GROUND LEVEL

5"

MAY 15

JUNE 1

NOVEMBER TO MAY

Like Galtonia, Hymenocallis bulbs are planted in the open garden only after warm weather is really established. It is amazing how fast the plants grow and bloom after setting, however. We have had buds shoot up on long scapes a mere week after planting. Set the bulbs in rich, well-drained soil, in sun, planting about 3 to 4 inches deep. The extremely handsome, glossy green strap-like foliage will be decorative in the bed and useful in arrangements long after bloom is over and probably until the bulbs are lifted. This should be done before frost. Dry off in an inverted position (foliage down), not cutting off the fleshy roots. Then store at 60 degrees. Many new offsets develop each season, so you will soon have enough bulbs to give away or swap for other plant material.

Polianthes tuberosa

This is the old-fashioned Tuberose of Grandmother's garden. After many years of semi-oblivion, it has again come into favor. The spikes of waxy white flowers, which reach a height of 3 to almost 4 feet, are overpoweringly fragrant, and the plant undoubtedly came into disfavor in the days when unwise home gardeners brought it indoors. If placed at the back of a white border or in a landscape group at some distance from the house or outdoor living room, the scent is really delightful, especially at night. The double form, Double Pearl, is the one usually grown, though the single Mexican Everblooming is preferred by many. Though Tuberoses are seldom planted out until early June, if you can find time to set them 3 inches deep in a well-worked sunny bed as soon as you feel sure all danger of severe frost is over, you will have earlier bloom. Or start them indoors in pots and set out in the open garden June first. Tuberoses require plenty of moisture during their growing season. Dig in autumn before the first frost. Bulbs should be stored at 65 to 70 degrees, but even when correctly carried over, they do not always bloom well the second season.

Tigridia

The Mexican Tiger-flower or Mexican Shell-flower is a charming Irid, easy to grow and most rewarding. The straight, Gladiolus-like stems, bearing but few leaves, produce in midsummer extremely showy fleeting flowers with three wide-spreading, flared perianth segments set off by six smaller ones forming a great spotted central cup. The colors range from flame red through orange and yellow to buff, with spotted centers. Though there are now many fine hybrids offering more refined color combinations, the bulbs are generally available in mixtures rather than in separate colors.

Tigridia Pavonia *or Shell Flower, flowering from July to frost, is brilliantly colored and dramatic. Likes full sun.*

Placed in groups in a sunny border among plants which, like themselves, prefer sandy, well-drained soil, Tigridias will give brilliant accents to the summer garden. Though the individual flowers last but a day, several appear on successive days from the same blooming stem, making them valuable for cutting as well as for garden display. Try them, too, at the seashore, where they are usually quite happy.

The culture of Tigridias is similar to that of Gladiolus. They are, however, considerably hardier and can, in many locations, be safely carried through outdoors with a mulch. Mr. Allan H. Wood reports them hardy near Boston.

Tritonia

Generally known commercially and by the home gardener as Montbretias, Tritonias are excellent companion plants for Tigridias and their near relatives, Gladiolus. More graceful than either of the above-named groups, Montbretias produce a few narrow sword-shaped leaves, deeply grooved, and 1- to 3-foot flower scapes bearing long, simple, or panicled spikes of red, orange, yellow, or copper tubular flowers, or combinations of these colors. The corms may be purchased in mixture, or you may order named varieties in separate colors. Among these are: Aurora, pure orange; Lady Oxford, pale yellow shading to peach; Prometheus, bronze gold with dark red center; Vesuvius, vermilion—to name but a few of the many available.

The culture of Montbretias, as with Tigridias, is similar to that of Gladiolus, except that they better endure light shade though they grow well in full sun. They also profit by a good feeding of well-rotted manure or bone meal worked into the soil before planting. See that they have good drainage, but be sure they get water in dry weather. South of Philadelphia they are hardy without protection and farther North can sometimes be carried over in a garden by mulching with strawy manure before hard freeze. It is safer, however, in the North to lift and store the corms as with Gladiolus. Or they may be over-wintered, heeled in in a deep frame.

Tritonia crocata is a small yellow or orange-red species which can be used in the front of the border; it also makes a satisfactory greenhouse or window-garden corm for winter flowering. Culture as for Freesias.

AUTUMN-FLOWERING

In the autumn-flowering group we have several distinct types, running from the hardy little Colchicums to the Hardy Amaryllis and its half-hardy sisters, *Lycoris aurea, incarnata,* and *radiata.* Once a gardener has come to depend on bulbs for a good part of his bloom through the spring and summer, he will want to carry on through the fall with these later-flowering species.

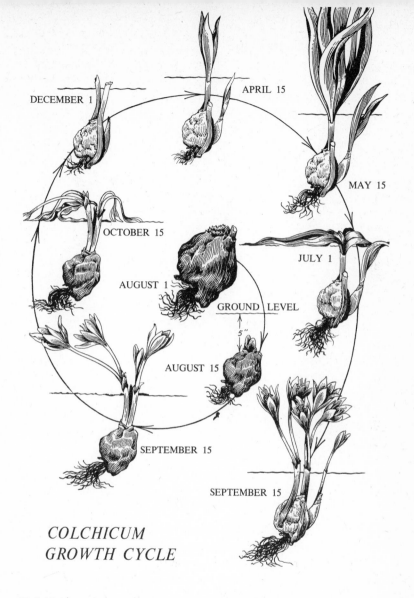

DECEMBER 1

APRIL 15

MAY 15

OCTOBER 15

JULY 1

AUGUST 1

GROUND LEVEL

5"

AUGUST 15

SEPTEMBER 15

SEPTEMBER 15

COLCHICUM
GROWTH CYCLE

Colchicums

Colchicums (Meadow Saffrons) are among the most charming of
the little bulbs. Though they look rather like autumn-blooming Crocuses, they belong to the Lily family and bloom on bare stems, un-
accompanied by foliage, which does not appear until the following

spring and which must be left uncut to mature if there are to be flowers in the fall. They are excellent material for the rock garden, for positions of light shade in front of shrubbery or under a specimen tree which is not too greedy for moisture, or in the front of a partly shaded border.

The color range of Colchicums is rather limited, running from white through the most delicate tints of lavender and orchid to deep purple-rose. It is the lighter tints, however, which show up to the best advantage in the autumn garden, where they blossom brightly in September and October. *C. autumnale* is an orchid-rose, and there is a white form, *album*. *Giganteum* is violet with a light center, very late to flower, while *speciosum* Autumn Queen and *speciosum* The Giant are rose-purple and lilac, respectively. Waterlily, also lilac, is double.

Colchicum corms should be planted as soon as delivered in August, as they are so anxious to come into bloom at that time of year that if they lie about for a few days the flowers begin to appear. Prepare the soil well and then plant the quite large corms only 3 or 4 inches deep. And remember next spring to keep the foliage growing until it has matured, even if it is so prolific as to be a nuisance.

Crocuses

At the head of the list of late-flowering bulbs come the autumn-flowering Crocuses. These have been discussed in Chapter 13.

Lycoris

The old garden favorite, *Lycoris squamigera* (*Amaryllis Halli*), the Magic-lily-of-Japan, is a fascinating garden subject. The bulbs are delivered from August on and should be planted at once, 5 inches deep, in rich, humusy soil, in part shade. The flower stems will be 3 feet tall, so select an appropriate spot in the shady border or in front of some evergreen shrub. Nothing more will be heard from your Lycoris until early spring, when strong, handsome strap-like leaves of gray-green will suddenly shoot out of the ground, rapidly reach a height of 2½ feet, quickly mature, and dry off and disappear completely. By late June you will be able to find the location of the Magic-lilies only by their labels.

When August arrives, keep your eye on the spot, especially after a

Lycoris squamigera, *sometimes called the Hardy Amaryllis or Magic-lily, appears suddenly in late July or August. Extremely hardy and long-lived.*

good soaking rain. One by one the flower spikes appear, striking up through the soil like strong green spearheads. In a remarkably short space of time, often only about a week, the solid scapes have shot up to their appointed 3 feet and are ready to open their clusters of pale orchid-pink, Lily-like flowers, six to nine to a scape. Handsome for garden display or for cutting, they are enhanced by a delicate fragrance. Plant them among Ferns in open woodland or, through the years, develop a long shady border of them which will be a real feature when they are in bloom. One old estate not far from our home boasts a 150-foot bed of Lycoris, 6 feet wide. What a sight it is at blossomtime!

Once planted, your Magic-lilies must not be disturbed. They will probably still be blooming in the same spot when you are no longer there to enjoy them. Though often called the Autumn-amaryllis, *Lycoris squamigera* blooms in August in many localities.

Lycoris radiata is a half-hardy relative of the Magic-lily, a species usually pot-grown for autumn bloom. The narrow leaves appear in spring and have the characteristic pale stripes down their centers. In September round heads of bloom appear on a solid scape. The many florets are starry red, orange, or white, with very long stamens, extremely showy. They are often used in flower arrangements as well as for decoration on the patio or porch. For many years *Lycoris radiata* was sold in the trade as *Nerine sarniensis,* the Guernsey-lily.

Pot the bulbs on delivery in Soil Mixture No. 4, leaving the top third of each exposed. When leaves appear, give more water, sun, and liquid fertilizer. After the foliage disappears in May, let them rest until late summer, giving little moisture. Then give more light, liquid fertilizer, and moisture until blooms appear. Repot only when necessary, as, like many other members of the Amaryllis family, *Lycoris radiata* flowers best when pot-bound.

By mulching heavily as for Bulbous Iris, *Lycoris radiata* can be grown out of doors in a sheltered location in the North. It is hardy to Washington, D.C.

Lycoris aurea, the Golden Spider-lily, with individual flowers larger than those of *radiata;* and *Lycoris incarnata,* with pink or rose Lily-like blooms similar to those of *L. squamigera* but on shorter stems (to 1½ feet); are two other half-hardy sorts well worth growing. Both can be treated like *L. radiata.*

Sternbergia lutea

This is far too pretty and dainty a little flower to go by such a long name, but it seems to have no common one. Mrs. Louise B. Wilder speaks of it as the Winter-daffodil, but we have never heard it so called. Certainly it is as brightly yellow as any Daffodil, but in appearance looks very much like a butter-yellow Crocus surrounded by plenty of handsome, glossy foliage. Long-lasting and weather-resistant, the blooms are bright for days on end, set off by the red October leaves which drift down off the trees to lodge in their rich foliage. (See illustration facing page 305.)

Plant the bulbs 4 inches deep, as soon as they are received, in well-drained soil in sun or very light shade. We have had a slowly increasing group growing for years under a clump of Gray Birches. They never seem to need dividing and replanting, but fend for themselves most successfully.

Zephyranthes

Last but not least of the less well-known fall-flowering bulbs are the airy Zephyranthes, Zephyr-, Fairy-, or Rain-lilies. Strictly speaking, some members of this group bloom in spring and summer also, but they are usually thought of as fall-blooming flowers. Natives of the Western Hemisphere, they come to us from South America, Cuba, Santo Domingo, Haiti, Mexico, and the Southeastern United States. The dainty, funnel-form, solitary flowers are white, yellow, red, pink, or bronze; the basal foliage is grass-like.

Z. *atamasco,* native to southern Virginia, is most often grown. Flowers, white or pale pink, appear first in early spring.

Z. *candida,* hardier than the above. White flowers in August and September.

Z. *citrina* is a South American species with bright yellow blossoms.

Z. *grandiflora* blooms after rains in summer and autumn. The Lily-like flowers are 4 inches across.

Z. *longifolia,* but 6 inches tall, has 1-inch yellow and copper blooms.

North of Washington, D.C., the Zephyranthes, with the possible exception of Z. *candida,* must be treated as tender bulbs. Plant in spring in a sandy soil mixture with good humus content, 2 inches apart, with the tips of the bulbs just below the surface of the soil. Lift before frost and store like Gladiolus.

They may also be forced for indoor bloom by potting six to a 5-inch bulb pan in autumn, using Potting Mixture No. 4. Keep moist until blooms fade. Then dry off for at least 8 weeks. With this interval of rest, a second and even a third flowering may be enjoyed within the year.

CHAPTER *20. Bulbs for Winter Bloom*

One of the easiest and most rewarding ways of providing the home with fresh flowers during the winter months is to grow bulbs indoors for winter bloom. Bulbous plants in living rooms or sun porch provide welcome color and fragrance. A sunny bay window and a glassed-in porch make the ideal combination for this sort of indoor gardening; the heat-loving plants in the former, those which insist on a cool temperature in the latter.

A greenhouse or conservatory is, of course, even better for the purpose, for here the temperature can be controlled to suit the preferences of the plants grown; but even without a greenhouse one may enjoy an almost continuous succession of flowers from Christmas to Easter. We use our greenhouse to grow bulbs (as well as other flowering plants) until the buds are ready to open, and then bring them into the house where we can enjoy the blossoms at close range.

A deep window sill or bay window edged with miniature Ivies or Oxalis, and with a few taller colorful foliage plants for a permanent display, can frequently be rearranged to provide a setting for bulbous plants which flower at the same time. These may include forced hardy bulbs, the "borderline" cases which must be grown very cool but which do not stand freezing, and the very tender tropical or semitropical subjects which like real warmth such as they would experience in a warm greenhouse.

Few gardening activities give greater satisfaction than bringing bulbs to bloom indoors. Of course it is easy to flower them the first year, for the embryo blossoms are already there inside the bulbs, ready to spring into growth as soon as they are planted and watered. To keep bulbous plants such as Amaryllis and Veltheimia blooming year after year in the window garden requires a certain groundwork of knowledge, though it is not a really difficult task.

CLASSES OF BULBS FOR WINTER BLOOM

The bulbs which may be brought to bloom indoors during cold weather can be considered in three groups, each of which must be treated differently.

1. *Hardy* spring-flowering bulbs which are forced or grown on in such a way as to produce flowers well in advance, of their normal season of bloom. Examples are Hyacinths and early Daffodils, which are often forced for Christmas; Tulips, Crocuses, Grape-hyacinths, and others, which can be brought to flower a little later.

2. *Half-hardy* types which cannot stand freezing but which must be grown in a very cool temperature. These are not forced but are grown indoors instead of in the open garden. Examples are Freesias, Ixias, and Ornithogalums.

3. *Tender* tropical or sub-tropical bulbs, corms, or tubers which either naturally bloom in winter or can be made to do so. As these are very tender, they must be grown as house plants the year round. Examples are members of the Amaryllis family, Fancy-leaved Caladiums, and Veltheimias.

A few species from the above groups can be forced into early bloom indoors by planting them in bowls or dishes with fiber, pebbles or one of the granular snow-like materials such as Flower Set, and water. Examples are Hyacinths and Paperwhite Narcissus, both of which can also be brought to early bloom in pots of soil, the former being hardy and the latter half-hardy or tender.

GENERAL CULTURE

Though each of the three groups mentioned above requires different treatment, and in some cases individual species have their peculiar likes and dislikes, there are general directions which apply to all.

Containers

For hardy bulbs and most of the half-hardies, bulb pans are the preferred containers. These are clay pots which are wide at the top and somewhat shallower (in proportion to the diameter) than ordinary standard pots. For some types, Azalea pots—deeper than bulb pans but not so deep as standard pots—are preferable. Rose pots, extra deep, can be used for Lilies.

When grown in quantity in a greenhouse or sun porch, the small half-hardy corms, such as Freesias and Ixias, may be planted in small flats instead of pots. Many of the large tender bulbs are set with the top third of the bulb exposed, and for these, 6- to 10-inch Azalea pots are the most satisfactory containers. For water culture, wide shallow ceramic bowls or dishes, with a depth of at least 2 inches, may be used.

Soil mixtures

For indoor bulb growing, the mechanical condition of the soil is even more important than its fertility, because the bulb itself contains sufficient stored-up food to produce good flower.

You will want, however, to get the best growth possible, and for that reason it is advisable to add some plant food or manure to the soil. After the various ingredients have been combined in a bushel basket or other large container, it should be *very thoroughly* mixed and pulverized.

NOTE: Measurements are by *bulk,* not by weight.

POTTING MIXTURE NO. 1

For hardy spring-flowering bulbs: Daffodils, Tulips, Hyacinths, etc.

⅓ sifted garden loam
If your garden loam is heavy clay, add to it ⅕ sharp sand.
⅓ pulverized peatmoss
⅓ sifted compost or well-rotted manure

Add to each bushel:
2 quarts mixed: ⅓ fine bone meal and ⅔ dried manure

POTTING MIXTURE NO. 2

For Liliaceae and others: Lilies, Gloriosa, etc.

½ rich sifted soil
¼ sharp sand
¼ sifted peatmoss (or leafmold)

Add to each bushel:
2 quarts mixed: ⅓ fine bone meal
and ⅔ dried manure

OR USE   ¼ sifted loam
½ sifted, well-rotted compost
¼ sharp sand

Add to each bushel:
1 quart mixed: 1 pint raw ground
bone meal and 1 pint dried manure

POTTING MIXTURE NO. 3

For Irids: Bulbous Irises, Moraea,
etc.

⅔ rich sifted loam
⅓ sharp sand

Add to each bushel:
1 quart bone meal

POTTING MIXTURE NO. 4

For tender bulbs indoors: Hippeastrum, Veltheimia, etc.

⅓ rich sifted loam
⅓ sharp sand
⅓ peatmoss

Add to each bushel:
2 quarts mixed: ⅓ fine bone meal
and ⅔ dried manure

POTTING MIXTURE NO. 5

For tender bulbs which require
rich, humusy soil: Tuberous Begonias, Achimenes, etc.

⅓ rich sifted loam
⅙ sharp sand
⅙ peatmoss or leafmold
⅓ old rotted cow manure

Add to each bushel:
1 pint bone meal

OR USE   ⅓ rich sifted loam
⅓ screened, well-rotted compost
⅙ sharp sand
⅙ peatmoss or leafmold

Add to each bushel:
2 quarts mixed: ⅔ dried manure
and ⅓ bonemeal

CULTURE STEP BY STEP

The bulbs

It pays to get good bulbs for any sort of planting. For bulbs to be grown indoors, care in this particular is even more important. This does not imply that you should obtain the most expensive ones you can find listed. In Hyacinths, for instance, we would much rather have first-quality medium-sized bulbs that produce graceful, somewhat informal spikes than the much more costly giant exhibition grade with their closely set, ramrod-like heads. Every bulb, of any sort, should be plump, sound, and heavy.

Care must be exercised also in the matter of varieties. Many Tulips and Daffodils that are beautiful in the garden do not force well. It is advisable to follow catalogue recommendations in this respect; most dealers indicate plainly which sorts are most suitable for forcing.

If you plan to grow more than a few pots for winter bloom, secure as much variety as you can. It is true that the flowering period of forced bulbs can be controlled by starting the top growth of different pots, of even the same variety, at different dates. A range of flower forms and colors, however, is much more interesting than having a succession of blooms of the same variety.

Planting

When you are ready to plant you will need to have at hand your bulbs, pots, flats, prepared soil mixtures, some broken pot shards, and some coarse screenings from the compost heap.

Place several pieces of broken pot shards over the drainage hole of each pot and cover with ½ to 1 inch of coarse compost screenings. Then place enough prepared soil in the pot so that when the bulbs are set on it their tips will come to about one inch below the top. (In planting an Amaryllid or some other bulb the top third of which is to be left exposed, more soil should be placed in the pot before setting the bulb.) The bulbs are then set. If several bulbs are to go in one pot, they can be placed shoulder to shoulder, but not touching. An inch to 1½ inches between bulbs is the usual distance. Pack the

Here's what you need for winter bulb gardening: compost, pots or bulb pans, drainage material (broken pots), labels, and first-quality bulbs. Then you are all set for exciting adventure!

soil in very firmly, first jarring the pot gently against a wooden surface to settle the soil, and then pressing it in around the bulbs so that there are no air spaces.

After planting, place the pots in a tray of water and let them remain there until the surface soil becomes moist. This is good practice even with bulbs which are kept on the dry side—after this initial watering —until growth starts.

Cross section of bulb pan, with bulbs (Hyacinths) in place.

When thoroughly watered, the potted bulbs are ready for their initial treatment, whatever that is to be. Hardy and half-hardy sorts requiring a period of preliminary root growth go outdoors in a trench or cold frame, or in a cold cellar. Tender species are placed under a greenhouse bench, under a table in a workroom indoors, or in a dark cool closet, until growth starts and good root development has occurred.

Flowering

When the time comes to start the potted bulbs into growth, they are brought gradually to more light and warmth. As growth develops, the amount of water is increased until the foliage is strong and of good color. At this time they can be placed in whatever light and temperature are ideal for the particular species. At this period most of them will require frequent watering.

When buds appear, the half-hardy and tender bulbs profit by a weekly feeding of liquid fertilizer. Forced hardy bulbs will not need this booster treatment. When in flower, the blooms will last longer if the plants are kept at a reasonably cool temperature and out of direct sunshine. Water as needed when the surface soil feels dry to the touch.

And after bloom is over, remove the faded flowers but do not reduce water until the foliage shows signs of maturing. As soon as the ground can be dug, hardy sorts can be set out in a garden row to grow on for a year, when they will have recovered their vigor. Half-hardy and tender species are coaxed to keep their green foliage as long as possible, but when it matures and dries off, the bulbs or corms are rested completely, either in their pots or removed from them and dried completely, as the case may require. Species with evergreen foliage, such as some of the Hippeastrums, are given just enough water to keep the foliage green until they start new growth the following fall. Types rested in their pots should have some slight moisture—just what they will get with the pots turned on their sides on the damp floor of a greenhouse or frostproof cellar.

There are a few bulbs—notably Paperwhite Narcissus, Narcissus Soleil d'Or, and Sprekelias—which cannot be made to bloom satisfactorily in our Northern climate a second year after being forced. These should be discarded after bloom.

FORCING HARDY BULBS

The word "forcing" used in this connection means growing to produce bloom well out of the plant's normal season for flowering. This does not imply, as many beginners are apt to assume, that the plants must be grown at a very high temperature. The more moderate the temperature, as a rule, the better the results. At no time during their growth are really high temperatures good for hardy bulbs. Keep in mind that these hardy species bloom naturally out of doors during the cool or even frosty days and nights of early spring.

In selecting varieties of hardy bulbs for forcing, use only varieties recommended for the purpose in the catalogues. Some fine garden varieties do not force well. Short lists of varieties are given below, but there are many others equally good.

Varieties marked with an * are fragrant.

Daffodils

YELLOW TRUMPETS:
Alaska
King Alfred
LARGE CUPS:
Deanna Durbin—white and orange
John Evelyn—white and yellow
SHORT CUPS:
Mrs. Barclay—primrose
Snow Princess—white, red cup

BUNCH-FLOWERED:
Geranium*—white, orange-red
Scarlet Gem*—yellow, red cup
CYCLAMINEUS HYBRID:
February Gold—yellow
TRIANDRUS HYBRIDS:
Silver Chimes—white
Thalia—white
DOUBLES:
Twink—primrose and orange
Cheerfulness*—white

Tulips

SINGLE EARLIES:
De Wet*—orange
Fred Moore*—orange-buff
Glory of Lisse*—orange
Prince of Austria*—orange-red
Princess Juliana—white and rose
Proserpine—carmine

White Hawk
DARWINS:
Demeter—violet-blue
Le Notre—rose-pink
Mrs. Grullemans—cream
Red Pitt—red
William Copeland—Lavender

COTTAGE:

Carrara—white
Ellen Wilmott*—yellow
Rosy Wings—salmon-pink

EARLY DOUBLES:

El Toreador—salmon and orange

Mme. Testout—rose-pink
Maréchal Niel—amber and orange
Tearose*—primrose

LATE DOUBLES:

Livingstone—cherry-pink
Snow Prince—white

Hyacinths (All are fragrant)

Bismarck—light blue
City of Haarlem—yellow
Edelweiss—white

Pink Pearl—pink
La Victoire—rose-red
French Roman Hyacinths (for pot
    or water culture)

Minor Bulbs

Calochortus, in variety
Chionodoxa
Colchicum
Crocus

Muscari armeniacum
Muscari Tubergenianum
Scilla sibirica Spring Beauty
Ranunculus, Florists'
Anemone, Florists'

Lilies

L. amabile
L. auratum
L. candidum
L. concolor
L. formosanum
L. Hansoni

L. Henryi
L. Martagon and hybrids
L. Maxwilli
L. pumilum
L. regale
L. speciosum and varieties
T. A. Havemeyer

Potting

For large Daffodil bulbs, select 6- or 7-inch bulb pans, placing three to five bulbs in each pot. Six or more Tulips can be fitted neatly into a 6-inch pan. For minor bulbs, species Tulips and Daffodils, a 6-inch bulb pan will hold six to twelve bulbs, depending on size. Lilies are potted as soon as delivered, one bulb to a deep 6- or 8-inch pot, or several may be planted in a tub.

If old pots are used, they should be first scrubbed vigorously with a stiff brush and clear water. Pot up in Mixture No. 1, following the

Method of watering after planting. Pots are placed in an inch or so of water until moisture shows on surface.

detailed instruction on planting given on page 264. Potting may be done any time between September and December; but with Daffodils especially, the earlier the better, as they begin to develop roots early in the autumn. Place one variety only in each pot, since different varieties may mature at different dates. Use narrow, 12-inch labels to mark each pot with its species and variety name or, attach wired labels to short bamboo stakes. These long labels will greatly simplify locating the varieties you may wish to bring in when the pots are covered with mulch.

After the bulbs are potted and marked, water them thoroughly by standing the pots in pans of water until the surface soil is uniformly moist.

Pre-rooting period

Since hardy bulbs must undergo a period of cold in order that they may develop a strong root system before top growth is started, the potted bulbs must be subjected to one of the following treatments:

1. Dig a trench 12 to 15 inches deep, 18 inches wide, and long enough to hold the pots. The trench should be dug in a well-drained part of the garden where there is no danger of water collecting in the

bottom. In heavy clay soil, place a 4-inch layer of cinders or coarse gravel in the bottom.

Set pans and pots in the trench, shoulder to shoulder, and pack damp peatmoss around and 2 or 3 inches deep over them. Just before hard freezing, place a heavy layer of straw or dead leaves over the

LEFT: *Pots are placed in trench, dug in shaded spot, to make root growth.* BELOW: *Pots in a cold frame. Long labels make it easy to find varieties wanted. Excelsior helps to keep soil cool. Pots showing top growth are ready to be brought in. Pot in background, having flowered indoors, has been returned to frame for foliage to mature normally.*

peatmoss, held down with evergreen boughs or burlap bags. This will prevent the pans from freezing hard in the peatmoss so that you cannot get them out. *Leave for at least six weeks,* or until roots begin to grow through the drainage holes of the pots.

2. Instead of a trench, use a well-drained cold frame, with the same packing and covering as that mentioned above. The mulching, however, will not be needed, as sash can be put on after the surface freezes.

3. Pack bulbs as above, in a *cold* cellar, omitting the covering of leaves or straw and boughs.

Wherever the bulbs are placed for this period of root development, all sorts (except Daffodils) *must be protected from mice.* The simplest method is to place wire screening over the tops of the pots.

As long as the potted bulbs stay outdoors, they will be developing strong roots without making much top growth. They can therefore be brought in any time after new roots begin to grow out of the drainage holes and form a mass around the insides of the pots. This will take from six to ten weeks, according to variety and conditions. Most people bring in a few pots at a time in order to have a succession of bloom. They can stay outdoors as long as you wish to leave them there and will be ready to start vigorous top growth whenever you bring them in.

Soil ball removed from pot ready to be brought in to heat: good mat of roots formed and tops started into growth.

A well-grown pot of Single Early Tulip Pink Beauty.

Bringing indoors

When first brought indoors, start them slowly in a cool atmosphere (40 to 50 degrees if possible) and in half light. They are being shifted from darkness and a freezing temperature and must not be shocked by too much light and heat all at once. First of all, water them by setting in pans of water as before. For a week or ten days, keep them under a bench in a cool greenhouse, partly covered on a cool sun porch, or under a table in a cool workroom, in half light.

At the end of this time, bring the bulbs into full sunshine, but if possible find a place for them where the night temperature never rises above 60 degrees (50 degrees is better). You will have stronger, healthier blooms if the bulbs are grown on at a cool temperature. Water them freely and give them just as much sunshine as you can until the flowers open. Then keep them out of direct sun for longer-lasting blooms. If they can be placed in a very cool room at night— even down to 40 degrees—the flowers will last longer.

Plant pests are not likely to appear except perhaps on Tulips, where aphids (page 113) may develop on foliage or buds.

After care

When bloom is over, *gradually* reduce water, but give enough to keep the foliage green. Pots may then be placed in a very cool room if above freezing. As soon as the ground can be worked in spring, set the bulbs out in flower borders or in garden rows to grow on for a year, when they will be ready to replant.

HALF-HARDY BULBS

The half-hardy bulbs are just as popular as the hardies for bringing to bloom indoors. This group cannot withstand hard freezing or is at least in danger of being injured if subjected to very low temperatures, but many of its members profit by a cooling period outdoors after potting and before hard freezing. As a rule, half-hardy bulbs bear smaller but more appealing flowers than the large Daffodils and Tulips, which are leaders among the hardies. For more detailed information on any bulb mentioned, consult the Catalogue of Bulbs, page 281.

The Irids

Many of the half-hardy bulbs which prefer an outdoor rooting period are members of the Iris family. The following species, which give attractive flowers when grown indoors, all require practically the same culture and can be potted in Soil Mixture No. 3.

Babiana	*Gladiolus tristis*	Moraea
Freesia	Iris, Bulbous	Sparaxis
Gladiolus, Herald	Ixia	*Tritonia crocata*
Gladiolus, Comet—red	Lapeirousia	Watsonia
Gladiolus, Rembrandt—red		

The Liliaceae

Half-hardy members of the Lily family which can be brought to winter bloom, using Soil Mixture No. 2, and which also require an outdoor rooting period are:

Albuca		*Leucocoryne ixioides*
Brodiaea	Lachenalia	Ornithogalum

The Amaryllids

Lycoris aurea	*Lycoris radiata*	Sprekelia
Lycoris incarnata		Zephyranthes

The above members of the Amaryllis family are also half hardy rather than tender. Nerines, Sprekelias, and Zephyranthes can be chilled outdoors before being brought to winter bloom. *Lycoris radiata,* as a fall bloomer, should not be exposed to freezing or very cold temperatures after bloom, but brought into a cool indoor temperature to dry off after flowering. Use Soil Mixture No. 4.

Others

Narcissus Paperwhite	French Roman	Anemone, Florists'
Narcissus Soleil d'Or	Hyacinths	Ranunculus, Florists'

The above two tender Narcissi and the dainty French Roman Hyacinths, long stand-bys for winter bloom, are treated just as the other half-hardies, potted in Soil Mixture No. 1, and placed in a frame outdoors until just before hard frost. They also lend themselves to water culture, with pebbles or plant fiber to hold the bulbs erect in the container. Hyacinths may be grown in special Hyacinth glasses which can be purchased for the purpose.

Bowl of Paper-whites grown in "florists' snow," without pre-rooting, but kept in moderate temperature—50° to 60°.

Anemones and Ranunculus may be forced as half-hardy or as hardy bulbs.

TENDER BULBS FOR WINTER BLOOM

The very tender bulbs, corms, and tubers which must be treated as house plants the year round are among the most showy and colorful flowers available in any class. Those discussed here either normally bloom in winter or can be coaxed into blossom during the cold months. Once the window gardener develops an interest in these exotic subjects, he will find many unusual and exciting plants to choose from, some of which give a long succession of flowers at a time of year when color is most needed indoors.

The culture of many of these tropical bulbs is quite similar, with but small variations. Since the members of one flower family are apt to require pretty much the same soil and treatment, we have divided them into family groups, as follows:

The Amaryllids*

Alstroemeria	Clivia	Haemanthus
Amarcrinum	Crinum	*Hymenocallis caribaea*
Amaryllis belladonna	Cyrtanthus	Nerine
Amaryllis (Hippeastrum)	Eucharis	

Culture

The members of this group are all planted in Soil Mixture No. 4, with the upper third of the bulb exposed, in pots which tend to encourage crowding of the roots. Bloom is apt to be bigger and better if the bulb is pot-bound. Amaryllids do not like to be disturbed after they are once established and are therefore repotted only when absolutely necessary.

From the time the bulbs are potted until growth starts, little water is given. The pots can be placed in half light, under a greenhouse

*For individual cultural notes, see Catalogue of Bulbs.

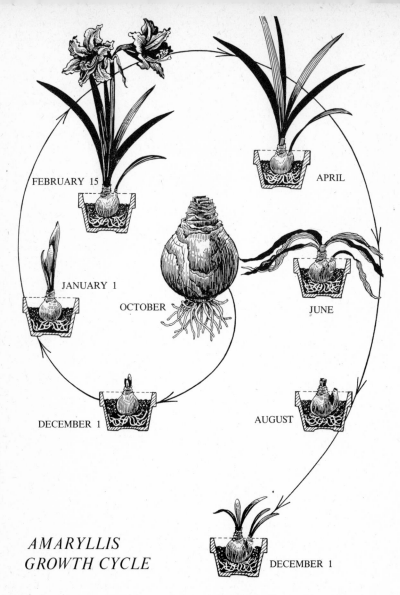

FEBRUARY 15

APRIL

JANUARY 1

OCTOBER

JUNE

DECEMBER 1

AUGUST

AMARYLLIS
GROWTH CYCLE

DECEMBER 1

bench or under a table in a workroom where they will be out of the way.

As soon as new growth appears, moisture is increased and the pots are brought to full light. When the flower scape appears, give weekly feedings of manure water or liquid fertilizer until the buds begin to show color.

After bloom, the flower scapes are cut off and water is gradually reduced until the foliage dries off (unless it is an evergreen species, in which case water sparingly during the resting period). When the foliage has withered, the bulbs are rested in their pots, which are turned on their sides under a greenhouse bench or in a damp, frost-proof cellar, until new growth begins late the following summer or early in the fall. During the summer months such pots can be stored outdoors with the bulbs in them, turned on their sides in the shade against a sheltering wall.

When repotting becomes necessary, knock the bulb out carefully without injuring or disturbing the roots. Remove what soil you can by gently dunking in a pail of water, and repot in a larger pot in Soil Mixture No. 4. Repotting is best done in late summer or early fall, before new growth begins.

Eucharis, the beautiful white florists' flower which rather resembles in form some of the white Triandrus hybrid Daffodils growing in a spray, is also an Amaryllid but requires somewhat different care. See under Catalogue of Bulbs.

Araceae

Members of the Arum family come from a more lush and humid habitat than the Amaryllids. They include:

Arum palaestinum	Hydrosme
Caladium, Fancy-leaved	Zantedeschia (Calla-lily)

These prefer a very rich yet well-drained humusy soil (Mixture No. 5) and insist on high humidity and sheltering shade. Most members of this family will not do well in a centrally heated living room, though they are ideal greenhouse subjects. If there are facilities for syringing the leaves in order to maintain humidity, some of the smaller Callas, however, can be successfully grown in the window garden.

Since individual requirements of the members of this group are quite different from one another, we refer you to their cultural notes under the Catalogue of Bulbs.

Liliaceae

Members of the Lily family for indoor bloom include:

Eucomis	Ornithogalum	Tulbaghia
Gloriosa		Veltheimia

All may be potted in Mixture No. 2, but as they require varying treatments to bring them into bloom, refer for details of indoor culture to the individual plants in the Catalogue of Bulbs.

Others

Other bulbs, corms, and tubers which give satisfactory winter bloom indoors are:

Cyclamen	Oxalis	Schizostylis (Kafir-lily)

For culture indoors, consult the individual plants in the Catalogue of Bulbs.

Begoniaceae and Gesneriaceae

A group of tender plants, all handled in the same way as exotic pot plants, and all very showy but unfortunately summer bloomers, includes the Tuberous Begonias, which belong to the Begonia family; and Achimenes and Gloxinia, both of which are Gesneriads.

By growing from seed or starting corms or tubers out of their regular season, it is possible to bring these three fine pot plants to winter flower, but they make the finest show if started in February to April for summer bloom. For details of culture, see Chapter 18, and the individual plants in the Catalogue of Bulbs.

PART THREE
—THE CATALOGUE OF BULBS

CHAPTER *21. Descriptions and Directions for Culture*

ACHIMENES [*Gesneriaceae*]

The tender tuber-like rhizomes of Achimenes rather resemble tiny pine cones which produce velvety Gloxinia-like flowers. They are grown under glass or as house plants. The showy red, violet, or white flowers in spring and summer are borne in the leaf axils on 1- to 2-foot stems. More striking than the African-violet and smaller and more appealing than the Gloxinia, Achimenes have many of the virtues of both these popular indoor subjects.

Of the many species, only three are in general cultivation: *A. grandiflora* with red-purple blooms and leaves reddish beneath; *A. longiflora,* flowers blue-violet with long tubes; and *A. patens,* with short-tubed, violet-blue flowers. There are many fine hybrids, among them:

Camille Brozzoni—violet and white
Gloria—violet-blue
Millon—red
Orchidee—orchid
Purity—white
Purple King—purple

For hanging baskets, choose Lavender Beauty and Edmund Vossier, white with purple.

CULTURE INDOORS: Start the rhizomes, as soon as received, at 60 degrees minimum. Plant ½ inch deep in a mixture of peatmoss and sand. Keep in subdued light until growth starts. Then transplant

(Mixture No. 5), crocking the bottom of the pot 1 inch deep. Place in north or west window or on shaded greenhouse bench. Water freely from below with tepid water and feed with liquid fertilizer once a week. Conditions and care suitable for the African-violet are satisfactory for Achimenes.

When flowering ceases, reduce water gradually until plants are dried off. Then remove the top of the plant and store the rhizomes in their pots in a damp cellar or under a bench in the greenhouse. When new growth appears, treat as before, bringing to light and giving ample water. Grow on in one pot through the second year, repotting when growth starts for the third time.

PROPAGATION: From seed or division of the roots; also by stem rhizomes formed on some varieties.

ACIDANTHERA [Iridaceae]

Acidanthera bicolor, the species most generally grown, comes to us from tropical Africa. The foliage is reminiscent of that of the Gladiolus but handsomer, and the delicate, fragrant white flowers with blackish centers poise like pale butterflies near the top of the 2-foot blooming stems. We usually plant them just behind the Hymenocallis and in front of the Galtonia in a bed of white summer-flowering bulbs.

CULTURE OUTDOORS: As for Gladiolus.

PROPAGATION: From cormels.

AGAPANTHUS [Liliaceae]

Agapanthus africanus (Blue African-lily; Lily-of-the-Nile) and A. africanus variegatus (which produces striped leaves) are usually grown in tubs or very large pots for bloom on patio or porch. They can be treated as garden subjects in the South, since they are summer bloomers. A. orientalis and its white variety, alba, are much grown outdoors in California. This is a more robust species, reaching 4 feet in height.

Twelve to thirty bright blue flowers, each 2 inches in length, are borne in terminal umbels on 3-foot naked flowering stems. The basal leaves are linear, pointed, dark green in color, to 3 feet in length. There are also several named hybrids, both dwarf and tall-growing.

CULTURE INDOORS: Pot (Mixture No. 5) from February to April, with crowns at soil surface. Feed with manure water while buds are developing, and keep moist until bloom is over. Will flourish in sun or light shade. After blossoming, reduce water gradually. When the tuberous roots are dried off, store in pot or tub, almost dry, in a cool place over the winter.

CULTURE OUTDOORS, SOUTH: Plant outdoors in spring in rich, moist soil, covering 2 inches deep. Keep well watered. Lift the tuberous roots before hard frost. May be left out the year round where temperature does not drop below 25 degrees.

PROPAGATION: By division.

ALBUCA [Liliaceae]

Albuca is a fragrant South African bulb which has become quite popular as a border plant in California A. *major* grows to 3 feet in height; A. *Nelsoni* to 6 feet; and A. *minor* to but 1½ feet. The racemes of white or yellow flowers are large and showy, borne in late spring or early summer.

CULTURE OUTDOORS, SOUTH: As for tender Ornithogalum, to which they are allied.

PROPAGATION: By offsets.

ALLIUM [Liliaceae]

This genus is a huge one which includes hundreds of species from many parts of the world, chiefly in the Northern Hemisphere. They vary in height from a few inches to several feet. The color range runs from white through pink to rose-red, lavender, and blue, and the flowering season from spring to fall.

Garden Alliums are usually hardy, and though most of them give forth an onion or garlic odor when the leaves or stems are crushed, few are objectionable in this respect if left uncut. Some of the blossoms, indeed, are pleasantly fragrant, with Heliotrope or Violet scent.

The flower heads are produced in globular or flattened umbels made up of many bell-like or star-shaped flowers, each borne on its own slender stem. The umbels vary in size from 1 or 2 inches in rock-garden species to great heads 8 to 12 inches across, as in A. *albopilosum,* the Giant Allium. Leaves are sometimes tubular, sometimes strap-like, broad or narrow. Roots may be strictly bulbous or rhizomatous. *A. caeruleum* is a tall-growing species with deep blue flowers in umbels 2 inches in diameter; *A. cyaneum,* a rock-garden subject, bears nodding blue flowers on short stems, while *A. moly* and *A. flavum* are yellow. *A. Douglasi* bears deep pink blossoms while *A. neapolitanum* is white. All four of the last-named species grow to about a foot in height. *A. stellatum,* 1½ feet, orchid, is an autumn bloomer. There are many varieties to choose from.

All authorities agree that nomenclature is still much confused among the Alliums, so that the collector may encounter difficulties in obtaining species in which he is interested. This, of course, only adds to the zest of the search, especially as so many of the genus are worth while in the garden picture.

So keen does the competition often become to secure rare varieties and species that even the most dignified herbist cannot always be trusted in a strange garden. An actor friend of ours who collected Alliums through the simple process of sending to Rex Pearce for seed and growing on whatever he received had a very unusual group of plants one summer. One early afternoon he was alone in the house, taking a shower, when he thought he heard the clinking of a spade outside. He threw his bath towel around him and ran to the door, to discover a former officer of the American Herb Society in the act of digging up his most precious species. "Why, Mrs. X," he called, "I'm surprised at you." The old lady was quite unabashed. "Well, I thought you weren't at home," she excused herself.

CULTURE OUTDOORS: Plant in spring in sun in well-drained, gravelly loam, with top of bulb near surface.

PROPAGATION: By seeds (many species self-seed freely) sown in spring and by offsets and bulbils taken in fall or spring.

ALSTROEMERIA [*Amaryllidaceae*]

South American members of the Amaryllis family, Alstroemerias are not generally hardy north of Washington, D.C., though the species *A. aurantiaca* (Peruvian-lily; Chilean-lily) can sometimes be brought through the winter outdoors as far north as Geneva, N.Y.

The showy red, purple, or yellow flaring, tubular flowers are borne in terminal umbels on leafy stems and bloom in spring in the South where they remain in the garden the year round. Half a dozen species are generally available.

A. *aurantiaca*—yellow, spotted brown, tipped green
A. *aurantiaca major*—larger than above, orange
A. *chilensis*—mixed pastel colors
A. *pulchella*—dark red, tipped green

CULTURE INDOORS: Pot in fall (Mixture No. 4). Water sparingly until growth starts, then give more moisture. After bloom, dry off gradually, and when foliage has matured, remove roots from soil in pots and replant.

CULTURE OUTDOORS, NORTH: Plant outdoors in spring when danger of frost is past, in rich, moist, humusy soil in a shady location. After bloom, when foliage has matured, lift and store in damp sand in a cool, frostproof place.

CULTURE OUTDOORS, SOUTH: Plant in autumn as described above. Mulch for winter in Upper South.

PROPAGATION: By seeds or division of roots.

AMARCRINUM [*Amaryllidaceae*]

The Amarcrinum is an Amaryllis-Crinum hybrid of outstanding beauty. The one usually available in commerce, *A*. *Howardi*, produces large clusters of soft pink Lily-like flowers on a thick, fleshy 2- to 4-foot stem in early autumn. At least two flower scapes are usually thrown up from a single bulb, the second appearing after the first is well along toward bloom. The trumpet-shaped blooms are long-lasting and deliciously fragrant. Because of its delicate pink color, fine form, and good lasting qualities, we consider it the most beautiful of our tender flowering bulbs. Visitors are always drawn to it.

CULTURE INDOORS, NORTH: Pot the bulb in fall with the upper third above the soil level (Mixture No. 4). Grow on indoors through winter. Pots can be sunk in a shady garden bed when warm weather comes and fed occasionally with manure water. After bloom, but before frost, bring indoors and gradually reduce water. After foliage matures, leave under bench in greenhouse or in cool cellar with pot turned on side until new growth starts. Then give more water and light, and begin feeding.

CULTURE OUTDOORS, SOUTH: Bulbs may be spring-planted in the garden for year-round growth. See Crinum culture.

PROPAGATION: By offsets.

AMARYLLIS—See HIPPEASTRUM

AMARYLLIS BELLADONNA [*Amaryllidaceae*]

The Belladonna-lily (*Brunsvigia rosea; Callicore rosea*) is a tender South African, a greenhouse subject. The strap-like leaves appear before or after the lovely Lily-shaped blooms, which are white and pink or rose-red and fragrant, to 3½ inches long, in umbels at the top of a 2-foot solid scape. There are purple and white forms as well. Bloom occurs in late summer or early autumn.

A. belladonna elata—rose-red

A. belladonna major—pink

A. belladonna speciosa purpurea—purple and white

CULTURE INDOORS: Pot while dormant in spring or early summer (Mixture No. 4). Use a small pot only a little larger than the bulb, the top half of which should remain exposed. When leaves appear, after bloom, give plenty of water and light until matured. Then gradually reduce water. Store bulb in pot laid on its side under greenhouse bench until new growth appears.

CULTURE OUTDOORS: As for Hippeastrum.

PROPAGATION: By offsets.

AMORPHOPHALLUS—See HYDROSME

ANEMONE [*Ranunculaceae*]

The Anemone tribe includes many fine tuberous-rooted garden subjects for various uses and blooming at different seasons. The largest and handsomest of the clan are the large-flowered Florists' Anemones, which can be brought to bloom outdoors or under glass. They come in white, brilliant red, rose, purple, and violet. A few of the many named varieties are:

Mr. Fokker—blue

His Excellency—scarlet

Rosette—double rose and white

St. Brigid—double strain, mixed colors

Sulphide—violet

The Bride—white

Tuberous-rooted hardy types, such as *A. apennina,* 9 inches, blooming in April; *A. blanda,* 8 inches, and varieties of these two species; *A. palmata,* 9 inches, yellow; *A. Caroliniana,* cream to purple, and

A. fulgens, red, are excellent in the rock garden. *A. ranunculoides,* 8 inches, the Yellow Wood Anemone, blooming in early spring, is a somewhat tuberous-rooted sort for naturalizing. *A. hortensis* and *A. tuberosa* are suitable for the border. There are dozens of fibrous-rooted species and varieties.

CULTURE OUTDOORS: Florists' Anemones. In the North, plant 2 inches deep and 12 inches apart in a sheltered bed or frame in humus-rich sandy loam in fall, and after first freeze, mulch with 8 inches of dead leaves. Remove mulch gradually in spring. Or plant in spring, lift roots after bloom is over and foliage matures, and store over winter.

In moist climates such as the Pacific Northwest, tubers multiply so rapidly that it is necessary to lift them every year in order to divide.

CULTURE INDOORS: Plant in Potting Mixture No. 2 in pots, and force as hardy bulbs. After bringing indoors, grow plants on at a cool temperature—from 35 to 50 degrees.

CULTURE, HARDY TUBEROUS-ROOTED TYPES: Plant in humus-rich, sandy, well-drained soil in sun or light shade.

PROPAGATION: By division in the spring and by seed.

ANOMATHECA—See LAPEIROUSIA

ANTHERICUM [*Liliaceae*]

Anthericum liliago, a native of the Alps, has been cherished in cultivation since late in the fifteenth century. This is the species known as St. Bernard-lily. Its raceme of dainty white flowers is borne on a 1-foot stem in early summer. It is a free-flowering and satisfactory tender bulb for the rock garden.

Anthericum liliastrum (now known as *Paradisia liliastrum,* St. Bruno-lily) is also an alpine, but is found in higher altitudes—6,000 feet or more. It is altogether a larger plant than its relative, with white, fragrant flowers which Louise B. Wilder described as "like small slightly disheveled Madonna Lilies."

CULTURE OUTDOORS: South of Philadelphia, plant in autumn in well-drained sunny position in the rock garden. Treat as Lilium.

CULTURE OUTDOORS, NORTH: Set out in spring as above. Dig and store before hard freeze in fall.

PROPAGATION: By stolons, divisions, and seeds.

ARISAEMA TRIPHYLLUM [Araceae]

Jack-in-the-pulpit or Indian-turnip is a familiar woodland plant, with its three ovate leaflets and the striped green Arum-like blooms. Later in the season a heavy head of bright red berries develops. Readily transplanted into the garden, this wild tuberous-rooted subject often reaches 3 feet in height when it finds beds with good soil and abundant food.

CULTURE OUTDOORS: Plant in rather moist woodland in part shade. Leave undisturbed.

PROPAGATION: By tubers and seeds.

ARUM PALAESTINUM [Araceae]

The so-called Black Calla is grown chiefly as a curiosity, since it certainly is not beautiful. Its 1-foot-tall, Calla-like bloom, with a deep purple spadix and surrounding black-purple and greenish spathe, is lemon-scented, a winter bloomer. The leaves are arrow-shaped, 8 inches long.

CULTURE INDOORS: Start tuberous roots in damp peatmoss, covering 1 inch deep, as the roots form near the top of the tuber. When roots develop, plant in pots (Mixture No. 5) and grow on in shade. For good bloom, the plant must be pot-bound.

PROPAGATION: By offsets.

BABIANA [Iridaceae]

Babiana is a dainty little half-hardy native of South Africa. There are a number of species bearing violet, pink, red, yellow, or white freesia-like blossoms in terminal racemes on 6- to 9-inch stems. The Iris-like leaves are plicate. Hybrids are available.

CULTURE INDOORS: Pot a dozen corms in a small bulb pan in Mixture No. 3 in autumn. Keep in a very cool sun porch or cold frame until growth starts. Then grow on with plenty of water on a cool window sill or in sun room. Bloom appears in February or March. After foliage matures, dry off corms and store.

CULTURE OUTDOORS, SOUTH: Plant out in sandy loam 3 inches deep in full sun in autumn for spring bloom. Divide every other year.

PROPAGATION: By cormels and seeds.

Dwarf Bedding Dahlias (Coltness Gem and Unwin Hybrids) are as readily grown from seed as annuals.

ABOVE: *Tuberous Begonias, the mockingbirds of flowerdom, come in an almost incredible range of hues and forms. Tubers last for many years.* BELOW: *"T.B.s" in a shady nook of the author's garden, where they provide more striking color than any other shade-tolerant plant.*

BEGONIAS [Begoniaceae]

Of the huge tribe of Begonias, two types are of interest here, the Tuberous-rooted, for which see Chapter 18, and *Begonia Evansiana,* the one hardy member of the family, whose tubers resemble perfect little bulbs about the size of a filbert. *B. Evansiana* produces large light green foliage, red beneath, and many tall spikes of pink blossoms on red stems in late summer. Once planted, it will increase of its own accord. It is a most valuable shade-loving perennial.

CULTURE OUTDOORS: Plant the bulb-like tubers of *Begonia Evansiana* in spring in a rich, humusy soil in shade. Keep well watered in drought.

PROPAGATION: By bulblets. These will increase in the ground and distribute themselves as they choose. Or they can be dug and replanted in early spring.

BELAMCANDA [Iridaceae]

Belamcanda chinensis, commonly called the Blackberry-lily because of its clusters of black seeds, is a hardy, showy member of the Iris family. It produces narrow 10-inch Gladiolus-like leaves on the 4-foot branched, flowering stems which bear clusters of red-spotted orange flowers. The black seed heads in autumn are prized by flower arrangers.

CULTURE OUTDOORS: Plant in fall in sandy loam in sun. Mulch after first hard freeze in the North. Leave undisturbed until bloom ceases.

PROPAGATION: By seeds or division.

BESSERA [Liliaceae]

Bessera elegans (Coral Drop) is a half-hardy Mexican bulb which makes a fine show forced in the window garden or grown out of doors for midsummer bloom. Growing 2 to 3 feet tall, with a few 2-foot leaves, each bulb produces several slender, naked flower scapes which bear in irregular umbels five to ten bright red 1-inch flowers marked with white. *Milla biflora* is sometimes sold as Bessera.

CULTURE INDOORS: Plant several bulbs to a pot (Mixture No. 2) and force as half-hardy bulbs. (See Chapter 20.)

CULTURE OUTDOORS: As for Gladiolus.

PROPAGATION: By offsets.

BRODIAEA [Liliaceae]

Brodiaeas are native American cormous plants from our far West, where they flourish in mountainous regions. Though perfectly hardy in the Pacific area and in the South, in the Northeast and Middle West they are difficult, and are grown successfully in Zone 6 (vicinity of New York City) only by giving them the very special conditions they prefer.

The bell-shaped or starry flowers are borne in umbels at the tips of frail scapes, while the foliage is grass-like. There are red, blue, violet, white, and yellow species as well as *B. volubilis,* the Snake-lily, a twining species to 8 feet with rose-pink flowers.

The following are but a few of the many species available.

B. *Bridgesi*—15 inches, violet-pink

B. *crocea*—9 inches, yellow

B. *grandiflora*—12 inches, purple-blue

B. *lactea*—12 inches, white

B. *Tubergini*—pale blue

B. *uniflora* (*Milla uniflora, Treteleia uniflora, Leucocoryne uniflora,* Spring Star Flower)—8 inches, white tinged with blue, solitary

Brodiaeas are most useful in the rock garden.

CULTURE OUTDOORS: Plant in fall in rough, gritty, well-drained soil, in sun. Mulch in the North after first hard freeze.

CULTURE INDOORS: Pot in early fall in soil as above and treat as hardy bulbs to be forced. Blossoms will appear in early spring.

PROPAGATION: By seeds and offsets.

BRUNSVIGIA—See AMARYLLIS belladonna

BULBOCODIUM [Liliaceae]

B. *vernum* (Spring Meadow Saffron) is a European member of the Lily family, and there is but one known species in the genus. Rather like a Crocus, it has narrow leaves and several large rose-violet flowers on 6-inch stems in very early spring.

CULTURE OUTDOORS: As for Crocus. Lift every third year and re-plant.

PROPAGATION: By offsets.

CALADIUM [Araceae]

As decorative foliage plants, Fancy-leaved Caladiums are grown in warm greenhouses, or as garden plants in the far South. They may also be treated as tender tubers for outdoor display in Northern states.

Hybrids are available in white ribbed with red, dark red edged in green, pink suffused with white or green, and in mixture.

Candidum—white leaves, green veins
Edith Mead—white leaves, red ribs, green edges
Itacapus—rust-red bordered green and with red dots
Keystone—green leaves, pink ribs and spots
Macahyba—moss green, mottled with lilac
Sorocaba—silver-pink and white with green ribs
Thomas Tomlinson—crimson with green edge

The arrow-shaped leaves are thin and delicate but large, making masses of exquisite color. The flowers are not particularly decorative.

CULTURE, NORTH: Start tubers under glass in flats of damp peatmoss at 70 to 85 degrees, covering roots 2 to 3 inches. Transfer to pots after roots have developed (Mixture No. 5). Pots may be sunk to the rim outdoors in semi-shade about June 15 or when the weather is settled and warm. Repotting may be necessary during the growing season. Keep well watered and sprayed with a fine mist in hot, dry weather. Reduce water gradually in early autumn and bring the tubers in before frost, dry off, remove from pots, and store at 60 degrees. Caladiums may also be grown under glass for winter color in the conservatory. They need a warm house and high humidity.

CULTURE OUTDOORS, SOUTH: Plant in rich, sandy, well-drained soil to which bone meal has been added, as soon as the weather has become reliably warm. Cover 1 inch deep, placing in semi-shaded, sheltered bed. Dig before frost and dry as described above.

PROPAGATION: By division and seeds.

CALLA—See ZANTEDESCHIA

CALLICORE—See AMARYLLIS belladonna

CALOCHORTUS [Liliaceae]

Here are other natives of our own West. Known as Mariposa-lilies, Globe-tulips, and Star-tulips, several species of Calochortus are to be found from southern California, through the high Sierras, to the Black Hills, Colorado, and on to Oregon. Though of easy culture in the West, they are difficult to acclimate to the East and Middle West, where they seem to resent the sudden changes of temperature, with consequent thaws and "heaving" of the cormous roots. When one has seen them growing in their thousands in native mountain meadows or woods, it seems futile to plant a dozen corms in a sunny rock-garden slope in New York or Massachusetts, to watch them struggle through a few seasons to slow death. They are most decorative, however, in the Northern rock garden, where they may last several years.

There are many species, varying in color from white through lavender to purple. Others are yellow and yellow-tinged with brown or orange. They are divided into three groups:

1. Star-tulips or Cat's-ears. Flowers erect on slender stems, most of them low-growing. The insides of the flower petals are hairy, giving them their common name of Cat's-ears. Star-tulips grow in sunny situations and better adapt themselves to Northeastern conditions than the other types.

2. Globe-tulips or Fairy Lanterns. Flowers nodding, lantern-shaped, with glossy petals, to 2 feet in height, borne on slender stems. These endure light shade when growing conditions are right.

3. Mariposa-lilies or Butterfly-tulips are the showiest of the Calochortus tribe. The slender stems rise from grass-like foliage from 1½ to 2 feet, bearing large (3- to 4-inch) flowers in white, red, purple, lavender, or yellow, or mixtures of these colors. Like the Cat's-ears, the petals are hairy at the base. Sun-loving.

In addition to the forty or more species which make up these three groups, there are hybrids giving stronger growth, larger flowers, more varied color, and greater adaptability to climatic conditions.

CULTURE OUTDOORS: Plant 2 inches deep in rather poor, light soil, porous and with perfect drainage. Though absolutely cold-hardy, they cannot stand alternate freezing and thawing. Mulch well in the North after first hard freeze. They need moisture in spring up to bloom but prefer to be quite dry through the summer.

CULTURE INDOORS: Treat as hardy forced bulbs.

PROPAGATION: By natural increase and seeds.

CAMASSIA [*Liliaceae*]—*See Chapter 14*

CANNA [Cannaceae]

This old-fashioned bedding flower is coming back into favor after having been banished with Victorian houses, iron deer, and stiff round or geometrical flower beds. The reason for its comeback is the introduction of many fine new hybrids which are compact in growth, with large flowers, many in pastel shades. In buying Canna roots, select named varieties with green or bronze leaves and of a height—they grow 2½ to 8 feet tall—to suit the location in which they are to grow.

GREEN LEAVES	BRONZE LEAVES
Gaiety—orange-yellow margins	America—dark red
President—red	Apricot—apricot
R. Wallace—canary yellow	Eureka—white
	Mrs. Alfred Conard—salmon-pink
	Tyrol—pink
	Wyoming—yellow-bronze

Latest addition to the Canna list is the Grand Opera Series, with extra-large flowers in lovely pastel shades.

CULTURE OUTDOORS: Start indoors in the North, as with Tuberous Begonias, four weeks before outdoor planting date; or set rhizomes horizontally, after danger of frost is past, 1½ to 2 feet apart, according to height, 3 to 4 inches deep in rich soil with plenty of moisture and in full sun, just covering the rhizomes with soil. During growth, side-dress with 5–10–5 fertilizer at the rate of 4 ounces per square yard. When frost blackens the foliage in fall, cut to within 6 inches of root, dig the rhizomes, dry off, and store upside-down in a cool place, not too dark, at a temperature of 50 to 60 degrees. In March, divide rhizomes, leaving several eyes on each, and start in flats of soil and peatmoss. Harden off in a cold frame for two weeks before setting in the garden.

PROPAGATION: By seeds—soaked in warm water for forty-eight hours, or filed, before planting—and by division.

CHLIDANTHUS [Amaryllidaceae]

The South American bulb C. fragrans (Delicate-lily) has strap-like, gray-green basal leaves and bears, on 6- to 10-inch solid scapes, umbels of fragrant yellow tubular flowers, each 4 inches long. Rock-garden subject. Late summer bloom.

CULTURE OUTDOORS, SOUTH: Treat as a garden plant.

CULTURE OUTDOORS, NORTH: Plant out 2 inches deep in early spring, in full sun, in humusy soil, well-drained and moist. Dig before frost and store bulbs above freezing; or start in small pots (Mixture No. 4) in late winter. After danger of frost is past in spring, sink pots in garden bed. Keep moist until after bloom. Then reduce water gradually until foliage matures.

PROPAGATION: By offsets.

CHIONODOXA [Liliaceae]—See Chapter 14

CLAYTONIA [Portulacaceae]

These gay little wild flowers of the early spring woods known as Spring Beauties adapt themselves well to naturalizing under shade, among Ferns, and in moist situations. Once a colony of their corms or tubers is established in a spot to its liking, it may be counted on to spread and increase.

C. virginica is the native species common in the northeastern United States, growing from Canada to Texas. The flowers are white, veined with pink, on 4- to 6-inch stems, the leaves grass-like and succulent. C. rosea and C. megarrhiza are both natives of the Rocky Mountains, while C. lanceolata and C. nivalis are from the Pacific Northwest. There are many species, including C. aurea, which is yellow.

CULTURE: Select a species native to your part of the country and naturalize in surroundings similar to those in which it grows in nature.

PROPAGATION: By natural increase.

CLIVIA [Amaryllidaceae]

Natives of South Africa, the Clivias or Kafir-lilies are popular greenhouse subjects, where the narrow evergreen leaves and showy umbels of 2- to 3-inch orange or orange-scarlet flowers on 2-foot stems are most colorful in early spring. They may also be grown successfully in the window garden or outdoors in the South. C. cyrtanthiflora, C. nobilis, C. miniata, and a number of hybrids are commercially available.

CULTURE INDOORS: Pot (Mixture No. 4) June to October and leave undisturbed for several years. Keep rather dry through summer and autumn. Start in January to give more water and regular applications of liquid manure. Keep at 65 degrees. After bloom, gradually reduce water until almost none is given through the fall.

CULTURE OUTDOORS, SOUTH: Plant in fall in a shady location in a rich, humusy, but well-drained garden bed.

PROPAGATION: By division.

COLCHICUM [Liliaceae]—See Chapter 19

COLOCASIA [Araceae]

Commonly known as Elephant's Ear, this giant foliage plant, 6 feet tall, was more popular in the home garden in the Victorian era than it is today. The huge, heart-shaped leaves—to 2 feet across—for which the plant is grown, provide a screen or a tropical-looking background for smaller garden subjects.

CULTURE: Start as Tuberous-rooted Begonias. Then transfer to shaded outdoor positions in very rich, damp soil. Dig and store before frost.

PROPAGATION: By division.

CONVALLARIA [Liliaceae]

This old-time favorite is still one of the most popular of our spring garden flowers. Flourishing and spreading as it does in deep shade, and providing masses of sweet-scented white flowers nodding like little bells on stiff flower stems, it is little wonder that the Lily-of-the-Valley keeps its popularity. The variety *rosea* bears pinkish flowers which, to us, seem rather unattractive. It is not bulbous but grows from rootstocks.

CULTURE OUTDOORS: Plant the roots in fall in rich, damp soil in partial or full shade. Leave undisturbed, but give a yearly fall application of well-rotted cow manure or compost.

CULTURE INDOORS: "Pips," for forcing indoors or under glass may be purchased from seed houses.

PROPAGATION: By division.

COOPERIA [Amaryllidaceae]

Native to Texas and Mexico, the dainty Rain-lily is often naturalized with Zephyranthes in the South or Southwest. The starry white or white, pink-tinged, solitary flowers on 10-inch stems are delightfully fragrant and appear after rains throughout the summer. They are hardy to Virginia.

C. *Drummondi*—white, tinged red in reverse
C. *pedunculata*—larger than preceding
C. *Traubi*—white, tinted pink in reverse
CULTURE: As for Zephyranthes.
PROPAGATION: By offsets.

CRINUM [*Amaryllidaceae*]

Crinums, known as Bengal-lilies or Milk-and-wine-lilies, are usually grown in the South, where they remain out of doors the year round and in one spot for many years without needing transplanting. In spite of their beauty, they are seldom grown under glass or indoors because of the space they require.

There are species with evergreen or deciduous foliage. Both throw up strong solid scapes 2 to 4 feet in height which, in September or October, bear umbels of long-tubed, Lily-like white, pink, or rose-red blooms, each 3 to 6 inches long. The following species are half hardy and may be grown as garden plants to Washington, D.C.:

C. *longifolium*—pink or white
C. *Poweli album*—white
C. *Poweli rosea*—rose

Tender varieties:

C. *amabile*—pink, late-blooming
J. C. Harvey—wine red, early blooming
Louis Bosanquet—white shading to pink, petals ruffled
C. *Moorei*—pink, requires shade
C. *virginicum*—white with rose stripes, early

CULTURE OUTDOORS, SOUTH: Plant outdoors in spring in sun (except C. *Moorei*) in rich, humusy, well-drained soil, setting the bulbs just below the soil surface. Water freely during the growing period. After bloom, reduce moisture gradually until foliage has matured in deciduous types. Less water is required after bloom in evergreen types also. Mulch tender varieties lightly in Middle South, heavily in Upper South.

CULTURE OUTDOORS, NORTH: Plant in spring, after danger of frost is past, 2 to 3 feet apart, in rich, humusy, well-drained bed. Water freely until after bloom, then reduce moisture. Lift and store before frost for deciduous types. In evergreen types, pot up before frost and keep in rather dry, semi-dormant condition until new growth starts.

CULTURE INDOORS: Pot (Mixture No. 4) as soon as delivered, with the top third of the bulb exposed. Feed with liquid fertilizer as flower scapes are thrown up and until color shows. After bloom, reduce water gradually. Repot only when necessary.

PROPAGATION: By natural offsets.

CROCOSMIA [Iridaceae]

As an autumn bloomer, the Crocosmia—sometimes called Copper-tip—is especially useful in the back of a sunny border, where corms may be set after danger of frost is past. The bright orange-yellow flowers, 2 inches in length, are borne in showy, long-panicled spikes which lift their heads to 4 feet—well above most other border material.

CULTURE: As for Gladiolus.

PROPAGATION: By offsets and seeds.

CROCUS [Iridaceae]—See Chapter 14

CYCLAMEN [Primulaceae]

The florists' Cyclamen (C. indicum), as a universal gift plant, is familiar to all. The heart-shaped, mottled leaves look almost metallic in their crisp beauty, while the many nodding flowers, with reflexed petals, are extremely striking. Purple, cerise, rose, red, and white varieties are available.

Tiny, hardy rock-garden Cyclamens are like miniature replicas of their florists' relatives. C. europaeum is native to the Swiss Alps and is perfectly hardy in the North. The leaves are mottled and the blooms rose-red. It is a summer bloomer. C. neapolitanum, with lovely silver-marked leaves and red or white flowers, is hardy in the Northeast. The leaves of these two dainty little species remain green through the winter.

CULTURE INDOORS: For florists' varieties, pot corm-like roots in a mixture of one part sifted loam, one part sand, and two parts leafmold. Give light but not too much direct sun, plenty of water, and a temperature not over 55 degrees. (Do not permit water to lodge and remain on leaves.) After bloom is over and foliage matures, lay pots on sides under greenhouse bench or out of doors for summer until growth starts again.

CULTURE OUTDOORS: For rock-garden varieties, plant in a shady part of the rock garden and leave undisturbed indefinitely.

PROPAGATION: By seeds or division.

CYPELLA [Iridaceae]

The Cypella is a bulbous Irid which comes to us from South America. The plants have basal and stem leaves and bear yellow, orange, or blue flowers in clusters on 2- to 3-foot stems throughout the summer.

CULTURE: As for Gladiolus.

PROPAGATION: By seeds and offsets.

CYRTANTHUS [Amaryllidaceae]

An Amaryllid from South America, Cyrtanthus (Ifafa-lily) bears funnel-shaped nodding flowers in umbels on bare stalks to 1½ feet, the basal leaves being evergreen in most cultivated species.

Red, white, and yellow species and varieties are available. Grown as a garden flower in the South, Cyrtanthus is a summer bloomer.

CULTURE: As for *Amaryllis belladonna*.

PROPAGATION: By offsets.

DAFFODIL—See Chapter 11

DAHLIA [Compositae]—See Chapter 16

ERANTHIS [Ranunculaceae]—See Chapter 14

EREMURUS [Liliaceae]

The Foxtail-lily or Desert-candle comes to us from Asia. It is not bulbous but produces a heavy, fibrous, star-shaped root. Its stately beauty makes it a striking subject for the back of the border where color is needed.

From rosettes of narrow leaves, flowering scapes 5 to 12 feet in height are thrown up, bearing heavy racemes 1 to 4 feet long of bell-shaped white, pink, yellow, or orange flowers. Many species and hybrids are available, among them:

E. *Elwesianus albus*—white

Him-Rob—7 to 9 feet, pink

Shelford Hybrids—pastel shades and named varieties in separate colors

CULTURE OUTDOORS: Plant the fleshy rootstocks in fall in rich but very well-drained soil, placing them just beneath the soil level and surrounding each with sand. Mulch heavily after hard freeze, as their uncertain hardiness seems due to late frosts destroying early spring growth. Remove mulch very gradually until danger of frost is past. Water liberally during the growing season.

PROPAGATION: By division or (slow) from seed.

ERYTHRONIUM [*Liliaceae*]

Except for a single European species, E. *dens-canis,* rose-red, the Erythroniums are natives of North America, where they are known under such names as Adder's Tongue, Trout-lily, and Dogtooth-violet. They are admirably hardy and most desirable rock-garden and woodland subjects, where their two basal bright green or more often dark-mottled leaves carpet the ground in early spring. The nodding, usually solitary flowers have pointed, recurved petals which give them a starry appearance. There are white, cream, yellow, and purple species, varying in height from 6 to 24 inches.

E. *albidum*. Eastern U.S.—white, leaves green or mottled

E. *americanum*. Eastern U.S.—yellow, leaves mottled

E. *californicum*. California—cream to yellow, cluster-flowered

E. *Hendersoni*. South Oregon—like above, but violet and maroon

E. *revolutum* (and varieties). Pacific Northwest—white to lilac, mottled leaves, cluster-flowered

Variety Pink Beauty—pink

Variety Rose Beauty—rose-pink

CULTURE OUTDOORS: Plant in partly shaded location, in soil rich in humus, 3 to 5 inches apart and 3 inches deep. Set, as soon as received, in moist soil and keep well watered until bulbs are established. Leave undisturbed.

PROPAGATION: By offsets or seeds.

EUCHARIS [Amaryllidaceae]

Eucharis grandiflora (*E. amazonica*), the Amazon-lily, is a popular florists' flower which has recently been "discovered" by flower arrangers and featured in many competitive cut-flower compositions displayed in the big flower shows. It can also be grown at home, preferably under glass, but with special care in the window garden. The blooming season is late winter and early spring.

The umbels of pure-white flowers are chastely beautiful and, in form, suggestive of some of the white Triandrus hybrid Narcissi.

CULTURE INDOORS: Plant in coarse, fibrous soil enriched with well-rotted or dried cow manure with a little bone meal added. Place four to six bulbs in an 8- or 10-inch Azalea pot, pressing in firmly, with necks of bulbs above soil. Water sparingly until new growth begins. Then give ample moisture and humidity during the growing season, with a temperature of 70 to 85 degrees. Keep from direct sunshine. Reduce water during the resting period, but do not dry so much as to lose the foliage, which should be kept green. Like most Amaryllids, the Eucharis blooms best when pot-bound.

CULTURE OUTDOORS, SOUTH: Pot as above and move, in pots, to partly shaded border for blooming period. Bring indoors during winter season.

PROPAGATION: By offsets in spring.

EUCOMIS [Liliaceae]

Eucomis, often called the Pineapple-lily, is a South African bulb, easy to grow as a tender summer-flowering subject in the North, as a Southern garden flower, or as a pot plant indoors.

From rosettès of basal leaves rise rather coarse scapes set with dense racemes of white or greenish-white, star-shaped flowers. Leaves crowning the tip of the raceme resemble the top of a Pineapple and give the plant its common name.

E. *comosa* (punctata)—leaves to 2 feet; brown-spotted on lower side; flowers greenish

E. *pedunculata*—leaves to 18 inches; flowers white, marked purple

E. *undulata*—leaves to 1 foot, strap-like; flowers greenish-white

CULTURE OUTDOORS: Plant in May in the North or in fall in the South in soil suitable for Lily culture, with bulbs near surface. If grown outdoors in the North, dig and store before hard frost. Hardy to Washington, D.C.

CULTURE INDOORS: Pot in fall (Mixture No. 2) and treat as half-hardy forced bulb. After flowering, gradually reduce water and rest the bulbs.

PROPAGATION: By offsets.

FREESIA [Iridaceae]

Few winter-blooming plants give greater satisfaction when grown under glass or in a cool sun porch than the fragrant Freesia with its loose spikes of dainty, colorful, funnel-shaped flowers. Among the many hybrids there is a large range of color, from white through yellow to mauve, lavender, pink, carmine, apricot, and copper.

Albatre—white

Buttercup—yellow, shaded orange

Charmante—pink and apricot

Flambeau—carmine

Maryon—lavender

Penerosa—pink, with yellow throat

Princess Marijke—bronze, orange, and yellow

CULTURE INDOORS: Plant at intervals of two weeks from October to January for continuous bloom—twelve corms to an 8-inch bulb or Azalea pan, using Mixture No. 3. Store pots in frame outdoors until hard frost threatens. Then grow on in very cool temperature—45 to 55 degrees—and water freely. Full sun. Bloom will appear ten to twelve weeks after planting. Dry off after flowering and store corms through the summer. Watch for aphids.

CULTURE OUTDOORS, LOWER SOUTH: Plant in sun in well-drained sandy soil in September or October.

PROPAGATION: By offsets and seeds.

FRITILLARIA [Liliaceae]—See Chapter 14

GALANTHUS [Amaryllidaceae]—See Chapter 14

GALTONIA [Liliaceae]—See Chapter 19

GLADIOLUS [Iridaceae]—See Chapter 17

GLORIOSA [Liliaceae]

One of the nicest things about the Gloriosa is the fact that the tuberous roots can be started into growth at any season of the year after a few months' rest. A root, 5 to 6 inches long and ½ inch in diameter, started in early spring, will bloom in late summer.

The showy 4-inch red and yellow Lilies with twisted petals are borne in the axils of the upper leaves, the petals being interestingly recurved in the manner of *Lilium speciosum*. The vine-like plant is supported by tendrils developed at the leaf tips, an ingenious method of climbing. The flowers are prized for arrangements and corsages.

CULTURE INDOORS: Use Mixture No. 2 and, when new eye appears on tuber, plant, one to each 6-inch pot, 2 to 4 inches deep, depending on the size of the tuber. Water well and leave undisturbed until active growth starts. Then keep consistently moist and grow on in a cool temperature which should never exceed 65 degrees. After bloom, gradually reduce water. New tuberous roots, angular in form, will have developed when the drying-off period is completed. Remove these carefully from the soil in the pot—they are very brittle—and store until a pink bud or eye is visible at end of tuber (approximately three months). Then replant as before. Two blooming periods a year may be had, as growth cycle is completed in six months.

CULTURE OUTDOORS: In southern Florida, leave in ground the year round. In the North, plant in the open ground, after frost danger is past, for bloom in July or August. Dig in the fall before frost.

PROPAGATION: By offsets or division of roots.

GLOXINIA [Gesneriaceae]—See SINNINGIA

HABRANTHUS [Amaryllidaceae]

The Habranthus is a small genus which until recently was confused with Hippeastrum and Zephyranthes, both of which it resembles. *H. Andersoni,* but 6 inches in height, produces solitary yellow flowers veined with red; *H. robustus* is 9 inches tall with rose-red flowers 3 inches long, and *H. texanus*—a native of Texas—is yellow with copper and purple markings on the outside of the 4-inch flowers which appear in summer. Most of the species are natives of South America.

CULTURE: As for Zephyranthes.

PROPAGATION: By offsets and seeds.

HAEMANTHUS [Amaryllidaceae]

The Haemanthus or Blood-lily is a tender South African bulb which flowers in late summer or early fall. Most of the species are rather low-growing, with decorative leaves to 1 foot in length and almost globular flower heads produced at the tips of sturdy scapes. Made up of many tubular starry flowers of white, red, or soft salmon-orange, each with six long star-like stamens, they are further enhanced by the even longer stamens, deeper in color and each bearing a conspicuous golden anther. In the specimen before us at this writing, there are two dozen fully opened blossoms surrounding a ring of half-opened blooms which enclose a heart of another two dozen still closed buds. This particular species, *H. Katharinae,* is of a delightfully soft salmon-pink color. There are a number of available species and varieties:

H. albiflos—white, to 1 foot; foliage evergreen; late summer

H. coccineus—red, to 2 feet; berries purple; late summer

H. Katharinae—soft salmon-pink, leaves 3 to 5 on short separate stem, appearing with the flowers; 1½ feet; August

H. hybridus Andromeda—salmon-red; very large; June

H. hybridus King Albert—red, to 1 foot.

H. puniceus—pale red flowers followed by scarlet berries which remain in good condition for months. Wavy leaves with reddish stems.

CULTURE INDOORS: Pot (Mixture No. 4) about March 1, leaving top half of bulb exposed. Water sparingly until top growth starts, then increase moisture and feed regularly with liquid fertilizer. Place in a partly shaded garden bed during summer and give complete shade while flowering. After bloom and when foliage has matured, withhold water entirely except in evergreen varieties. Repot only when necessary.

PROPAGATION: By offsets.

HIPPEASTRUM [Amaryllidaceae]

Hippeastrum is the botanical name for our common "Amaryllis"— a large tribe with glossy strap-like leaves and two to four large Lily-like flowers appearing in an umbel at the tip of a hollow scape. In some species and varieties the leaves appear after the flowers, but with most, they come with the bloom. In some cases, too, the foliage is persistent, growing throughout the year.

Most Hippeastrums in commerce today are improved hybrids, many of them blooming several times a year. These come both in strains like the Royal Dutch and Giant California Hybrids, and in named varieties, and under color. Among these are:

Brilliant Star—dark red	Orange
Irene—pink with rose veining	Salmon-orange
Madame Curie—salmon	Scarlet
Mont Blanc—white	White—with pink veins
Pure pink	

Hippeastrums are good subjects for the cool greenhouse, sun porch, or window garden, where they bloom in winter and early spring; or they can be used as summer-flowering bulbs in the North and as garden subjects in the South.

CULTURE INDOORS: One of the oldest and easiest of house plants to bring into bloom, Hippeastrums are planted in early winter (Mixture No. 4) with the upper third of the bulb exposed. Water sparingly until growth begins. Then increase water. Grow on through summer in pots in garden bed. After leaves mature in fall, dry off gradually and rest in pots until new growth again begins. Repot only when necessary.

CULTURE OUTDOORS, NORTH: Plant in shady garden beds after danger of frost is past and lift bulbs before frost, storing in damp peatmoss and sand. In the far South, the bulbs may be left in garden beds the year round.

PROPAGATION: By offsets, seeds, and, with hybrids, by bulb cuttings.

HYACINTHUS [*Liliaceae*]—*See Chapter 14*

HYDROSYME [*Araceae*]

Grown as a curiosity, *Hydrosyme Rivieri* is rather like a giant, dark, evil-smelling Calla-lily. The reddish spathe, often a foot long and borne on a 2- to 4-foot spotted stalk, gives the plant its common name of Devil's-tongue. Worthless as the flower is, however, the broad, palm-like foliage, which appears after the flower has faded, on mottled stems (giving the common name of Snake-palm), is very interesting and produces an unusually tropical effect. Well worth trying.

CULTURE INDOORS: Pot 2 to 3 inches deep in very early spring (Mixture No. 5). After leaves have matured, reduce water and rest

ABOVE: *A group of the new Buell Gloxinias, an American strain far surpassing older forms in size and variety of coloring.* BELOW: *The Tigerflower (Tigridia) from Mexico, which is now to be had in a wide range of pleasing colors.*

ABOVE: *Most dramatic of the autumn-flowering bulbs are the Colchicums, which suddenly appear as if by magic. The Giant (illustrated) has flowers over 6 inches across.* BELOW: *"Farewell to summer" is the theme song of the Sternbergias—or should it be, "Hail to another spring"?*

through winter in a cool greenhouse or sun porch. When new growth starts, increase water.

CULTURE OUTDOORS: Set out in late May.

HYMENOCALLIS [*Amaryllidaceae*]—*See Chapter 19*

IRIS, BULBOUS [*Iridaceae*]

The Bulbous Irises are separated into three main groups: the Junos, the bulbs of which keep their roots during the resting season; the xiphiums (Spanish Iris) and the xiphiodes (English Iris), both with smooth bulbs without roots when resting; and the reticulatas, the bulbs of which are covered with a characteristic netting.

Juno Irises are not always commercially available in this country and are as a rule considered more unusual than beautiful. The plants rather resemble cornstalks with flowers in the leaf axils. They bloom with the "Dutch" bulbs in spring.

The following species represent a selection of those considered of interest by Iris growers:

I. bucharica—yellow with golden falls; 30 inches
I. persica—blue, purple, green, and gold; 6 inches
I. Rosenbachiana—rose, purple, white, and gold; dwarf with 3-inch flowers
I. sindjarensis—blue and white; 10 inches

CULTURE OUTDOORS: Plant in well-drained sandy soil in full sun and leave undisturbed. In the North, mulch with evergreen boughs after first hard freeze.

Iris reticulata includes a number of dwarf varieties blooming in early spring. Much more decorative and appealing than the Junos, the reticulatas are beloved of rock gardeners. They produce single blossoms in shades of blue, violet, or purple with orange markings, and many are delightfully fragrant. Blooming as they do in early spring, they are often planted with *Arabis albida* and other early low-growing perennials.

I. r. cyanea and *I. r. coerulea* are blue varieties.
I. r. Krelagei and *I. r. purpurea* are purple.

CULTURE: Plant in light, well-drained neutral soil in sun. Mulch well with evergreen boughs and straw after first hard freeze in the North.

Iris xiphium (Spanish Iris) is a clan which includes many named varieties, as does also *I. xiphiodes,* or English Iris. The so-called "Dutch" Irises, so named because they were bred and are grown in Holland, are hybrids of *I. xiphium* and other species. They have heavier stems and larger blooms than their Spanish parent. These are the Bulbous Irises sold as cut flowers in florists' shops. They make fine garden flowers, too, for those who care to meet their simple requirements.

The xiphiums, xiphiodes, and Dutch Hybrids all produce heavy single-flower stems 1½ to 2 feet in height, the xiphiums with narrow, channeled leaves a foot in length, the xiphiodes with larger foliage equaling the stem in length, and the Dutch rather like the xiphiums but more robust in every way and with larger flowers. The flowers of all three types, in which there is a fine color range, are showy and Orchid-like, with many fine porcelain blues.

There are dozens of named varieties, only a few of which are mentioned in the following lists:

DUTCH HYBRIDS—BLOOMING LATE MAY OUTDOORS

Alaska—orange-yellow
Belle Jaune—yellow
Blue Champion—large blue
David Haring—white, tinged lilac
Gold and Silver—white standards, gold falls
Golden Harvest—golden yellow
Jacob De Wit—dark blue
Saxe Blue—delft blue
Violet Queen—lilac
Wedgwood—porcelain blue
White Superior—white
Yellow Queen—bright yellow

SPANISH IRIS (XIPHIUMS)—BLOOMING EARLY JUNE

King of the Blues—blue
Cajanus—yellow
L'Innocence—white
Thunderbolt—violet-bronze
British Queen—white

ENGLISH IRIS (XIPHIODES)—BLOOMING IN LATE JUNE

Lucinda—light blue
Mont Blanc—white
Othello—dark blue
Ruby—purple-red
Sir Wm. Mansfield—purple-blue

CULTURE OUTDOORS: As for *I. reticulata,* except that xiphiums require full sun and a sheltered location with excellent drainage, while xiphiodes require summer moisture (like Japanese Iris) and a rich, moist, humusy soil. Plant in fall and mulch—preferably with evergreen boughs—after first hard freeze. *This is obligatory* in the North.

All the Bulbous Irises (except the Junos) may be lifted yearly after bloom and stored, to be replanted in fall; but if left in the ground and winter-mulched or grown in a frame, they need not be disturbed for six or eight years.

CULTURE INDOORS: Force as hardy bulbs.

PROPAGATION: By offsets.

ISMENE [Hymenocallis]—See Chapter 14

IXIA [Iridaceae]

Ixias (Corn-lilies) are stand-bys for the Southern summer garden and in the North are often grown under glass for winter and spring bloom. They may also be spring-planted in the open for summer color out of doors. Thin wiry flower stalks, varying in height from 1 to 3 feet, depending on the species or variety, bear hanging, bell-shaped flowers above grass-like foliage. Among the many named hybrids there is a range of color from white through cream to yellow, orange, red, pink, and violet. In most cases the flowers are marked with contrasting colors, as red on white, yellow with a lavender eye, etc. Listed here are a few named varieties:

Afterglow—orange	Hogarth—yellow, purple eye
Azure—blue	Hubert—copper-red
Bridesmaid—white, red eye	Wonder—double pink

CULTURE INDOORS: Plant as directed for forcing half-hardy bulbs (Chapter 20). Bring indoors before first hard freeze and keep at 55 degrees. After foliage matures, remove corms from pots, dry thoroughly in sun, and store.

CULTURE OUTDOORS, SOUTH: Plant in November in moist, well-drained soil in sun or part shade; mulch after first hard freeze with 4 to 8 inches of dead leaves, depending on severity of winter climate. Remove mulch gradually in early spring.

CULTURE OUTDOORS, NORTH: Plant in garden beds in early spring. After bloom, when foliage matures, lift corms and store as Gladiolus.

PROPAGATION: By offsets.

IXIOLIRION [Amaryllidaceae]

A little-grown spring-flowering bulb from Asia, the Ixiolirion, or Siberian Bluebell, sends up in May 12- to 18-inch flowering spikes bearing sprays of true-blue or lilac starry flowers.

CULTURE OUTDOORS: If planted in light, well-drained soil, 3 inches deep, Ixiolirion is hardy. It cannot, however, survive poor drainage. Bulbs can be dug before frost and stored over winter.

PROPAGATION: By offsets.

LACHENALIA [Liliaceae]

Lachenalias (Cape-cowslips) form a large group of small bulbous flowers for culture indoors or under glass. There are many hybrids as well as an impressive list of species, the latter all natives of South Africa.

The spikes of long tubular flowers rise from two or more basal leaves and range in size from the tiny *L. orchioides* in white, yellow, red, or blue, with blooms but ⅓ of an inch long, to *L. pendula superba* (the most satisfactory sort for indoor culture), with large red, yellow, and purple flowers borne on stiff 12-inch peduncles. *L. aurea* is bright orange-yellow, and *L. luteola* is lemon-yellow, but both of these are smaller than *L. pendula superba*.

CULTURE INDOORS: Bulbs should be potted in August (Mixture No. 2), a dozen bulbs to a 6-inch pot or bulb pan. Place in a cold frame in full sunshine until just before hard frost. Then remove to sun porch or greenhouse at 50 to 60 degrees and grow on in full sun, increasing the water supply. After flowering, reduce water gradually until bulbs mature. Dry off and store.

CULTURE OUTDOORS, LOWER SOUTH: Plant in September or October. After bloom and when foliage has matured, dig, dry, and store until following fall.

PROPAGATION: By offsets and seeds.

LAPEIROUSIA (Anomatheca) [Iridaceae]

There are several available species of this little-grown corm from South Africa. They are low-growing plants suitable for the summer rock garden or, forced, for bloom indoors. The bright but fleeting violet, rose, red, or white flowers are closely set in short panicles on 12-inch stems. They are half hardy.

CULTURE INDOORS: Use Mixture No. 3. Treat as Freesias.

CULTURE OUTDOORS: As for Gladiolus.

PROPAGATION: By seeds or cormels.

LEUCOCORYNE [Liliaceae]

The Leucocoryne is a small Chilean genus producing narrow basal leaves and blue or white tubular flowers in a terminal umbel. The bulbs are tender.

L. ixioides, the species generally available, produces large, sweet-scented blue flowers, white-centered, on 18-inch stems in spring.

CULTURE INDOORS: As for Freesias.

CULTURE OUTDOORS, LOWER SOUTH: As for Freesias.

PROPAGATION: By offsets and seeds.

LEUCOCRINUM [Liliaceae]

Leucocrinum montanum (Sand- or Star-lily) is a single species, a hardy native of our own West, with large, pure-white, fragrant flowers in stemless clusters in early spring. Though each flower lasts but a day, many appear in succession. It is a valuable addition to the rock garden.

CULTURE OUTDOORS: Plant the rhizomes in early fall in a sunny, sandy, well-drained position in the rock garden.

PROPAGATION: By seeds.

LEUCOJUM [Amaryllidaceae]—See Chapter 14

LILIUM [Liliaceae]—See Chapter 15

LIRIOPE [Liliaceae]

Lily-turf is a common name for both the Liriopes and the Ophiopogons, closely allied genera. Both are useful ground covers in sun or shade, where the roots form mats or sods so dense as to suggest their common name.

L. muscari, the Big Blue Liriope, has leaves to 18 inches and lilac-purple flowers. There is a variegated form with yellow-striped leaves. L. spicata, the Creeping Liriope, bears narrow grass-like leaves and pale violet or white flower spikes.

CULTURE OUTDOORS: Plant in ordinary garden soil in sun or shade. Has proved hardy with us north of New York City.

PROPAGATION: By division.

LYCORIS [*Amaryllidaceae*]—*See Chapter 19*

MILLA [*Liliaceae*]

Milla biflora is a bulbous species native to our Southwest, and is commonly called Mexican Star. Fragrant, wax-white 2½-inch flowers are borne in spring in clusters at the top of a 1½-foot scape, while leaves are basal. It is sometimes sold commercially as *Bessera elegans.*

CULTURE INDOORS: Plant several bulbs in a bulb pan in Mixture No. 2 in fall and treat as half-hardy bulbs for forcing.

CULTURE OUTDOORS, NORTH: Plant out in early spring and lift before freezing weather. Far South it may be treated as a garden plant.

PROPAGATION: By offsets.

MONTBRETIA—See TRITONIA

MORAEA [*Iridaceae*]

The Moraeas are popular garden plants in the South and Southern California, where they are grown like Irises. They may also be treated as window garden plants, especially those species which are either constant bloomers or which blossom several times a year.

Foliage is narrow and basal, while the showy but fleeting flowers, appearing in clusters and opening successively, are white, violet, or blue, some with splotches of yellow or orange.

FOR INDOORS:

M. iridioides Johnsoni—flowers large, white with lavender and orange; blooms several times in the summer months; 2 feet

M. polystachya—lilac with yellow markings; blooms for six weeks or more; 2 feet

FOR OUTDOORS:

M. ramosa—yellow, large; 3 to 4 feet

M. Oakhurst hybrid—Cream-white; 4 feet

M. Robinsoniana—white with yellow and violet; 6 feet

CULTURE INDOORS, CORMOUS TYPES: As for Ixias.

CULTURE INDOORS, RHIZOMATOUS TYPES: Pot (Mixture No. 3) and keep very moist until after bloom. Then reduce, but do not withhold water.

CULTURE OUTDOORS, SOUTH: Plant out in early autumn.

PROPAGATION: By seed or division.

MUSCARI [Liliaceae]—See Chapter 14

NAEGELIA [Gesneriaceae]— See SMITHIANTHA

NARCISSUS [Liliaceae]—See Chapter 11

NERINE [Amaryllidaceae]

The Guernsey-lily (so called because this South African bulb established itself in Guernsey after the bulbs were cast up there from a wrecked ship) makes a beautiful fall display indoors or under glass in the North. *Nerine sarniensis* produces narrow light green leaves which appear *after* the flowers. These, bright red or crimson with long bright red stamens, are produced in umbels at the top of an 18-inch solid scape and look as if sprinkled with gold dust. (For many years *Lycoris radiata* was sold as *Nerine sarniensis*.) *N. filifolia* is a smaller species, also with red flowers, and with 8-inch leaves occurring with the blossoms. Other species commercially available are: *N. Bowdeni,* tall-growing, with large pink flowers marked with rose, and *N. magnifica,* a still larger pink.

CULTURE OUTDOORS: As border flowers in the South. Plant in early fall. Keep moist in winter, dry in summer.

CULTURE INDOORS: Pot up (Mixture No. 4) when received in autumn. Grow on through winter with plenty of water to encourage growth of foliage. As spring approaches, reduce water gradually, and when leaves turn yellow, rest completely in pots turned on their sides in dry sunny location until bloom appears in early fall. Leaves will follow bloom, and these must be kept green through winter with ample moisture.

PROPAGATION: By offsets.

OPHIOPOGON [Liliaceae]

A close relative of the Liriopes, the Ophiopogons are also commonly called Lily-turf because both form dense mats of roots and foliage which create a satisfactory ground cover in sun or shade.

O. jaburan has narrow leaves to 2 feet and spikes of white flowers. *O. jaburan vittatus* has striped leaves. Other varieties with variegated foliage are *O. aureus* and *O. variegatus*. *Liriope muscari,* which has blue or violet flower spikes, is often misnamed *O. jaburan*. *O. japoni-*

cus is a dwarf variety with tuber-bearing roots and foot-long, very dark green leaves. Flowers are light blue. This is the best species for use as turf.

CULTURE: As for Liriope.

PROPAGATION: By division.

ORNITHOGALUM [*Liliaceae*]

There are two groups of these star-like bulbous flowers, commonly known as Star-of-Bethlehem: the hardy species which may be planted outdoors to give spring bloom, and the tender sorts grown under glass.

O. umbellatum, 6 to 12 inches tall, with green-margined racemes of white star-shaped flowers and grass-like foliage, makes itself so much at home in Northern gardens that it often becomes a serious pest. Other hardy species are *O. pyramidale,* to 2 feet, also with green-margined white flowers, and *O. nutans,* to 2 feet, with nodding white and green blossoms.

O. arabicum, a tender species for the window garden, produces racemes of white flowers with black pistils on scapes 2 feet in height. *O. caudatum,* another window-garden subject, has green-centered white flowers to 3 feet. *O. thyrsoides* produces long-lasting white or pale yellow blossoms in long, dense racemes. Its variety, *O. aureum,* is one of the best for indoors.

CULTURE OUTDOORS: Plant as any hardy garden bulb.

CULTURE INDOORS: Plant 6 bulbs to a large bulb pan (Mixture No. 2) as soon as delivered. Keep in cold frame until roots appear in drainage holes. Then bring in to a temperature not exceeding 60 degrees. Treat as Freesias.

PROPAGATION: By offsets.

OXALIS [*Oxalidaceae*]

Oxalis may be had in red, rose, pink, violet, yellow, white, and striped species and varieties, which are greenhouse or indoor favorites, for winter and early spring bloom. The clover-like, glossy leaves are also decorative. Native, hardy summer-blooming sorts are small-flowered.

For indoor growing or greenhouse culture, and as garden subjects in the South:

O. Bowieana—rose-purple, large flowers; summer

O. cernua (Bermuda Buttercup)—bright yellow; spring

O. hirta—pink, large flowers, most satisfactory; winter

O. rubra—pink or rose color, dark veining; winter

CULTURE INDOORS: In September or October plant bulbs near the surface, six to a 6-inch bulb pan, in Mixture No. 2. Place in dark, cool place, giving little water, until growth starts. Then bring to full light, increase water, and feed with liquid fertilizer. After bloom, reduce water gradually until foliage matures. Then store in pots and let rest until early autumn. Divide and replant.

CULTURE OUTDOORS, SOUTH: Plant in fall 2 inches deep and 3 inches apart at the front of a sunny border.

PROPAGATION: By offsets, root division, or seeds.

PANCRATIUM [*Amaryllidaceae*]

P. maritimum is a charming summer-blooming tender bulb which comes to us from the Mediterranean region and closely resembles Hymenocallis (Spider-lily or Peruvian-daffodil). The blue-green, strap-like but twisted leaves are evergreen, while the very fragrant flowers with 3-inch tubes and 1½-inch perianth-like petals make the blossoms resemble a large white Daffodil. *P. canariense* is a species from the Canary Islands bearing six to ten flowers on long pedicles.

CULTURE OUTDOORS, SOUTH: Plant bulbs near surface in sandy, well-drained soil which can be kept rather dry. Do not water until after bloom is over. Then keep moist until foliage matures.

CULTURE OUTDOORS, NORTH: (Mixture No. 4.) Set out in late spring, sinking pots to rim in dry, sandy bed. After bloom is over, water and bring indoors, in pots, before first frost, keeping moist until foliage stops active growth.

PROPAGATION: By offsets and seeds.

POLIANTHES [*Amaryllidaceae*]—*See Chapter 19*

POLYGONATUM [*Liliaceae*]

P. biflorum and *P. commutatum* are North American natives, with fleshy creeping underground stems, found in rich woods. Commonly known as Solomon's-seal, the pendent, bell-like greenish flowers in the axils of the leaves in spring are followed by shining fruits which turn rose-color in autumn. There are several species native to other parts of the world.

CULTURE OUTDOORS: Naturalize in rich, fairly moist woods.

PROPAGATION: By division and seeds.

PUSCHKINIA [Liliaceae]

Puschkinia (Striped Squill) is a close relative of the Scilla and is perfectly hardy. The gray-blue flowers appearing in spring on short (to 1 foot) stems make good rock-garden subjects. *P. scilloides libanotica* is the variety generally offered.

CULTURE OUTDOORS: As for Scilla.

PROPAGATION: By offsets.

RANUNCULUS [Ranunculaceae]

This is a large family, with some members scarcely 2 inches tall (as *R. creticus*) and others 4 feet (as *R. Lyalli*). Many are hardy perennials, some suitable for the rock garden, others for the mixed border. *R. bulbosus,* which has a bulbous root and grows to 1 foot, is an escape from Europe which has become one of our most common wild flowers—the Buttercup.

The so-called florists' Ranunculus, *R. asiaticus* (tuberous-rooted), produces the showiest blooms. Growing to 1½ feet, it has flowers 1 to 4 inches in diameter. There are double forms with yellow, orange, scarlet, crimson, pink, and white blooms. Listed in catalogues are Persian, French, Turban, and Peony-flowered strains.

CULTURE: As for Anemones.

PROPAGATION: By division and seeds.

SCHIZOSTYLIS [Iridaceae]

S. coccinea (Crimson Flag; Kafir-lily) is a member of the Iris family sometimes grown indoors or under glass for winter bloom and as a cut flower. The long grass-like leaves are up to 2 feet in length, and the slender-tubed deep red flowers are borne on 1½-foot spathes in early winter.

CULTURE INDOORS: Plant in March (Mixture No. 3) and water

plentifully until after bloom. Then gradually reduce moisture and rest in pots with only an occasional watering until the following spring. The potted plants may spend the summer sunk to their rims in a garden bed but should be brought in before the first frost.

PROPAGATION: By division of the rhizomes.

SCILLA [Liliaceae]—See Chapter 14

SINNINGIA [Gesneriaceae]

Sinningias, commonly called Gloxinias, are among the showiest of tender, shade-loving summer flowers. The great velvety leaves are suggestive in texture of giant Saintpaulia foliage; the large bell-shaped flowers of violet, purple, salmon, rose, red, white, and two-color combinations are startingly beautiful.

The hybrids generally available are imported from Europe and have varied very little in recent years. These may be had in named varieties in separate colors. A few are:

Fire King—carmine-red   Emperor William—blue and white
Montblanc—white

Recently, however, a remarkable new American strain has appeared. These wonderful Gloxinias, known as the Buell Hybrids, are bred by a Connecticut hybridizer who has, in a few years, produced many outstanding new shades, forms, and color combinations. Mr. Buell is already working up stock for named varieties in separate colors, and these should be eagerly watched for by Gloxinia enthusiasts.

CULTURE: Start tubers any time from February to May in flats in a mixture of moist peatmoss and sand, the tops just exposed. Keep at 60 to 70 degrees in the shade until several leaves develop. Then pot in coarse, fibrous, humusy soil with an inch of charcoal in the bottom of each pot. Five-inch pots are suitable for average-size (1½-inch) tubers. Grow on in a window, sun porch, or greenhouse where the night temperature never drops below 60 degrees. Though Gloxinias like plenty of moisture, it is best to water thoroughly until soil in pots is moist all the way through, then not again until the surface soil feels dry to the touch. Avoid wetting the foliage. Feed regularly with liquid fertilizer.

When summer comes, the plants will require some shade. They can remain in the window garden or on a porch well sheltered from wind and rain. In August, begin to reduce water gradually until the foliage matures and dries off. Store, in the pots, under a bench in the greenhouse or on dampish cellar floor until new growth begins. Then bring to light and increase water. Repot if necessary about every third year. For succession of bloom, start tubers at two-week intervals from February to April.

For winter bloom, plant seeds in spring and grow on into the following winter, or hold tubers dormant until later in season, starting them only when new growth begins to develop.

PROPAGATION: From seed and leaf cuttings, as for African-violet.

SMILACINA [Liliaceae]

The False Solomon's-seals are native woodland wild flowers of North America. One species, S. trifolia, is native also in Siberia, while S. stellata is found in both North America and Europe. The terminal racemes or panicles of greenish or white flowers are borne on long curving stems, to 3 feet, with alternate leaves. It is for the round red berries which follow the flowers that the plants are prized, however. For naturalizing in moist, open woodland, Smilacinas are ideal subjects.

CULTURE OUTDOORS: Plant in drifts or colonies in moist woodland in part shade.

PROPAGATION: By division and seeds.

SMITHIANTHA [Gesneriaceae]

Smithianthas (Naegelias, as they are usually listed in the catalogues) have hairy, velvety leaves and tubular red or yellow flowers in terminal panicles 1 to 3 feet. In S. cinnabarina the foliage hairs are red and the flowers red, spotted with white. S. zebrina has leaves marked with plum or brown, and red flowers spotted yellow. Smithianthas make showy plants for the greenhouse or window garden.

CULTURE INDOORS: Plant one root to a pot, covering 1 inch deep (Mixture No. 2). Keep relatively dry until growth starts. Then increase water and feed with liquid fertilizer. After bloom, reduce water gradually and rest three months in pots.

PROPAGATION: From stolons or offsets.

SPARAXIS [Iridaceae]

Sparaxis (Wand Flowers) are tender cormous plants from South Africa producing in spring short spikes of yellow, purple, or rose-colored flowers rising to 1 or 2 feet from narrow basal leaves.

S. *bulbifera*—yellow, solitary flowers to 1 foot

S. *grandiflora*—yellow or purple to 1 foot

S. *grandiflora alba*—white

S. *Pillansi*—rose and yellow to 2 feet

S. *tricolor*—purple, yellow, and white to 1½ feet

Named varieties and mixtures are also commercially available.

CULTURE: As for Freesias.

PROPAGATION: By offsets.

SPREKELIA [Amaryllidaceae]

Variously known as Aztec-lily, Jacobean-lily, and St. James-lily, this Mexican bulb is grown indoors or under glass in the North, and out of doors as a garden plant in the South. It may also be treated as a tender summer-flowering bulb in the North. S. *formosissima* produces solitary 4-inch bright red spidery flowers on 1- to 2-foot stems. The three upper petals are erect, while the three lower ones are rolled or curled.

CULTURE INDOORS: As for Hippeastrum.

CULTURAL OUTDOORS: As for Hymenocallis.

PROPAGATION: By offsets.

STERNBERGIA [Amaryllidaceae]—See Chapter 19

TIGRIDIA [Iridaceae]—See Chapter 19

TRICYRTIS [Liliaceae]

Tricyrtis or Toad-lilies come to us from Asia, where a number of species are native. T. *hirta,* a Japanese species which is hardy to Massachusetts, produces many creamy flowers splotched with purple. Borne on 2- to 3-foot stems, the small flowers are typical of the Lily family, bell-shaped and graceful. Appearing in late September and October, they are especially welcome. T. *flava,* also from Japan, is a dwarf with yellow flowers. T. *macropoda* is another hardy species which flowers in summer. The pale violet, spotted flowers appear in a long, terminal corymb.

CULTURE OUTDOORS: Plant the rhizomes in humusy, well-drained soil in partial shade, in the rock garden or elsewhere; the dainty flowers make little show in a mixed border. After the first hard freeze, mulch lightly with salt hay or dry leaves.

CULTURE INDOORS: Pot in late winter (Mixture No. 2), and in spring sink pots in shaded garden beds. Before hard freeze, take indoors, dry off gradually, and store.

PROPAGATION: By division.

TRILLIUM [*Liliaceae*]

Trilliums are native to our American woods and are easily recognized because of their three whorled leaves and three-petaled flowers.

There are many species, but *T. grandiflorum,* with 3-inch white flowers, is the showiest. *T. sessile rubrum,* which bears the common name of Wake-robin, has deep red-purple flowers. *T. undulatum,* the Striped Trillium, has 1½-inch flowers of white veined in pink or purple and is a native of the Eastern seaboard, where it is found from Canada to Georgia and west to Missouri.

CULTURE OUTDOORS: Plant thick roots in rich, moist woods soil after flowering and when foliage has matured.

PROPAGATION: By seeds.

TRITELEIA—See BRODIAEA

TRITONIA [*Iridaceae*]—See Chapter 19

TULBAGHIA [*Liliaceae*]

Tulbaghia is another South African genus grown indoors; as a tender summer bulb in the North; and outdoors in the South, where it blooms from June to September. (Hardy to North Carolina.) In California, flowers are produced in both winter and summer. Tulbaghia is a relative of both Agapanthus and Allium. Urn-shaped flowers are borne in a terminal cluster, while leaves are linear, from 8 inches to 1 foot in length.

T. violacea—violet   *T. fragrans*—pinkish-lavender,
T. cepacea—lilac   fragrant

CULTURE INDOORS: As for Agapanthus, but all species must have full sun.

CULTURE OUTDOORS: Plant in sandy soil in full sun. In the North, dig and store before frost.

PROPAGATION: By offsets and seeds.

TULIPA [Liliaceae]—See Chapter 12

VELTHEIMIA [Liliaceae]

V. viridifolia has recently gained in popularity as a window-garden plant, even though it has not as yet taken to itself a common name. Blooming in late winter, this Veltheimia is decorative all through the cold weather because of its beautiful glossy basal foliage, 3 inches wide, crimped and ruffled along the edges, and growing out from the bulb in a symmetrical circle of handsome leaves, which are invaluable for use in flower arrangements.

The small tubular flowers, rather like those of the Tritoma but paler in color, are produced in an erect dense, tapering raceme at the top of a stalk 2 feet in height. There is something fascinating about following the rather slow development of the flower stalk and head, and we always bring the plant to a position in the window where we can watch it closely as soon as the bud appears. The flower head will keep in good condition for three weeks or longer after it first begins to show color.

CULTURE: As for Hippeastrum. Repot only when necessary (Mixture No. 4).

PROPAGATION: By offsets.

WATSONIA [Iridaceae]

Watsonias, popular in California gardens, are in many ways similar to Gladiolus. W. Meriana, to 4 feet, produces bright rose-colored flowers. A white form is W. iridifolia O'Brieni. W. coccinea is scarlet. There are many species and varieties, including a group with evergreen foliage, Beatricis hybrids with a range of color from salmon and orange to pink, and Tubularis hybrids in shades of orange.

CULTURE OUTDOORS, NORTH: As for Gladiolus, but foliage should be encouraged to remain green as long as possible. Because more time is required for foliage to mature, Watsonias cannot be planted out for succession of bloom as late in the season as Gladiolus. Can be wintered over in frame.

CULTURE OUTDOORS, SOUTH: As for Gladiolus. See above, but can be left in open over winter. Evergreen varieties shipped in damp moss, are planted at once with plenty of moisture.

CULTURE INDOORS: As for Ixia.

PROPAGATION: By cormels.

ZANTEDESCHIA [Araceae]

The Calla-lily (formerly Richardia, as it still is often listed) is primarily a greenhouse plant for winter blooming. It can be grown successfully in the window garden or as a tender bulb out of doors, for which use it is far too little appreciated in Northern sections. The medium-sized yellow Calla, Z. Elliottiana, with spotted foliage, and the pink Z. Rehmanni, or its improved form, Rehmanni superba, dwarfs to 1 foot, are especially suitable for indoor bloom. Z. aethiopica, the commonly grown greenhouse species, reaches 3 feet or more. Z. a. devoniensis is a whiter, more free-flowering variety. Godefreyana is a smaller form of Z. aethiopica but blooms more freely, while Childsiana is a miniature white, to 1 foot. These last two must be grown in shade.

In the Pacific Northwest and other mild moist climates, Callas may be seen blooming in many a dooryard in spring.

CULTURE INDOORS: Plant, when received, in 6-inch pots (Mixture No. 5), the upper third of the rhizome protruding. Keep in a cool, damp, dark place until growth starts, watering sparingly. When growth begins, bring to light and warmth (65 degrees minimum) and water plentifully. Feed once a week with manure water. After flowering, mature foliage gradually, then dry off bulbs and store. Repot each year.

CULTURE OUTDOORS, SOUTH: Plant in rich humusy soil, 3 to 4 inches deep, in light shade, spring or fall. Keep well watered.

CULTURE OUTDOORS, NORTH: Start indoors in March or April, or plant in open when soil is warm. Enrich bed with plenty of rotted manure, or humus plus dried manure; apply liquid manure frequently. After frost, store as for Tuberous Begonias.

PROPAGATION: By offsets, and Z. Elliottiana by seeds.

ZEPHYRANTHES [Amaryllidaceae]—See Chapter 19

LISTS

BY

Season of bloom
Height

FOR

Hot, dry situations
Moist situations
Shade
Woodland

Mixed borders
Features or landscape groups
Naturalizing
Rock garden
Edgings
Patio, in pots or tubs
Greenhouse, or as house plants
Fragrance
Cuttings and arrangements

NOTE

H indicates: hardy
HH: half hardy
T: tender

BULBS BY SEASON OF BLOOM

SPRING	SUMMER	AUTUMN	WINTER
Achimenes T	Achimenes T	——	——
——	Acidanthera T	——	——
——	Agapanthus T	——	——
Albuca T	Albuca T	——	——
Allium H; HH	Allium H; HH	Allium H; HH	Allium H; HH

SPRING	SUMMER	AUTUMN	WINTER
Alstroemeria HH; T	Alstroemeria T	——	——
——	Amarcrinum HH; T	Amarcrinum T	Amarcrinum T
——	Amaryllis bella-donna HH	Amaryllis bella-donna HH	——
Anemone HH	Anemone HH	Anemone HH	——
Arisaema tri-phyllum H	Anthericum HH	——	——
——	Arum palaes-tinum HH	——	Arum pal-aestinum T
Babiana T	Begonia Evan-siana H	Begonia Evan-siana H	——
Bulbocodium H	Begonia, Tuber-ous T	Begonia, Tuber-ous T	——
——	Belamcanda H	——	——
——	Bessera HH; T	——	——
——	Brodiaea HH	——	——
Camassia H	Caladium T	Caladium T	Caladium T
Chionodoxa H	——	——	——
Claytonia H	Calochortus H; HH	——	——
Clivia H	Canna T	Canna T	Clivia
Convallaria H	Childanthus T	Colchicum H	——
——	Colocasia T	——	——
Cooperia T	Cooperia T	Crocosmia T	——
Crinum T; HH	Crinum HH; T	——	——
Crocus H	——	Crocus H	——
Cyclamen H	——	——	Cyclamen T
——	Cypella T	——	Cyrtanthus T
——	Dahlia T	Dahlia T	——
Eranthis H	Eucomis T	——	Eucharis T
Eremurus H	——	——	——
Erythronium H	——	——	——
Eucharis T	——	——	——
Freesia T	——	——	Freesia T
Fritillaria H	——	——	——

SPRING	SUMMER	AUTUMN	WINTER
Galanthus H	Galtonia HH	——	——
——	Gladiolus HH; T	Gladiolus HH; T	Gladiolus T
Gloriosa T	Gloriosa T	Gloriosa T	Gloriosa T
Hyacinthus H	Habranthus T	——	——
——	Haemanthus T	Haemanthus T	——
——	Hippeastrum T	——	Hippeastrum T
——	Hydrosyme T		——
——	Hymenocallis T	——	——
Iris, Bulbous H; HH	Iris, Bulbous H; HH	——	——
Ixia T	Ixia T	——	Ixia T
——	Ixiolirion T		
Lachenalia HH	——	——	Lachenalia HH
——	Lapeirousia HH	——	Lapeirousia HH
Leucocoryne T	——	——	
Leucocrinum H	——	——	——
Leucojum H	Lilium H	Lilium H	Lilium H
——	Lycoris squamigera H	Lycoris radiata HH	
Muscari H	Moraea HH	——	Moraea HH
Narcissus H	——	——	Narcissus, H Paperwhite T
Nerine T	——	——	Narcissus Soleil d'Or T
Nomocharis H; HH	Nomocharis H; HH	——	Nerine T
Ornithogalum H; T	——	——	——
Oxalis HH; T	Oxalis HH; T	——	Oxalis HH; T
Polygonatum H	Pancratium T	——	——
Puschkinia H	Polianthes T	——	——
Ranunculus H; T	Ranunculus H; T	——	Rohdea T
Scilla H	Sinningia T	Sinningia T	Schizostylis T
Smilacina H	——	——	
Smithiantha T	——	——	Smithiantha T

SPRING	SUMMER	AUTUMN	WINTER
Sparaxis T	Sparaxis T	Sternbergia H	——
Sprekelia T	Sprekelia T	——	Sprekelia T
Trillium H	Tigridia HH; T	——	Tritonia crocata HH; T
Tulip H	Tricyrtis H; HH	Tricyrtis H; HH	Tulbaghia T
——	Tritonia HH; T	——	——
——	Vallota T	Vallota T	Veltheimia T
——	Watsonia T	——	——
Zantedeschia T	Zantedeschia T	——	Zantedeschia T
——	Zephyranthes HH; T	——	——

BULBS ACCORDING TO HEIGHT

LOW TO 1 FOOT	MEDIUM TO 2½ FEET	TALL 3 TO 8 FEET
——	Achimenes T	Agapanthus T
——	Acidanthera T	Albuca T
Allium H; HH	Allium H; HH	Allium H; HH
——	Alstroemeria T	Alstroemeria HH
——	Amaryllis belladonna T	Amarcrinum T
Anemone H	Anemone H; HH	Anemone H; HH
Anthericum HH	——	——
Arum palaestinum T	——	——
Babiana T	Begonia, Tuberous T	Begonia Evansiana H
Brodiaea HH	Bessera HH; T	Belamcanda H
Bulbocodium H	——	Bessera HH; T
	Caladium T	——
Calochortus H	Calochortus H	——
——	Camassia H	Camassia H
Chionodoxa H	——	——
Chlidanthus T	Clivia T	Canna T
——	——	Colocasia T
Claytonia H	Crinum T; HH	Crinum T; HH
Colchicum H	——	——

LOW TO 1 FOOT	MEDIUM TO 2½ FEET	TALL 3 TO 8 FEET
Convallaria H	——	Crocosmia T
Cooperia T	Cyrtanthus T	Cypella T
Crocus H	——	——
Cyclamen H	Cyclamen T	——
——	Dahlia T	Dahlia T
Eranthis H	Erythronium H	Eremurus H; HH
Erythronium H	Eucomis T	——
Eucharis T	——	——
——	Freesia T	——
Fritillaria H	Fritillaria H	——
——	——	Galtonia HH
Galanthus H	Gladiolus T	Gladiolus T
——	——	Gloriosa T
Habranthus T	Haemanthus T	——
——	Hippeastrum T	
——	——	Hydrosyme T
——	Hymenocallis T	Hymenocallis T
Iris H; HH	Iris H; HH	Iris H; HH
——	Ixia T	
Lachenalia HH	——	——
Lapeirousia HH	——	——
Leucocoryne T	——	——
Leucocrinum H	——	——
Leucojum H	Leucojum H	——
Liriope H	Lilium H	Lilium H
——	Lycoris radiata HH	Lycoris squamigera H
Moraea HH	Moraea HH	Moraea HH
Muscari H	——	——
Narcissus H	Narcissus H; T	——
——	Nerine T	——
——	Nomocharis H; HH	——
Ophiopogon H	——	——
Ornithogalum H; T	Ornithogalum H; T	——
Oxalis HH; T	——	——

LOW TO 1 FOOT	MEDIUM TO 2½ FEET	TALL 3 TO 8 FEET
Puschkinia H	Pancratium T	Polianthes T
	Polygonatum H	Polygonatum H
Ranunculus H; HH	Ranunculus H; HH	——
	Rohdea T	
Scilla H	Schizostylis T	——
	Sinningia T	——
	Smilacina H	——
	Smithiantha T	——
	Sparaxis HH	——
Sternbergia H	Sprekelia T	——
	Tigridia HH; T	——
	Tricyrtis H; HH	——
Trillium H	Trillium H	——
	Tritonia HH; T	Tritonia HH; T
	Tulbaghia T	——
Tulip species H	Tulip H	Tulip H
	Vallota T	Vallota T
	Veltheimia T	——
		Watsonia HH; T
Zephyranthes HH; T	Zantedeschia T	Zantedeschia T

FOR HOT, DRY SITUATIONS

Bessera HH; T
Brodiaea HH
Calochortus (spring moisture needed) H
Cooperia T
Gladiolus HH; T

Ixia T
Tritonia (Montbretia) HH; T
Tigridia HH; T
Tulipa (species) H
Watsonia T
Zephyranthes HH; T

FOR MOIST SITUATIONS

Alstroemeria T; HH
Arisaema triphyllum H
Caladium H

Canna T
Claytonia H
Clivia T

Colocasia T
Convallaria H
Erythronium H
Iris xiphiodes HH
Leucojum
Lilium canadense H

Lilium superbum H and others
Polygonatum H
Schizostylis T
Smilacina H
Trillium H
Zantedeschia T

FOR SHADE

Achimenes T
Allium H
Agapanthus T
Amarcrinum T
Amaryllis belladonna HH
Anemone (rock-garden varieties)
    H; HH
Arisaema triphyllum H
    (Jack-in-the-pulpit)
Begonia, evansiana H
Begonia, Tuberous T
Caladium, Fancy-leaved T
Camassia H
Chlidanthus, T
Claytonia virginica H
    (Spring Beauty)
Clivia T
Colocasia T
Crinum, Moorei HH
Eranthis hymenalis H
Erythronium H
Eucharis T
Fritillaria H
Galanthus H

Gloriosa T
Hippeastrum T
Hydrosyme T
Leucojum H
Lilium: Bellingham Hybrids H
    canadense H
    Henryi H
    martagon H
    philadelphicum H
Lycoris squamigera H
Muscari H
Ornithogalum H; T
Polygonatum biflorum H
    (Solomon's-seal)
Sanguinaria canadensis H
    (Bloodroot)
Scilla H
Smilacina H
    (False Solomon's-seal)
Tricyrtis HH; T
Trillium H
Vallota T
Zantedeschia T
    (Calla-lily)

FOR WOODLAND

Allium moly H
    and others
Arisaema triphyllum H
Calochortus H

Camassia H
Claytonia virginica H
Convallaria H
Erythronium H

Galanthus H
Leucojum H
Lilium H
   amabile
   auratum
   canadense
   giganteum
   Henryi
   martagon
   philadelphicum

   rubellum
   superbum
   and others
Polygonatum biflorum H
Sanguinaria canadensis H
Scilla campanulata H
Scilla nonscripta (nutans) H
Smilacina H
Trillium H

FOR THE MIXED BORDER

Acidanthera T
Albuca T
Allium H; HH
   moly, 12 inch, yellow, July
   neapolitanum, 15 inch, white,
      May, June
Alstroemeria T
Anemone HH
   Florists'
   hortensis
   tuberosa
Belamcanda H
Bessera HH
Calochortus H
Camassia H
Canna T
Cooperia T
Crocosmia T
Cypella T
Cyrtanthus T
Dahlia T
Eremurus H; HH
Eucomis T
Fritillaria imperialis H
Galtonia candicans HH
Gladiolus T; HH
Hyacinth H
Hymenocallis T

Iris, Bulbous HH
Ixia T
Ixiolirion T
Lachenalia HH
Leucojum H
Lily H
   Aurelian hybrids
   auratum hybrids
   candidum
   concolor
   Fiesta hybrids
   Golden Chalice
   Rainbow hybrids
   martagon
   speciosum
   tigrinum
   umbellatum
   and others
Lycoris radiata HH
Lycoris squamigera H
Montbretia T; HH
Moraea HH
Muscari H
Narcissus H
   Alasnam
   Bernarino
   Cheerfulness
   Dawson City

Narcissus (cont.)
  Deanna Durbin
  Fortune
  Geranium
  Golden Sceptre
  Golden Pedestal
  La Vestale
  Irene Copeland
  Mary Copeland
  President Carnot
  Spring Glory
  Tresserve
  Trevithian
  Twink
Nomocharis H; HH
Ornithogalum H; T

Oxalis T; HH
Pancratium T
Polianthes T
Ranunculus H; T
Scilla campanulata H
Scilla sibirica H
Sprekelia HH
Tigridia T; HH
Tritonia (Montbretia) HH; T
Tulip H
  Double Early
  Single Early
  Lily-flowered
  Peony-flowered
  Parrots
Watsonia T; HH
Zephyranthes T; HH

FOR FEATURE PLANTING AND LANDSCAPE GROUPS

Acidanthera T
Amaryllis (Hippeastrum) T
Anemones, Florists' HH
Begonia, Tuberous T
Belamcanda H
Caladium T
Camassia H
Canna T
Clivia T
Colchicum H
Colocasia T
Crinum T; HH
Crocus H
Dahlia T
Eremurus HH; H
Fritillaria imperialis H
Galtonia candicans T; HH
Gladiolus T
Haemanthus T
Hyacinth, Dutch H
Hymenocallis T

Iris, Dutch HH
  English (xiphiodes)
  reticulata H
  Spanish (xiphium)
Lilies, in variety H
Lycoris squamigera H
Moraea HH
Narcissus H
  Alcida
  Adventure
  Beersheba
  Dick Wellband
  Daisy Schaffer
  Diana Kasner
  Francisca Drake
  Gertie Millar
  Mrs. John Bodger
  Music Hall
  Monique
  Red Cross
  Rose of Tralee

Narcissi H (cont.)
Scarlet Elegance
Tunis
and others
Polianthes T
Tigridia T
Tritonia (Montbretia) T
Tulip H
Breeders

Darwins
Lily-flowered
Mendels
Parrots
Species Cantate
Species Princeps
Species Red Emperor
Triumphs

FOR NATURALIZING

Allium H; HH
Arisaema triphyllum H
(Jack-in-the-pulpit)
Brodiaeas HH
Bulbocodium H
Calochortus H
Camassia H
Chionodoxa H
Claytonia virginica H
(Spring Beauty)
Colchicum H
Convallaria H
Cooperia T
Crocus H
Eranthis H
Erythronium H
Fritillaria meleagris H
Galanthus H
Leucojum H
Lilium H
Bellingham Hybrids
canadense
Hansoni

martagon
philadelphicum
superbum
tigrinum
and others
Lycoris squamigera H
Muscari H
Narcissus H
Actaea
Edith
February Gold
Firetail
Hera
jonquilla
Mrs. Nette O'Melveny
Peeping Tom
poeticus
Queen of the North
Star of the North
Sunrise
Thalia
Trevithian

FOR THE ROCK GARDEN

Allium H; HH
Anemone H

apennina
blanda and varieties

Anemone H (cont.)
  caroliniana
  fulgens
  palmata
  ranunculoides
Anthericum T
Arisaema triphyllum H
Babiana T
Brodiaea (see Triteleia) HH
Bulbocodium H
Calochortus HH
Camassia H
Chionodoxa H
Chlidanthus T
Claytonia virginica H
Colchicum H
Cooperia T
Crocus H
  Dutch
  Species
  Autumn fl.
Cyclamen H
  europaeum
  neapolitanum album
Eranthis H
Erythronium H
Fritillaria meleagris H
Galanthus H
Lapeirousia HH
Leucocrinum H
Leucojum H
Lilium H
  amabile
  concolor
  pumilum and varieties
  scottiae and hybrids
  umbellatum Thalia
Muscari H

Narcissus H
  albus
  bulbocodium citrinus
  bulbocodium conspicuous
  campernell
  cyclamineus
    February Gold
    March Sunshine
  gracilis
  Johnstoni, Queen of Spain
  jonquilla simplex
  minimus
  nanus
  odorus Orange Queen
  rupicola
  triandrus albus
  triandrus calathinus
    Agnes Harvey
    Moonshine
    Thalia
  Watieri
  W. P. Milner
Nomocharis HH
Oxalis T
Puschkinia H
Sanguinaria canadensis H
Scilla bifolia H
  sibirica and varieties
  Tubergeniana
Sparaxis HH
Sternbergia H
Tricyrtis HH
Trillium H
Triteleia Brodiaea HH
Tulip H
  Species
  Species hybrids
Zephyranthes T

FOR EDGINGS

Allium moly, 12 inches H
Allium neapolitanum, 15 inches H
Chionodoxa H
Galanthus H
Hyacinthus, amethystinus H
   amethystinus albus H
    Dutch H
    Roman H
Leucojum H
Liriope H
Muscari H
Narcissus H
   February Gold
   Louis Capet
   Pearly Queen
   W. P. Milner
   Thalia
Ornithogalum H; T
Oxalis HH; T
Ranunculus H; T
Scilla H
Brodiaea (Tritelia) HH
Tulip H
   Single Earlies, species, and hybrids

FOR PATIO AND PORCH BOXES

Achimenes T (hanging baskets)
Agapanthus T (tubs)
Amarcrinum T (pots)
Amaryllis, belladonna T (pots)
Begonia, Tuberous T (pots and hanging baskets)
Caladium T (pots or boxes)
Clivia T (tubs)
Crinum T (pots or tubs)
Eucomis T (pots)
Gloriosa T (pots—a climber)
Haemanthus T (pots)
Hippeastrum T (pots or boxes)
Nerine T (pots)
Oxalis T (boxes, hanging baskets)
Sinningia (Gloxinia) T (pots)
Vallota T (pots)
Zantedeschia (Calla-lily) T (tubs)

FOR GREENHOUSE, OR AS HOUSE PLANTS (H)

Achimenes
Agapanthus
Alstroemeria
Amarcrinum
Amaryllis belladonna
Arum palaestinum
Babiana
Begonia, Tuberous
Caladium
Chlidanthus
Clivia
Crinum
Cyclamen, Florists'
Cyrtanthus
Eucharis
Eucomis
Freesia
Gloriosa
Haemanthus
Hippeastrum

Hydrosyme
Hymenocallis
Ixia
Lachenalia
Lapeirousia
Leucocoryne
Lilium in variety
Lycoris radiata
Moraea
Narcissus
  Paperwhite
  Soleil d'Or
Nerine

Oxalis
Ranunculus
Schizostylis
Sinningia (Gloxinia)
Smithiantha
Sparaxis
Sprekelia
Tritonia crocata
Tulbaghia
Vallota
Veltheimia
Zantedeschia (Calla-lily)
Zephyranthes

NOTE: All tender or half hardy. For details of culture, see Catalogue of
  Bulbs.

FOR FRAGRANCE

Acidanthera HH
Amarcrinum T
Amaryllis belladonna T
Brodiaea (Triteleia) HH
Chlidanthus T
Convallaria H
Cooperia T
Crinum T
Daffodil (see Narcissus)
Freesia T
Hyacinth H
Hymenocallis T
Iris reticulata H
Lachenalia HH
Leucocoryne T
Leucocrinum H
Lilium, in variety H
Lycoris squamigera H
Narcissus H
  Poetaz varieties
  Mary Copeland
  Jonquil and Hybrids
Ornithogalum H; T

Pancratium T
Polianthes T
Tulbaghia T
Tulip H
Single Earlies:
  Apricot Yellow
  Bellona
  De Wet
  Fred Moore
  Jonköping
  Prince Carnival
  Prince of Austria
  Proserpine
  Rising Sun
  Scarlet Admiral
  Thomas Edison
  Yellow Prince
Cottage:
  Alaska
  Dido
  Mrs. Moon
  Orange King
  Orange Queen

Darwins and Breeders:
  Alice Keith
  Dom Pedro
  Lucifer
  Pride of Haarlem
  Prince of Orange
  William Copeland

Species:
  australis
  persica
  sylvestris

FOR CUTTING AND ARRANGEMENTS

Allium H; HH
Alstroemeria HH
Amarcrinum T
Amaryllis belladonna HH
Anemone, Florists' HH
Belamcanda T
Bessera HH; T
Caladium* T
Canna* T
Chlidanthus T
Clivia T
Convallaria H
Crinum T
Cypella T
Cyrtanthus T
Dahlia T
Eucharis T
Freesia T
Gladiolus T
Gloriosa T
Haemanthus* T
Hippeastrum T
Hyacinth, Roman H
Hymenocallis* T

Iris in variety* HH
Ixia HH
Ixiolirion T
Lachenalia T
Leucocoryne T
Lilium, in variety H
Lycoris aurea HH
Lycoris incarnata HH
Lycoris radiata T
Lycoris squamigera H
Muscari H
Narcissus, in variety H; T
Nerine T
Ornithogalum H; T
Pancratium T
Ranunculus H; T
Scilla H
Smithiantha* T
Tigridia T
Tritonia (Montbretia) T
Tulips, in variety H
Veltheimia* T
Watsonia T
Zantedeschia (Calla-lily)* T

*Indicates decorative foliage.

Recommended Varieties of Garden Bulbs

CROCUSES

Spring-blooming, Dutch

BLUE	WHITE	YELLOW
Early Perfection— violet-blue	Jeanne d'Arc	Golden Goblet
Enchantress—China blue	Kathleen Parlow	Golden Yellow
Queen of the Blues— lilac	King of the Whites	Largest Yellow
Striped Beauty—blue, striped white	Snowstorm	
The Bishop—purple		
The Sultan—purple-blue		

Species

Biflorus (Scotch Crocus)—striped blue & white (naturalizing)	*Fleischeri*	*aureus*—orange-yellow
Imperati—lilac		*sulphureus concolor*— pale yellow
Sieberi (very early)— blue		*chrysanthus* and varieties
Tomasinianus, and varieties—lavender to purple		*Korolkowi*—golden-orange
versicolor—white, feathered blue		*susianus*
		susianus minor (rock garden)

Autumn-blooming Species

Aitchinsoni—pale blue	*Aitchinsoni albus*— white, tinted rose
asturicus—purple-lilac	*cancellatus albus*
medius—lilac-purple	*Cartwrightianus albus*
sativus (Saffron Crocus) —lilac, feathered violet	*laevigatus*
speciosus—blue and its varieties	*speciosus albus*
	zonatus albus—white, flushed pearl

DAFFODILS

Trumpet (*Division* I)

YELLOW	BICOLOR	WHITE	PINK
Adventure	Chula	Ada Finch	Antibes
Aerolite	Eskimo	Beersheba	Lady Bird
Alasnam	Jefta	La Vestale	Lovenest
Diotima	Pres. LeBrun	Mt. Hood	Menton
El Capitan	Silvanite	Pres. Carnot	Mrs. R. O.
Hunter's Moon	Spring Glory	(small)	Backhouse
Unsurpassable		Roxane	Pink Favorite
		Silverine	

Large Cups (*Division* II)

Carlton	Asmode	Hera	Beauty Glow
Croesus	Brookville	Ludlow	Champagne
Damson	Daisy Schaffer	Silver Star	Ecstasy
Fortune	Deanna Durbin	Tunis	Pink Fancy
Golden Pedestal	Dick Wellband	Zero	Pink Rim
Red Cross	E. H. Wilson		Siam
Scarlet Elegance	Francisca Drake		Spring Mist
Wodan	Gertie Millar		
Yellow Poppy	John Evelyn and		
Zarah Leander	hybrids		
	Selma Lagerlof		

Small Cups (*Division* III)

YELLOW	BICOLOR	WHITE
Bath's Flame	Firebird	Chinese White
Brightling	La Argentina	Mrs. Nette O'Melveny
Crocus	Lady Diana Manners	Polar Ice
Mrs. Barclay	Mystic	
Rene de Chalons	Magic Fire	
Rose Marie	Queen of the North	
Scarlet Leader	Sunrise	

Doubles (*Division* IV)

Holland's Glory	Irene Copeland	Cheerfulness
Indian Chief	Mary Copeland	Daphne
Inglescombe	Poeticus plenus	
Twink		

Triandrus Hybrids (*Division* V)

Hawera	Agnes Harvey
	Lady Kesteven
	Moonshine
	Shot Silk
	Silver Chimes
	Snowbird
	Thalia

Cyclamineus Hybrids (*Division* VI)

ALL YELLOW

Beryl	March Sunshine
February Gold	Peeping Tom
Garden Princess	

Jonquilla Hybrids (*Division* VII)

LARGE CUPS, *yellow*	SMALL CUPS, *yellow*	WHITE
Golden Goblet	Lanarth	Cheyenne
Golden Perfection	Orange Queen	
Golden Sceptre	Trevithian (Tall)	
Sierra Gold		

Tazetta (*Bunch-flowered, fragrant*) (*Division* VIII)

YELLOW (*orange cup*)	BICOLOR (*white perianth*)	WHITE
Admiration	Anna Brita	Cheerfulness
Early Perfection	Geranium	
Klondike	Glorious	
Red Guard	Helios	
Scarlet Gem	Laurens Koster	
Yellow Cheerfulness	Orange Wonder	
	Winter Pride	

Poeticus (*Division* IX)

WHITE, *with red-rimmed cups*

Actaea	Red Rim
Dulcimer	Sarchedon

Species (*Rock Garden*) (*Division* X)

YELLOW	inches	WHITE	inches
bulbocodium citrinus	8	minimus	3
bulbocodium conspicuus	6	triandrus albus	7
cyclamineus	12	triandrus calathinus	7
gracilis	12	Watieri	4
jonquilla	15		
junctifolius	4		
W. P. Milner	8		

DAHLIAS

Large Dahlias

CLASSIFICATION: ID, Informal Decorative; FD, Formal Decorative; SC, Semi-Cactus; IC, Incurved Cactus; C, Cactus; STC, Straight Cactus

RED

Abbot STC—cherry-red
Adolph Mayer FD—black-red
Ann Benedict IC—dark red
Gen. Eisenhower IC—turkey-red
Son of Satan SC—scarlet
Supreme Command FD—cherry-red

PINK AND ROSE

Clara Carder ID
Jersey Beauty FD—pink to chamois
Mary Taylor SC—flesh-pink and gold
Mrs. I. de Ver Warner FD—mauve-pink
Pink Elephant ID—rose-pink
Pink Mum IC—Phlox-pink

YELLOW AND ORANGE

California Idol ID—yellow
Enchantress C—bronzy orange
Gay FD—primrose-yellow
Jane Cowl ID—bronze-buff-gold
Kirsten Flagstad FD—chrome and rose
Salem Sunshine ID—yellow
Sherwood's Peach ID—orange-apricot
Sparkler FD—primrose-yellow
Treasure Island FD—apricot and gold

PURPLE AND LAVENDER

Bedford Beauty IC—lavender
Blue Jersey FD—purple
King David FD—purple
Purple Heart STC
Purple Knight SC
Vivianne Coppens STC—lavender
Zenith SC—purple

WHITE

Alice May ID
Ida Perkins FD
Jersey Dainty STC
Madonna ID
Snow Ball IC
White Beauty FD
White Wonder ID

BLENDS AND BICOLORS

Crystal's Surprise ID—buff and red
Flash IC—crimson, white tips
Jeanette FD—purple, tipped white
Miss Elsie Jane SC—shrimp, shaded cream, violet tips
Miss San Diego STC—yellow and pink blend
Silver Lady ID—white, flushed rose
W A A C FD—lemon suffused with salmon rose

Small Dahlias

CLASSIFICATIONS: M, Miniature; POM, Pompon; B, Bedding; D, Dwarf; S, Single

RED

Bishop of Llandaff M PEONY—dark red, golden rays, plum-red foliage
Ike D—blood-red
Little Nemo MFD—crimson, tipped white

PINK AND ROSE

Estelle MSC—Amaranth-rose
Fairy MFD—peach-pink
Joyce MFD—pink
Little Peaches C—salmon and rose
Rapture MID—rose shading to yellow
Wild Rose MID—rose-pink

WHITE

Snow MFD
Snowsprite MSC
White Fawn MFD

YELLOW AND ORANGE

Andries Orange MSC
Buckeye Babe MFD—buff-yellow-red
Daisy Mae MSC—primrose-yellow
Myall Sonne STC—lemon-yellow
Peach Glow MSC—burnt orange
Peggy Lindley MFD—golden-orange
Yellow Kitten MFD—yellow, tipped pink

LAVENDER

Betsy MC—lilac
Fairy MFD—violet-rose and mauve
Fuchsia Gem MS
Miss Plumb MFD—red-purple

Pompons

RED

Atom
Belle of Springfield
Ebony—black-red

PINK AND ROSE

A. D. Livoni—shell-pink
Betty Anne—rose-pink
Pink Perfection

WHITE

Bob White—white, yellow cast
Mrs. J. Telfer—white, yellowish cast

PURPLE AND LAVENDER

Betty Malone—white, tipped purple
Margaret Williams—mauve and pink
Mary Munns—red-purple
Morning Mist—white, tipped lavender
Sherry—deep purple

Dwarf (Bedding)

Unwin's Dwarf—mixture   Coltness Hybrids—mixture   Mignons—mixture

GLADIOLUS

RED

Dieppe—salmon-scarlet
Firebrand—deep red
Firegleam—scarlet
Red Charm—deep red
Red Wing
Velvet Mantle—very dark
War Paint—scarlet

PINK AND SALMON

Chinook—salmon
Evangeline—rose-pink
Friendship—pink
Heart's Desire—pink
Lady Wayne—salmon-pink
New York—deep rose
Pandora—geranium-pink
Picardy—light salmon
Pink Paragon—pink, cream throat
Spic and Span—pink
Spitfire—deep salmon
Tivoli—light rose

SMOKIES

Sahara
South Seas
Stormy Weather
Voodoo

BLUES

Elizabeth the Queen—lavender
Great Lakes—blue
Havelock—purple
King Lear—purple
Sherwood—purple
Treasure Island—orchid
Wedgwood—lavender

BUFF, YELLOW AND ORANGE

Boise Bell—yellow and pink
Butterscotch—buff
Donna—gold-buff
Lantana—orange and yellow
Sahara—russet
Sundance—yellow

WHITE AND CREAM

Florence Nightingale—snow-white
Leading Lady—cream
Margaret Beaton—white
Silver Wings—cream-white
White Goddess—creamy white

OTHERS

Buckeye Bronze
Frans Hals

Small decoratives

RED

Atom—scarlet, white-edged
Ito—orange-red and yellow
Kewpie
Ruby
Tweedledum
Tweedledee

PINK AND SALMON

Aria—dark pink
Bo-Peep—pink
Filigree—buff-pink
Little Sweetheart—pink
Nadia—salmon-pink
Pink Ribbon
Rosette—rose

BLUE

Athena—orchid
Fairy—light lavender

YELLOW AND ORANGE

Flicker—orange
Lemon Lass—yellow
Little Gold—orange-gold
Marionette—yellow, flushed red
Old South—buff
Orange Butterfly—orange
Twinkles—salmon, orange, and yellow

WHITE AND CREAM

Fairy Fancy—cream
Snow Baby—white
Starlet—white

Face-ups

RED

Red Button

PINK

Airy Fairy—pink and white
Peri—pink
Pinkie Dot

YELLOW

Bright Eyes—yellow, red throat

WHITE

Piccolo—white with red markings
White Satin
Woodbury—white, red throat

LILIES

NAME	COLOR	DATE OF BLOOM
amabile	red, spotted	June
amabile luteum	yellow, spotted	June
auratum, and varieties	white, spotted crimson	July–Sept.
Aurelian Hybrids	white-yellow or apricot centers	July–Aug.
Bellingham Hybrids	yellow-orange, spotted	June–July
Shuksan	yellow-orange, spotted	July
Browni	white, purple reverse	July
bulbiferum	orange-red, spotted	June
canadense, and varieties	yellow-orange, spotted	July
candidum	white	June
Cascade Strain	white	June
salonikae	white	June

NAME	COLOR	DATE OF BLOOM
centifolium	white, green-striped	July
Hybrids	white, flushed pink, rose, or ice-green	July
chalcedonicum	scarlet	July
columbianum	golden-orange, spotted	June
concolor	scarlet-orange	June–July
cordatum	greenish-white, spotted	July
Davidi	red, spotted	July
elegans, and varieties	apricot to red, mostly spotted	June–July
Fiesta Hybrids	yellow to red	July
Fire King	scarlet, spotted	June
formosanum, and varieties	yellow, red, white	Aug.–Oct.
giganteum	white, red-purple throat	June
Golden Chalice Hybrids	yellow to orange	June
Grayi	red, shaded orange, spotted	July
Green Mountain Hybrids	white with green to brown throat	July
Hansoni	yellow, spotted	June
Henryi	orange-yellow, spotted	Aug.
Humboldti	orange-yellow, spotted	July
Leichtlini Maximowiczi	orange-red, spotted	July
Lillian Cummings	orange, spotted	July
longiflorum, and varieties	white	June–July
Lyla McCann	golden-orange, spotted	July
martagon, and varieties	purple, wine-red, white	June–July
Maxwill	orange-red, spotted	July
Mid-century Hybrids	salmon-buff to red	June–July
Enchantment	nasturtium-red	
Fireflame	mahogany-red	
pardalinum	orange-red to crimson, spotted	July
giganteum	crimson to gold, spotted	July
parvum	orange-red, spotted	June
Philadelphicum	bright red, spotted	June
pumilum (tenuifolium)	scarlet	June
Golden Gleam	yellow	June
Rainbow Hybrids	yellow to red	June–July
Flamingo	pinkish-orange	June
regale	white, yellow throat, rose reverse	June–July
rubescens	white to pink-purple	June–July
Sargentiae	white, yellow throat, reverse brown-purple	July–Aug.
Scottiae	orange, spotted	May–June
speciosum, and varieties	white to crimson	Aug.–Sept.
superbum	orange-yellow, spotted	July–Aug.
T. A. Havemeyer, and seedlings	cream to orange-buff ivory to burnt orange	Aug.–Sept.
tenuifolium, and varieties	yellow to scarlet	June
testaceum (excelsum)	yellow, flushed pink	June
tigrinum, and varieties	yellow, salmon, orange	Aug.
umbellatum, and varieties	yellow to red	June
Wilmottiae	orange-red, spotted	July

TULIPS

* Fragrant

Single Earlies

PINK

La Reine maxima—white, pink
Pink Beauty—pink and white

ROSE

Flamingo
Ibis
La Reve (Hobbema)
Proserpine

RED

Brilliant Star—scarlet
Couleur Cardinal—orange-scarlet
Keizerskroon—scarlet, yellow edge

WHITE

Diana
Pelican
White Hawk

YELLOW

Apricot Yellow*—red and orange
Golden Mascot
Joffre
King of Yellows
Mme. Gevers
Rising Sun*

ORANGE

Fred Moore*—terra cotta
General de Wet*
Glory of Lisse*
Prince of Austria*—orange-red

PURPLE

Van der Neer—violet-purple

Double Earlies

PINK

Murillo—white, tinged pink
Peach Blossom—rose-pink
Salmonetta—salmon-pink
Spinel—cherry-pink
Triumphator—deep pink

YELLOW AND ORANGE

Bonanza—orange-yellow
El Toreador—orange
Maréchal Niel—canary with orange
Mr. Van der Hoef
Orange Nassau—orange-brown
Tea Rose*—yellow

RED

Dante
Electra
Scarlet Cardinal
Willemsoord—red, white edge
William of Orange

WHITE

Schoonoord (Purity)

OTHERS

Goya—salmon with yellow
Lac van Haarlem—violet

Triumphs

RED

Alberio—wine-red, white edge
Crater—bright red
Piccadilly—carmine
Red Matador—scarlet
Spring Song—cochineal

YELLOW AND ORANGE

Bruno Walter—orange
Orange Wonder
Pride of Berlin—orange
Rhineland—orange
Ursa Minor—yellow

WHITE

Kansas

PINK

Elizabeth Evers—white base
Mr. Kerbert

BLUE

Telescopium—red-violet

Mendels

ROSE AND RED

Early Queen—rose
Hildegarde—deep red
Mozart—bright pink
Scarlet Admiral
Sonja—cherry, shot with orange
Zenith—rose

WHITE

Athlete
White Sail

ORANGE AND ORANGE-RED

John Gay—orange-red
Orange Early Queen
Orange Wonder—bronze-orange

WHITE AND PINK

Her Grace
Mozart
Rose Marie
Weber

Peony-flowered (Double Cottage)

PINK

Clara Carder
Eros

WHITE

Mt. Tacoma

BLUE

Bleu Celeste
Uncle Tom—purple-red

RED

Symphonia

Cottage

PINK

Barbara Pratt
Rosabella
Rosy Wings
Smiling Queen

RED

Advance
Dido*—cherry
G. W. Leak—geranium-red
Marshal Haig—scarlet

WHITE

Albino
Blanca
Carrara
Mt. Erebus
White City

YELLOW

Arethusa
Belle Jaune
Inglescombe Yellow
Yellow Emperor

ORANGE

Beverley—orange-flame
Orange King*

OTHERS

Geisha—dove-gray and violet
Marjorie Bowen—buff and salmon
Ossie Oswalda—white and rose
Princess Margaret—rose-yellow,
    edged orange-red

Darwins

RED

Allard Pierson—crimson-maroon
Campfire—dark red
Charles Needham—scarlet
City of Haarlem—deep red
Gloria Swanson—crimson
Red Pitt
Utopia—cardinal red
William Pitt—strawberry

PINK AND ROSE

Clara Butt—clear pink
Eunice—pink, white center
Kathleen Parlow—silver-pink and
   mauve-rose
Mme. Krelage—lavender-pink
Queen Astrid
Rose Copeland

WHITE AND CREAM

Annie Speelman
Glacier
Helen Gahagan—cream
White Giant

YELLOW

Golden Age—deep yellow
Niphetos—lemon-yellow
Sunkist—golden-yellow
Yellow Giant—gold

PURPLE AND BLACK

Demeter—plum
Faust—blackish-purple
Frans Hals—deep purple
Jubilee—pansy-violet
La Tulipe Noire—black-purple
Queen of Night—almost black
The Bishop—bluish-purple

MAUVE AND LILAC

Insurpassable—lilac
Invincible—mauve
Rev. H. Ewbank—heliotrope
William Copeland*—mauve-lilac

Breeders

RED

Astarte—red, flushed violet
Dillenburg—flame
Indian Chief—copper-red
Panorama—terra cotta
President Hoover—orange-scarlet

VIOLET AND BLUE-BRONZE

Bacchus—violet-blue
Cardinal Manning—purple and
   bronze
James Watt—pansy and bronze
Louis XIV—purple and gold-bronze
Meridian—carmine-violet
Titanic—violet and bronze
William the Silent—royal purple

YELLOW

Dixie Sunshine
Garden Magic—yellow, flushed
   purple
Kathryn Truxton—yellow and rose
Tantalus

ORANGE AND BRONZE

Admiral Tromp—orange
Brigadier—bronze with orange
Don Alma—bronze and buff
Dom Pedro—dark mahogany*
Indian Chief—copper-bronze
Lucifer—red-orange*
Orange Beauty—orange-bronze
Prince of Orange*

Parrots

BLUE AND VIOLET

Blue Parrot
Discovery
Gadelan
Violet Queen

RED

Early Wonder
Firebird
Red Champion
Therese

PINK

Fantasy
Laetitia
Pink Champion

YELLOW

Sunshine*

ORANGE

Orange Favorite*

VERY DARK

The Black Parrot

Lily-flowered

RED

Columbus
Captain Fryatt
Sidonie—wine-red

PINK

China Pink
Marcellina—rose
Martha—carmine-pink
Rhodes—satiny pink
Rosy Wings

WHITE

The Bride
White Crown
White Triumphator

YELLOW

Alaska—canary
Golden Duchess
Mrs. Moon—deep yellow*
Sebastian—gold

ORANGE

Paola
Stanislaus

OTHERS

Astor—bronze, tinged amber and
    pink
Maytime—mauve, white edge
Philemon—sulphur to cream

Species

acuminata—yellowish and red
australis—yellow, flushed red on
    outside*
chrysantha—yellow, red outside
clusiana—white, pink striped out-
    side
Eichleri—scarlet, black and yellow
    center
Fosteriana:
    Cantate—red
    Princeps—red
    Red Emperor—huge red
    and others
Kaufmanniana:
    Caesar Frank—cream, exterior
    red

Elliot—white, exterior red
Gaiety—white, exterior red
Scarlet Elegance—scarlet, multi-
    flowered
The First—cream, exterior red
Vivaldi—cream yellow, exterior
    crimson
    and others
Marjoletti—primrose, exterior rose
praestans
    Fusilier—red, multi-flowered
pulchella humilis—violet-pink, yellow
    base
sylvestris major—golden-yellow*
turkestanica—white, orange-yellow
    center

Index

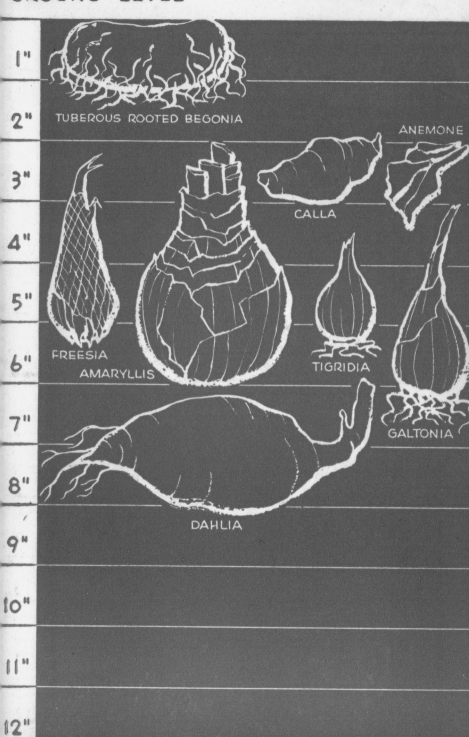

GROUND LEVEL

1"

2"   TUBEROUS ROOTED BEGONIA

ANEMONE

3"   CALLA

4"

FREESIA

5"

TIGRIDIA

6"   AMARYLLIS

GALTONIA

7"

8"

9"   DAHLIA

10"

11"

12"